NEW GENESIS

Also by Robert Muller

MOST OF ALL THEY TAUGHT ME HAPPINESS

NEW GENESIS
Shaping a Global Spirituality

———◆———

Robert Muller

Doubleday & Company, Inc.
Garden City, New York
1982

"The UN's Prophet of Hope" by Pam Robbins originally appeared in the September 1979 issue of *Sign* Magazine, copyright © 1979 by Passionist Missions, Inc. Used by permission of the publisher.

"My Five Teilhardian Enlightenments" originally appeared in *The Spirit of the Earth*, by Jerome Pulinski (Seabury Press, 1980). Reprinted by permission of the publisher.

Library of Congress Cataloging in Publication Data

Muller, Robert.
New Genesis.

1. Spirituality.   I. Title.
BV4501.2.M76   261.8
AACR2
ISBN: 0-385-18123-X
Library of Congress Catalog Card Number 81–43925

I dedicate this book to the innumerable good people of this planet who want to live in peace, friendship, freedom and justice, and to enjoy the miracle of life under the generous rays of our sun and the good guidance of the God of the universe.

It is dedicated to all peacemakers who try to heal the antiquated quarrels, divisions and insanity of those who refuse to recognize the oneness of our planetary home and of the human family.

It is dedicated to all my comrades from Alsace-Lorraine who died in the flower of their age during World War II while God granted me the privilege of survival.

It is dedicated to the United Nations, the first universal organization of this planet, from which I have learned so much.

It is dedicated to Dag Hammarskjöld and U Thant, my spiritual masters.

It is dedicated to all those who have given me peace, happiness, love and knowledge during my sojourn on earth.

May the kind divine providence help us start a new history and prepare the advent of a new age, a new world, a new philosophy and new human relationships, as we approach the bimillennium.

Let us all coalesce with all our strength, mind, heart and soul around a New Genesis, a true global, God-abiding political, moral and spiritual renaissance to make this planet at long last what it was always meant to be: the Planet of God.

Robert Muller

Contents

PART IV: MY PERSONAL GLOBAL
TRANSCENDENCE

FOREWORD

The UN's Prophet of Hope
by Pam Robbins

Pam Robbins is a free-lance journalist writing on religious and humanistic subjects. She lives in Springfield, Massachusetts.

NEW YORK CITY—His office on the twenty-ninth floor of the United Nations Secretariat building gives him a view of more than the skyline. For over thirty years he has witnessed conflicts, crises, natural and man-made disasters around the world.

But Robert Muller remains undaunted. His round face is smiling and his blue eyes serene as he declares cheerfully, "A new world is in the making."

This is not the assessment of one whose ignorance is bliss. Currently serving as Secretary of the UN's Economic and Social Council, Muller has filled numerous posts for the organization, including that of aide to three Secretaries-General. He holds degrees in law and economics from the universities of Strasbourg and Heidelberg and from Columbia University. A native of Belgium who was raised in Alsace-Lorraine, he fought in the French Resistance and was briefly imprisoned by the Nazis.

Muller has collected some of his adventures and insights in a book titled, *Most of All They Taught Me Happiness*.[1] "People who live in the world of action," he explains, too often postpone writing until some future date which never arrives. "Rather than leave nothing behind," he decided to record "a few perspectives, recipes for happi-

[1] New York: Doubleday & Co., Inc., 1978.

ness. I have tested them and maybe one will be appropriate for you."

Despite the well-cut gray suit, striped tie, crisp white handkerchief peeking from his breast pocket, and a golden Crucifix given to him by Pope John Paul II, there is a simplicity about the man. He could as easily be the hatmaker his father was. The austere office he occupies is enlivened by pieces of sculpture on walls and surfaces, and by his own energy and enthusiasm.

Like his book, his conversation is pervaded by unbounded optimism. "I saw a film on television last night, *The Grapes of Wrath*. It is a description of what happened during the thirties in the dust bowl. When you see it, you immediately realize what a distance has been covered. That could not happen today." It is the observation of a man who persists in believing the glass is half full, while all around him call it half empty. "Never in human life is the situation completely satisfactory, but you must have the ability of looking back and forward. People are often dissatisfied because they do not take stock of what they have accomplished.

"In 1948, when I first came here, there was not a single black nurse in any hospital in New York, not a single black teller in any bank. I was appalled. We have made tremendous gains in racial equality." Reading the will and testament of George Washington recently, he discovered that the first President had bequeathed a number of slaves to his wife. "And that was George Washington! We are still far from a perfect world, but we must keep at it. Progress, even if it is not satisfactory, is nonetheless progress. Every hour six thousand people die, but that doesn't prevent doctors from trying to save lives."

For Muller, optimism is more than an inherent disposition; it is an obligation, a responsibility. "In order to model a happy and beautiful world," he has written, "we must believe in it, we must work at it; we must be in love with it." Teachers and others will say "some children are optimistically or pessimistically inclined. As with all life, you are born with certain natural tendencies, but you can change them. If you could not, you could just forget about education.

"When you sit in my position, you know what is going on in the world and the time is getting ripe to restore confidence." His book, he points out, is only one of several on similar topics of hope and positivism and his friend Norman Cousins (of *Saturday Review* fame) "is going all over the United States making speeches in which he says the world is divided not into East and West, or rich and poor, or black and white, but into optimists and pessimists." He chuckles as he recalls his attendance earlier this year at a conference of missionaries from various religions. "When I finished my speech, one missionary said, 'How can you be so optimistic? What are your reasons!' I looked at him. 'I am not an expert on optimism,' I told him. 'You are. It is called the miracle of faith. All the religions are based on that.'"

The linking of optimism and faith may explain Muller's fascination with religion and his conviction that it is through the world's religions and their belief that life is sacred that global problems can be solved.

"My great personal dream is to get a tremendous alliance between all the major religions and the UN. U Thant used to say we would not be able to solve our problems without seeing our place in relation to the universe."

Muller is a Catholic and considers himself a good one. "But I am not so fanatical as not to respect other faiths. I would never fight with another religion about the superiority of mine." He recalls one of his four children asking him, "What is the best religion?" His reply is the one he gives anyone who asks a similar question. "You have about five thousand religions on the planet," he says. "You'd be dead before you studied them all to decide which is the best. You are born into a religion and it will give you full satisfaction. Be interested in all religions, in what they have in common, but there is no compelling reason to switch.

"I have a little file of things on particular religions that would be good for everyone." He picks up a folder and begins thumbing through until he locates a paper on Moslem dietary rules. "They explain the prohibition of alcohol because intoxication hinders people from remembrance of God and the proper observance of their prayers." His excitement is obvious. Deeply troubled by the worldwide tide of alcohol abuse, Muller believes the only answer lies in "linking it to God, saying, 'If you want to be in communion with God, you cannot be intoxicated. Period.'" Moslems pray at least five times a day, he continues. "You know how they explain it? They say that you drink water several times a day; you have the same need to drink the water of God. Common sense." He remembers a world conference on water during which he longed to hang a sentence from the Koran above the assembly hall: "Do not waste a drop of water, even if you are sitting on the bank of a river." A simple statement, he says, "but it says it all. Scientists and people in government would be well advised to turn to religions to ask their perceptions and guidance. And religions should urgently assimilate the tremendous results of science and accelerate their ecumenic, global cooperation. They are far behind nations in that respect."

People often evaluate the United Nations and the Catholic Church in the same light, he says, since both are world-wide in scope, prize human life, and seek what is ultimately good for humanity. Critics often dismiss both as lofty, unrealistic and ineffective in achieving their goals of peace and brotherhood. Muller disagrees. "In my opinion, they are both extremely effective—in the long run. They are part of building the ethics and evolution of humanity." Neither body can offer instant remedies, but that does not mean they achieve nothing. He uses a UN example. "Say you begin to notice that the actions of all the nations are damaging the seas and oceans. You call a world conference and governments immediately begin to wake up. There are now ministries of the environment everywhere. You don't see things improve overnight, but the rate of deterioration begins to diminish." Full improvement only comes with time, but historians, he maintains, "will say that at the turning point of the nineteen hundred seventies, when so many global problems arose, humanity was lucky to have global organizations.

"I would hate to think what the world would be today if, during the last thirty years of population explosion, atomic bombs, increased science and technology, nations hadn't had a place to meet. We would have had at least two world wars in that period." He admits that the UN has often failed. In preventing conflicts, for instance, he rates its success as fifty-fifty, not very good for a peace-keeping organization. But, in the tremendously dangerous period when Asian and African states sought independence, the UN reduced bloodshed by ninety per cent, and the picture of racism would be far uglier if there were none of the black delegates speaking out in the UN forum.

The organization has provided an enormous service in preventing the coalition of poor countries by giving them a place to let off steam and to obtain help. This outlet has prevented a splitting of the world into rich and poor, which would mean world disaster. Both the political center in New York and the thirty-two agencies of the UN are writing the future. "What you are reading on the front page of the newspapers is being forged here," Muller says.

His positive evaluation of the UN's past is matched by an equally upbeat forecast for the organization and the world it serves. "There will be no third world war between the big powers," he says matter-of-factly. "They are so interlinked and armed that a war is unthinkable. But there will be conflicts between poor countries. One of my major recommendations is to foster cooperation between the developing countries, to turn their energies away from territory and power to more constructive objectives."

He does not, however, see quick disarmament. Nations are "too insecure for that. Several decades will pass before that progress can be made." Again, he expects a gradual shift, beginning with a slow de-escalation of arms build-up. Also on a negative side, he predicts "continued human rights violations in many countries. Another major problem—until the year 2000—will be the poor. Population will increase from four and a half billion to six billion and ninety per cent will be born in developing countries. Not even an economic miracle will solve that." Generally, the world will have to deal with global problems—population, environment, natural resources. "We have to manage our planet with more intelligence. By the year 2000 we will be fully into the business of making a new world." The task of doing so does not require any form of world government, he stresses, although narrow nationalism will shrink and countries will become "like Vermont and California are now. Things do not come into being in terms of world law, but at the end of a meeting on terrorism or the law of the sea, for example, delegates go home and write national legislation. They prefer to do it that way, and it doesn't matter. We can do the job with that. It is the result that counts."

Muller often refers to an exchange of letters between Albert Einstein and Sigmund Freud, in which a frustrated Einstein asked the psychologist if he could offer any answers to the problems of armament, aggression and war. Freud's reply noted that humans are divided between instincts of aggression and love. Peace would require the development of ties of sentiment among people. "The love of country has succeeded in binding people at the national level. The great new historical challenge is to develop love among all earth inhabitants, and for the earth itself."

Muller firmly believes such unity among humankind can be

achieved. "This was the message of God—you can do it, but it's up to you to do it," he says. One of the most significant aspects of Christ's message to the world, he believes, is that Christ "always, uncompromisingly was on the side of light, not darkness, good, not evil. There was no yin and yang in Christ." He also remained true to his message "right to the end. He let himself be killed," Muller says, stabbing the air with a forefinger for emphasis, "rather than fight his killers with their own methods."

It is a lesson which Muller has taken to heart. His world view has earned him various epithets, even from his admirers. But those who say he is somehow "different" are only "seeking an excuse" for not embracing his positive attitude. As he told one woman, "There are 40,000 international civil servants. Even if you came to me and said 39,999 are no-good bureaucrats, I am not going to change one little bit. Why should you let yourself be reduced by the behavior of others? You have one power, the power over yourself. As an individual, you might be pushed down or pushed forward."

Dealing in global proportions has made him even more convinced of the power and responsibility of each person. "The most important act of the individual is to take good care of his own life. We have a planet of four and a half billion people. It will be a good planet if there are four and a half billion good, peaceful and happy people. The total situation depends, in the end, not on governments and on the UN but on the people. You cannot expect the world to change before you change yourself."

Such self-determination must be rooted in a spiritual value system and Muller has found ample inspiration in the lives of people he has known, including Dag Hammarskjöld and U Thant. Hammarskjöld was a dedicated servant of Sweden before coming to the UN. But it was there that he became "one of the great mystics of our time. I read every day the same book he read, *The Imitation of Christ*, a recipe for spiritual life for a man of action, an ideal book for an international civil servant. Hammarskjöld showed the world that the way to sanctity passes through the world of action."

U Thant, a Buddhist whom Muller calls "a master in the art of living," never drew distinctions between his public and spiritual lives, but instead lived the former in accordance with the precepts of the latter. Muller attempts to do the same. "A man must care to know during his lifetime how he wants to be remembered in death. This will mold his entire life," he has written, and he wants to be remembered as "having tried to convince everybody I could that to be alive on this planet is a miracle."

Muller is fully aware of the uniqueness of his life and the people he has known during it. That awareness compels him to write and speak. "I will retire in a few years, and if God allows, I see my life very clearly. Now that I am getting older, I have to leave to others the lessons left to me. I have had a complete adult life in the first universal organization, working only for the world and humanity, according to the oath I took when I entered the United Nations. I am not the same being as in 1948, when I first came here. I have been given so much and it is absolutely my duty to give it back in digested form—speeches, articles, books. My great duty is to conclude." He glances out the wide window at the New York panorama. "There is," he says simply, "a lot of happiness in store for me."

NEW GENESIS

PART I

The Global Transcendence
of Humanity

1

The Need for Global Education

In order to prepare our children properly for tomorrow's world, we must discern among the agitations and headlines of the day those trends and tendencies which are fundamental to our time and put aside whatever is accidental, secondary, ephemeral and anachronistic.

What strikes us most in recent years is that, since the last world war, humankind has entered a totally new era of history, perhaps even of evolution. During this period man has advanced dramatically into the infinitely large and the infinitely small. More scientific progress has been achieved in the last thirty years than during the entire previous history of mankind. Instruments, linked by instant communication to our planet, have been sent farther and farther away into the universe. Humans have set foot on the moon and have returned safely to earth. Outer space is being used for unprecedented systems of world-wide communication and study of the earth's resources and physical conditions. More than two thousand satellites and space objects are circling around the earth. Transportation has expanded from land and sea to the atmosphere, with ever larger and faster planes. Man has reached with his tools the abyss of the seas. We have witnessed the harnessing of atomic energy, the birth of electronics, of cybernetics, of laser technology and the unlocking of many mysteries of the infinitely small. Microbiology has opened up new exhilarating and frightening vistas of scientific advance with the synthesis of genes. Never on this planet has there been such intensive research and discovery by so many scientists in so many lands.

The Industrial Revolution and its recent scientific and techno-

logical acceleration have had far-reaching consequences for humankind. The first effect was an unprecedented improvement in living
conditions on our planet. This improvement is spreading progressively to the entire world despite regrettable discrepancies and de-
lays.

Length of life has increased, reaching more than seventy years in
many affluent societies. Even in India life expectancy has increased
from forty to fifty years in two decades. Diseases which caused great
epidemics not long ago have been wiped out. Gigantic efforts are
being made to attack the remaining principal causes of early death.
Thus humanity's death rate has been reduced from 17 per 1,000 in
1950–55 to 13 per 1,000 in 1965–77. The world is able to feed more
than one million additional people a week. During the last twenty
years more than six hundred million newcomers have been added to
the world's literate population.

The goods placed at the command of people for their sustenance
and enjoyment have reached phenomenal quantities in some societies. Thus, to sustain a person in the United States over an average
life span, 56 million gallons of water, 37,000 gallons of gasoline, 5½
tons of meat, 5½ tons of wheat, 9 tons of milk and cream are
required. In the poorer parts of the world the level of consumption
is only a fraction of such figures. But there, too, the amount of
goods placed at the disposal of the individual is on the increase. The
scientific and technical revolution which started two hundred years
ago has spread to most continents and it will encompass, in the not
too distant future, our entire planet.

Its second effect has been the advent of an entirely new period in
world history, namely, the era of mass phenomena due to the multi-
plication of human lives. Lower death rates, longer lives and better
lives have brought about the well-known accelerated growth of the
human race.

People on our planet have increased from 2.5 billion in 1951,
when the UN published the first world statistics, to 4.5 billion in
1980. We will be more than 6 billion people in the year 2000 and a
child being born today might live in a world of 8 billion at the age
of sixty. It is as if the child were to witness the landing of several billion more people on this planet during his lifetime.

The statistics published by the United Nations and its specialized
agencies show a doubling or tripling of most world data during the
past twenty years. World industrial production has tripled. The vol-

ume of world exports has quadrupled. Agricultural production has increased 1.7 times. The phenomenal growth in the production of certain commodities is illustrated by petroleum, which has increased 5 times, plastic, which has increased 15 times, aluminum 5 times, cement 4 times, crude steel 2.8 times, motor vehicles 2.7 times. There were only 11 cities of more than one million inhabitants in 1923; there are 160 today and there will be more than 300 in the year 2000, 40 of which will have more than 10 million inhabitants.

While the population increase is greatest in the poorer countries and the consumption explosion greatest in the developed ones, the Industrial Revolution will continue its world-wide spread. Higher population figures will then be accompanied by higher consumption everywhere, yielding staggering results. This is the new world into which we have entered. These are the real causes of the various crises which have lately beset our planet: pressures on the environment, on resources, the energy crisis, the food crisis, the urban crisis, and inflation.

The third effect has been the advent of an intricate and extremely dense network of world-wide interdependencies among societies which until recently were living in relative isolation from each other. Beyond nature's interdependencies which have always characterized our planet (the water cycle, the oxygen cycle, the carbon cycle, the nitrogen cycle, and many other internal links of the biosphere), the world has suddenly been seized in a rapidly growing web of man-made interdependencies. Thousands of planes are constantly in the air, and at certain airports they sometimes wait in queues for the opening of an air channel. Thousands of ships and trains are carrying huge quantities of goods from one country to another. Some seaports cannot catch up with the increase in world trade. International tourism, congresses, meetings, assistance and studies are mushrooming. Colossal transnational companies have a foot in many countries, combining money, labor, resources and technologies across national boundaries on a world-wide scale, and taking the globe as a single market. They begin to dwarf many nations, thus opening yet another page in the history of power.

These interdependencies have forced governments into new collective thinking and cooperative arrangements which would have been inconceivable only a few decades ago. The United Nations, as a result, has profoundly changed. The world organization, strengthened by thirty-two specialized agencies and world programs, is today concerned with practically every global problem on earth.

Through its world-wide data collection, studies and conferences—political, economic, social, scientific, cultural and environmental—the United Nations has become the greatest observatory and warning system of planet Earth. Through it, governments are making an honest effort at cooperation in many fields, although such cooperation would warrant infinitely more heart, effort, vision and generosity.

Under such dramatically changed circumstances, which deeply affect our lives, there is an urgent need for more *global education*. This is very important for the future of humanity. How can our children go to school and learn so much detail about the past, the geography and the administration of their countries and so little about the world, its global problems, its interdependencies, its future and its international institutions? People are astonished by the sudden emergence of global crises. They wonder how environmental deterioration could have developed to the point of endangering life on this planet. They wonder why there is an energy crisis which had not been foreseen by their governments (but had been foreseen by the United Nations, which convened, as early as 1961, the first world conference on new sources of energy). They ask themselves why bad crops in faraway countries should make the prices of the food on their tables shoot up and why there is a sudden world food shortage after so many years of agricultural surpluses (again nations had been warned of the danger by the UN's Food and Agriculture Organization). A child born today will be faced as an adult, almost daily, with problems of a global interdependent nature, be it peace, food, the quality of life, inflation, or scarcity of resources. He will be both an actor and a beneficiary or a victim in the total world fabric, and he may rightly ask: "Why was I not warned? Why was I not better educated? Why did my teachers not tell me about these problems and indicate my behavior as a member of an interdependent human race?" It is, therefore, the duty and the self-enlightened interest of governments to educate their children properly about the type of world in which they are going to live. They must inform the children of the actions, the endeavors and the recommendations of their global organizations. They must be prepared to assume responsibility for the consequences of their actions and help in the care of several billion more fellow humans on earth. Many governments have begun to realize this. In 1974 they created a United Nations University located in Tokyo, with affiliates in many countries. In 1979 the UN General Assembly welcomed the decision by the government of Costa Rica to establish a University of Peace. Institutes for global education have sprung up, and the UN and UNESCO are convening meetings of educators to develop global curricula. In many countries, especially the United States, educators feel that this is a new educational trend whose time has come.

The United Nations and its specialized agencies have a wealth of data and knowledge on every conceivable world problem. This source must be systematically tapped by educators. Time is running short. Global events are moving fast. It would be more beneficial to teach children around the world to close their water faucets a few seconds earlier, and to conserve our resources, than to adopt intricate legislation or endlessly drill new holes in the ground. The world will be in great trouble and will not be able to solve its global problems if citizens are not taught properly from their earliest youth. This is a great new challenge, a new historical dimension, and a thrilling objective for educators everywhere in the world.

Beyond the turmoil, the divisions and perplexities of our time, humanity is slowly but surely finding the ways, limits and new codes of behavior which will encompass all races, nations, religions and ideologies. It is the formulation of these new ethics which will be the great challenge for the new generation. It will concern not only man's material fate but also his mental and spiritual lives. The fulfillment of a human person's earthly destiny, of his happiness during his short span of life, of his right place in creation, depends in great degree on his comprehension of the total web of life and his personal part and comportment in it. Former Secretary-General U Thant, a teacher, when discussing these problems, always came back to his fundamental belief that education held the keys to the future, and that mental fulfillment was superior to material life, moral qualities superior to mental qualities, and spiritual fulfillment superior to mental life. In a speech he made on his religious beliefs in Toronto in 1966, he said:

"The law of love and compassion for all living creatures is again a doctrine to which we are all too ready to pay lip-service. However, if it is to become a reality, it requires a process of education, a veritable mental renaissance. Once it has become a reality, national as well as international problems will fall into perspective and become easier to solve. Wars and conflicts, too, will then become a thing of the past, because wars begin in the minds of men, and in those minds love and compassion would have built the defences of peace."

In his farewell address to the United Nations in December 1971, he said:

". . . I have certain priorities in regard to virtues and human values. An ideal man, or an ideal woman, is one who is endowed with four attributes, four qualities—physical, intellectual, moral and spiritual qualities. Of course it is very rare to find a human being who is endowed with all these qualities but, as far as priorities are concerned, I would attach greater importance to intellectual qualities over physical qualities. I would attach still greater importance to moral qualities over intellectual qualities. It is far from my intention to denigrate intellectualism, but I would attach greater importance to moral qualities or moral virtues over intellectual virtues—moral qualities like love, compassion, understanding, tolerance, the philosophy of 'live and let live,' the ability to understand the other person's point of view, which are the key to all great religions. And above all I would attach the greatest importance to spiritual values, spiritual qualities. I deliberately avoid using the term 'religion.' I have in mind the spiritual virtues, faith in oneself, the purity of one's inner self which to me is the greatest virtue of all. With this approach, with this philosophy, with this concept alone, will we be able to fashion the kind of society we want, the society which was envisaged by the founding fathers of the United Nations."

Yes, global education must transcend material, scientific and intellectual achievements and reach deliberately into the moral and spiritual spheres. Man has been able to extend the power of his hands with incredible machines, of his eyes with telescopes and microscopes, of his ears with telephones, radio and sonars, of his brain with computers and automation. He must now also extend his heart, his sentiments, his love and his soul to the entire human family, to the planet, to the stars, to the universe, to eternity and to God.

He must perceive his right, miraculous place in the splendor of God's creation. We must manage our globe so as to permit the endless stream of humans admitted to the miracle of life to fulfill their lives physically, mentally, morally and spiritually as has never been possible before in our entire evolution. Global education must prepare our children for the coming of an interdependent, safe, prosperous, friendly, loving, happy planetary age as has been heralded by all great prophets. The real, the great period of human fulfillment on planet Earth is only now about to begin.

A PARABLE[1]

Once upon a time there was a class
and the students expressed disapproval of their teacher.
Why should they be concerned with
global interdependency, global problems
and what others of the world were thinking, feeling and doing?
And the teacher said she had a dream in which she
saw one of her students fifty years from today.
The student was angry and said,
"Why did I learn so much detail about the past
and the administration of my country
and so little about the world?"
He was angry because no one told him
that as an adult he would be faced
almost daily with problems of a
global interdependent nature, be they
problems of peace, security, quality
of life, food, inflation, or scarcity
of natural resources.
The angry student found he was the
victim as well as the beneficiary.
"Why was I not warned? Why was
I not better educated? Why
did my teachers not tell me about
the problems and help me understand
I was a member of an interdependent human race?"
With even greater anger the student shouted,
"You helped me extend my hands with incredible machines,
my eyes with telescopes and microscopes,
my ears with telephones, radios, and sonar,
my brain with computers,
but you did not help me extend
my heart, love, concern
to the entire human family.
You, teacher, gave me half a loaf."

[1] By Jon Rye Kinghorn, based on the preceding essay, from A *Step-by-Step Guide for Conducting a Consensus and Diversity Workshop in Global Education.* A Program of the Commission on Schools, North Central Association and the Charles F. Kettering Foundation.

2

Of Right Human Relations

Someday our planet will be a world spiritual democracy. Today's international community is only an assemblage of powers. How the governors came to power is seldom questioned. At this stage of history, all one can hope for is peace, restraint and cooperation among the tenants of power. But at some point in our evolution the question of the proper representation of the people in the management of our globe will certainly pose itself, as will the spiritual quest for our proper place in the universe and in the eternal stream of time. There is urgent need to determine the cosmic or divine laws which must rule our behavior on earth.

A Sun Safe and Stable

I have now worked in the world organization for over thirty years. I have learned from it more than I would have learned from any university or school on earth, and I continue to learn every day, for the UN has become the greatest laboratory of human affairs that ever was. It is an entirely new event, a paradigm in evolution. I am in charge of the coordination of the specialized agencies. There are today thirty-two specialized agencies and world programs. This is a fact of momentous historical importance. These agencies cover a large array of human concerns, from aviation to the atom, from children to workers, from agriculture to industry, from navigation to trade, from economic development to the environment, from health and science to art and culture. As a result, governments possess today the embryo of a world system of diagnosis, consultation, monitoring, prognosis and action which allows them to deal with old as well as newly emerging planetary problems. These instruments and agencies provide humankind with the most up-to-date, enlightened perceptions. Thus, recently, when reading a document on extra-terrestrial messages published by the UN Outer Space Committee, I learned something quite fundamental. In it, astrophysicists calculated the likelihood of other civilizations in the universe. They started from the billions of galaxies and the more than two hundred billion stars or suns in our own galaxy. They calculated the probability of planets in belts located at a certain distance from stable suns, i.e., stars whose light hydrogen explosions have reached stability.

This is the case of our sun, which will remain safe and stable for another six to eight billion years. In addition to stable solar radiation, life requires a certain size of planet to retain a favorable atmosphere, a certain chemical composition of the surface of the planet and a rather narrow range of temperature, i.e., the planet must be located neither too near nor too far from a sun. After reviewing these factors, the astrophysicists introduce another: the number of civilizations in the universe further depends on the length of life of such civilizations. The longer civilizations are able to survive and to develop, the larger their total number will be in the universe. And then comes this fundamental statement: *the length of life of a civilization depends on its capability to solve environmental and social problems;* the civilization must not destroy itself, soon after it masters the technical means to do so. Our own civilization stands now at this precise crucial threshold. Two momentous questions have indeed been put to us during the last decades:

– How are we going to deal with our environment, how will we manage it and survive and develop in it without destroying certain vital conditions inherited from billions of years of prior evolution?
– How will we manage to live peacefully and cooperatively together among races, nations, cultures and so many other human groups and interests? In particular, will we be able to refrain from using the life-annihilating arms developed to protect, assert, and foster those specific groups produced by history and called nations?

For the astrophysicists, the problem is very simple: either you do it or you don't. If you don't, you will disappear and the universe will not change a bit.

I will deal here with this second problem, namely, that of "right human relations."

At the United Nations I am faced with so many problems, the complexity of which increases every day, that I had to choose between giving up or developing a canvas which permitted me to see a specific problem at its right place within a logical scheme, so that the totality makes sense, as do our individual beings, our planet and our universe despite their respective complexities. To coordinate requires to discern a sense of direction in the complexity. This is quite fundamental. It is like the coordination of our body's movements: out of the complexity of the surrounding environment and the multiple possibilities of the body we must make sense and decide on the right movement. The human body—from eyes to nerves via the brain—has reached such an advanced stage of coordination that these movements are often "automatic," "unconscious" or "instinctive." Someday humanity will reach the same degree of almost instantaneous adaptations, but we are only at the very beginning of that new evolution and learning process. The United Nations has an important part in it.

The framework which I have adopted to classify and store each problem which reaches my desk consists of the following three categories:

- the physical, non-human cosmos;
- the human, social cosmos;
- the personal, individual cosmos.

The physical, non-human cosmos

I include in that cosmos not only the entire physical world but also all other life forms except humans. In other words, we are human beings, members of a well-defined species with its definite characteristics which lives in the particular circumstances and environment of a given planet. Our first knowledge, our first great adventure in evolution, has to do with this outside world, the surroundings, the totality of our planetary conditions and our relations with the sun. We must know our house, our dwelling, our place of abode in the universe and what it has to offer, favorable or detrimental to human life. On that score, the human race has made prodigious progress over its history and more particularly during the last thirty years. Humanity has extended its knowledge of the far reaches of the universe hundreds of times during the last decades and it has penetrated ever deeper into the infinitely small, the atom, the cell, the genes. At each level, at each layer of this prodigious spatial distribution of the physical universe, scientists, technologists, thinkers and researchers are working relentlessly to extend our knowledge and further uncover "reality."

The totality of our current knowledge culminates in the United Nations and in its specialized agencies where governments thus obtain a planetary view of the human environment. As a result, we are beginning to have a pretty comprehensive grasp of our relationships and place on our planet, of the planet itself, and of its place, structure, and functioning in relation to the sun and to the universe.

I am sometimes tempted to draw an enormous table on one of the walls of my office, presenting in a vertical form the layers of our prodigious knowledge from the infinitely large to the infinitely small and showing for each layer how humans are cooperating in their world organizations, where they draw a synthesis and conclusions from all we know. The table would reach from astrophysics and interplanetary science to solar science and outer space, the earth's atmosphere and its layers, the biosphere, the seas and oceans, the continents, the earth's surface and soils, the climate, the world's waters, energy, the earth's crust (minerals, underground water, heat, oil, etc.), the bottoms of the seas, other living species, the microbial, genetic and planktonic world, the infinitely small realm of the atom, its particles and subparticles, etc. Practically nothing has been left out by humans in their search for total comprehension and possible mastery of the surrounding world. A complete Copernican tapestry is thus emerging for which humanity deserves a high mark among the civilizations in the universe. We have taken stock on an all-planetary scale of this total knowledge in a series of remarkable world conferences held during recent years: on outer space, science and technology, the world's seas and oceans, the environment, water, food and deserts, to mention only those which were concerned with our physical environment. They were the first world conferences ever held on this planet. The fact that all nations on earth were able to cooperate in these tremendous ventures augurs well for our future civilization. They mark the beginning of a science of planetary management which has become all the more necessary now that our actions are able to change the earth so profoundly.

The Human or Social Cosmos

We have also accomplished progress with regard to the human or social cosmos. All the people on earth constitute together an entity, a family, a society. Regarding the quantitative aspects of that society, we have made considerable progress: we had a world population conference; we know how many we are; we know where we live; we know how long we live; and we have projections of the future for the next hundred years. The UN's work on demography is another signal achievement of the new global institutions.

The UN has surveyed every possible quantifiable aspect of humanity: sexes, races, children, youth, old age, the number of malnourished, the handicapped, standards of living, nutrition, literacy, longevity, etc. In many instances, world conferences and international years have been used to arouse the people's awareness: the UN World Population Conference, the two World Women's Conferences, the World Youth Conference, the World Racism Conferences, the World Assembly on Aging, various economic and social conferences, a World Employment Conference, the International Year of the Child, the International Year of Disabled Persons, etc.

Much less progress has been achieved on the qualitative aspects of the human family. We do not even possess the rudiments of a comprehensive physiology, sociology, psychology or philosophy for the human race as a whole.

Even more troublesome is the fact that little attention has been paid to the reasons why humans associate, assert a group, fight for it, glorify it, place it above other groups, including humanity, seek advantages, belittle and denigrate others. The total cosmos of these social groups is so complex that it seems almost unmanageable. People coalesce in a race, a nation, a language, a religion, a culture, a region, a continent, an alliance, an ideology, a company, a profession and they behave as if that group were the most important one on earth. We have at this moment a multitude of groups founded on old as well as new beliefs, interests and common characteristics. Many of them think that they hold the ultimate truth, that others are wrong and that the rest of the world should accept *their* truth, way of life and beliefs. The sociology of this cosmos has barely retained humanity's attention. I will return to this when trying to determine how "right human relations" can be established and what progress is being made.

The Personal or Individual Cosmos

Finally, the last cosmos which is of importance to you and to me is the personal or individual cosmos, that miracle of temporary consciousness, matter, energy, spirit, mind and heart, linked with the rest of the world and the heavens, but also self-contained, autonomous and well defined, as are all other cosmoses from the infinitely large to the infinitely small.

Regarding the physical aspects of individual life, humanity has made enormous progress. Our material life has improved immensely: food, health, shelter, security, mobility are available to more humans than at any previous period of evolution. Our lives are longer than ever before. Of course, this progress has not yet reached equally all regions of the world, but there is constant progress as is evidenced in the UN agencies and forums concerned with the problems of health, food, nutrition, industry and housing. We have made enormous progress in eradicating major diseases and epidemics, in better understanding the nutrition and functioning of the human body, how it can be improved, lengthened and perhaps someday arrive at near perfection. New problems of course also arise as we change the environment. In the affluent countries, the major killers are now brought about by the new environment: cancer, heart diseases and accidents.

In the realm of the mind, each of us knows more today than any king or emperor in the past. For a few dollars we can buy a paperback describing the universe. Never have there been so many literate people on this planet. The fulfillment of the human person from the point of view of knowledge has been prodigious, to the point that the environment again is moving in on us: too many ideas, too many writings, too much news, too many claims of truth, quality and novelty, a saturation of a complexity which bewilders, creates anxiety and unhappiness, and often drives the individual away from his civilization.

There has been considerably less progress on the moral, sentimental and spiritual planes, although some advances are noticeable on fundamental human rights, world solidarity and altruism, as well as a revival of spirituality. But the science and arts of living have lagged considerably behind, neglecting to explore and develop the immense possibilities offered by the human heart and soul. This transcendence is not even discussed in the world forums. The scientific and industrial revolutions have paid little attention to the fundamental questions: "Why am I on earth? How do I relate to the universe, to creation, to the eternal stream of life and time? What are the meaning and purpose of life? What is the sense of it all?" These philosophical and spiritual questions have not yet reached the United Nations as an institution, but they were powerfully incarnated in individuals such as Dag Hammarskjöld and U Thant.

In short, one could say that as a species we have achieved considerable progress in our knowledge and piercing of the surrounding world; that good progress is being made towards the increased fulfillment and flowering of the miracle of individual life, especially in the material and intellectual fields; but that progress is lagging farthest behind in the political and social spheres. For example, while the world abounds with religious, moral, ethical and legal precepts for the behavior and conduct of the individual, there is barely the beginning of similar ethics for the conduct of institutions, including the most powerful of all, namely, armed nations. For a private person to kill another human being is a crime. For a nation to kill wholesale is heroism. Is this situation hopeless? Can we ever emerge from the sea of contradictions and complexities inherited and unlocked by ourselves on our strange little planet twirling in the universe? This is the main challenge of our time and we will need much optimism, vision and determination to keep civilization on its upward path.

A Gigantic Biological Process

For science the future is bright: there remains so much to be uncovered and investigated in innumerable fields. For the human being, progress is needed with regard to interiority, morality and spirituality, and more generally for the achievement of happiness, which is the culmination of the miracle of life. But what can be done with regard to the social cosmos?

In this respect, nobody knows today how the world will look in a hundred years. Existing groups are protecting themselves, among other ways, with frightful arms, and are trying to gain ground over each other in a thousand overt and covert ways. New groups such as the transnational corporations are being born and progressing rapidly. Is this situation hopeless? Will we ever see decent, harmonious, happy, peaceful, orderly, satisfying human relations on this planet? Yes, I think so. Someday it will all work out for the best of the human race, but we do not know when and how, for this gigantic biological process of adaptation has only begun. In this regard we can discern a few basic trends and hopeful signs.

The first and fundamental task is to prevent these groups from slaughtering each other and blowing up our planet and life in the process. This is the most immediate priority. The first thing to do at this juncture of evolution, whenever a conflict is about to break out or whenever power—new or old—is beginning to grow excessively, *is to build bridges*. This is one of the fundamental and historical tasks of the United Nations: constantly to build bridges and to let off steam so that tensions and pressures, be they territorial claims, poverty, injustice, inequality, violation of human rights, etc., are prevented from creating havoc. Thus, each year at the end of three months of General Assembly, statesmen and -women have learned something from each other, they have become a little wiser, they better understand the other side's point of view. There is a little more give and take, and as a result, progressively, we are moving closer towards each other in the consideration and understanding of our common fate on planet Earth.

This is the most important task we must perform for the moment and it is taking place in dozens of world agencies and innumerable meetings on practically every conceivable subject, difference and tension. Once the last conflicts have disappeared, the leaders of nations will discover a completely new world in the making, a new age of which they had no idea but which they themselves helped to prepare in the network of international organizations they created. These are becoming a sort of brain, heart, nervous system and soul for the human species. Yes, the UN's first and paramount task is to build bridges, to help avoid the gigantic and murderous conflagrations which could well erupt during the present Promethean period of change.

Another source of hope for the improvement of human relations is the fact that governments and other large entities are beginning to discover that *they cannot win it all* and that within our biosphere, our planet, our solar system and the universe they are after all not so great and powerful. They are beginning to understand that there are innumerable forces at work in the present stage of evolution and that within the framework of our given reality and resources they cannot pursue very far their dreams of total dominion. I have accompanied the Secretary-General on several state visits. Everywhere, leaders of nations considered the environment to be one of the most important problems of our planet. They were right. They knew that this new preoccupation was moving in on us and that it provided them with opportunities to cooperate and put somewhat aside the old ideologies and values inherited from their predecessors and in which they often no longer believe. Ecumenism is a major phenomenon of our time: it is a new philosophy which helps religions to stop hating and fighting each other in the name of God. It will also help nations to stop slaughtering each other in the name of the goddess National Sovereignty. Thus, planetary understanding of the global conditions of human life on earth is one of our greatest chances. The new conditions will change the political scene and political thinking for ages to come. World cooperation has become a powerful asset, brought about by the deep forces which are at work in the present phase of evolution.

It is vitally necessary to take advantage of the period of physical stability of our planet and of stable energy flows from our sun. The current human quarrels and atomic endangering of our planet are totally incomprehensible if we think of our geophysical and astrophysical luck in the universe. It just cannot be that billions of years of evolution should have had as their sole purpose to see an atomic holocaust put an end to all life on our planet!

If Christ Came Back to Earth

There is another area where considerable progress can be made by the peoples themselves, by the individual as an autonomous free-willed cosmos with a profound influence during his lifetime on his family, community, nation, religion or profession: the emergence and advancement of the notion of the *human family*. In the midst of the deafening claims of so many groups, who speaks for the human family as Christ did two thousand years ago? I admit that all races are important, that all nations are important, that all religions are important, that East, West, North and South are important, but what about *humanity as a whole*? What attention, what priority does that supreme family of all receive in our civilization, in the media, in the schools, in literature, in the arts, in churches, in our homes? As for me, after having lived through a horrible war and an uncertain peace, after having seen my own family torn between two nations, I have decided long ago that the only realities that matter for me are God, planet Earth, humanity, my family and myself. All other groups are in constant change: their borders, their priorities, their power, their allegiances change. But God, the planet, humanity, the natural family and the miracle of individual life are permanent realities in our cosmic presence and adventure. We do not do enough for the human family. Therefore, if you are an anthropologist, I would beg you to help develop a science of total human anthropology and study the new global concerns and institutions of the human race. If you are a psychologist, please help develop a science of world psychology. Why do we have a world youth problem simultaneously in most countries? Why are there world scares? Why do people experience a psychological togetherness in world Olympics? Could we not develop world musical and other art festivals? There are so many beautiful and useful things the world's peoples could do together. There *is* a world psychology, because there is a world public opinion, owing to rapid communications. The same is true of world philosophy, world sociology and world spirituality. Where are the philosophers who have the courage to speak out for the whole human race? If Kant were alive today he would come to the United Nations and rewrite his *Project for Perpetual Peace*. If Christ came back to earth, his first visit would be to the United Nations to see if his dream of human oneness and brotherhood had come true. He would be happy to see representatives of all nations, North and South, East and West, rich and poor, believers and nonbelievers, young and old, Philistines and Samaritans, trying to find answers to the perennial questions of human destiny and fulfillment. But how many disappointments and criticisms would he have? Would he not say that, without seeing ourselves as one family and asking ourselves the fundamental questions of life and of our relations with the Creator and the universe, we will never make it?

A World-wide Bimillennium Celebration of Life

I have observed during my lifetime that it is difficult to hold together any human group for long if there is not a vision, an ideal, an objective, a dream. To bind the human family together, to foster its further ascent, to prevent it from losing ground and falling into the abyss of despair, we must have a constant vision, a dream for the human family. We will not swim forever in the present sea of complexity if we are not shown a shore. Unfortunately when one looks at the curricula of schools and universities, at the media and literature, one does not find any shores. The dreams of peace, of world fraternity and of the United Nations are all too often scoffed at and ignored as childish and hopeless fantasies. Of course, they become hopeless by the mere disbelief of the people. Peace and right human relations are not solely matters for governments and international agencies. They are the concern of every human being. There is an immense power for peace and good in the four and a half billion people of this planet. We each have our sphere of influence. No government can forever remain insensitive to the people's demands. The defense of peace, good human relations and the United Nations rests largely in the hands of the people. Nothing prevents them from joining United Nations associations or citizens' groups for peace. Never should one underestimate the real power of the people and of their dreams, if they really want to be heard. This is why, on the occasion of Earth Day, I proposed that humanity should hold in the year 2000 a world-wide Bimillennium Celebration of Life preceded by unparalleled thinking, perception, inspiration, elevation, planning and love for the achievement of a peaceful, happy and godly human society on earth.[1]

Beyond the Imperialism of Reason

I would like to point out another domain where there is good hope for a further ascent in human relations: *the world of the heart.* During the last three hundred years humanity's progress has been essentially of an intellectual and material nature. The imperialism of reason had little room or respect for sentiment. Scientists and thinkers believed that everything could be solved, explained and furthered by means of pure physical manipulation and intellect. We seem to have come to the end of that belief. How many times do we see in the United Nations that world problems are insoluble because of the excessive intelligence of the antagonists? Piles of arguments mount endlessly on each side with no solution in sight. Usually it takes a great statesman to brush it all aside and to decide that he will see his adversary, sit down with him, forget about all arguments and find a peaceful solution simply because he is determined to find one. In diplomatic and political science courses young people are being taught the intricacies of intellectualism and systematic falsehoods: lies are called "negotiating positions" and the truth is called

[1] See Sister Margaret McGurn, I.H.M., "Global Spirituality, Planetary Consciousness in the thought of Teilhard de Chardin and Robert Muller, with a proposal for a Bimillennium Celebration of Life," World Happiness and Cooperation, Ardsley-on-Hudson, 1979.

a "fallback position." With such immorality we will go nowhere. Freud pointed to the right path in his famous reply to Einstein in 1932, when he said that the instinct of aggression in man could only be counteracted by the development of love or sentiment. Hence his recommendation that ties of sentiment or love for the earth, for all its people and for international institutions be developed. He considered the League of Nations to be an experiment without precedent which would call into play certain idealistic attitudes of mind, an identification with the totality of the group, and in the end might hold the world together. What he said then is even truer today.

Humanity has done marvels in the last few hundred years in developing human senses and comprehension through stupendous scientific and technological inventions. This march of knowledge and intelligence will go on, uncovering a heretofore unknown reality which has existed all around us since the beginning of time. But there is no reason for downgrading the heart and the soul. The miracles of science must be repeated now in the fields of sentiment and interiority. Human beings must again be seen as total beings, able to fulfill themselves and to act with the full capacity of the qualities deposited in us by God and evolution. Once this is done, most problems will fall into place and become soluble. In order to see right, to think right and to act right we must visualize our place in the total universe and in time, as all great prophets, spiritual leaders and philosophers have told us since the beginning. We must absolutely restore the great moral forces of love, compassion, truthfulness, optimism and faith in human destiny which have always been at the root of civilization. They alone will enable us to see the light and the great simplicity of the pattern of evolution foreseen by God amidst the complexities, obscurities and anxieties of the present time.

Learning to Live Together

The greatest avenue to right human relations is *education*. The human family is continuously renewed: every hour about 6,000 people die and 15,000 babies are born. All these newcomers must be educated in the perception and art of living, so as to fulfill the miracle of life they have been given. In this chain, our knowledge and wisdom are transmitted constantly at higher levels. Education starts with the mother and in the home, and is later continued in educational institutions. Babies are born with blank minds and then are "wired in" by education and their social environment. It will become increasingly important, if we wish to establish right human relations, to give the children the right universal education. This is probably the most important problem we face on this planet. Children are "wired in" with slanted values and distorted information about our globe, its people, the human destiny and our place in the universe and in time.

We cannot obtain right human relations if we do not give the children an honest view of the world into which they are born. We must give them a global view of the planet's marvels and conditions, of the human family and its rich diversity, we must give them to understand that they are a cosmos of their own endowed with the miracle of life among innumerable brethren and sisters on our planet. We must tell each child that he is a unique happening in the universe which will never be repeated in exactly the same form. Right human relations require that we tell the children how they should relate to the skies, to the stars, to the sun, to the infinite, to time, to the human family, to their planet and to all their human brethren and sisters. We must tell them that they have only a few years to live and that they must think what will become of them after they die. We must tell them a story which no longer has anything to do with idealism but which reflects common facts derived from the collective efforts of the human family to learn, to understand and to elevate itself.

This will require a real revolution in education, which will happen sooner or later. Education is really the key to our future. Former Secretary-General U Thant, who was a teacher, often said to me: "Robert, we are too old to bring about the necessary changes in the world. Only the younger generation can do it. And, for that, education is the key." This was why he supported so strongly international schools and proposed the creation of a United Nations University, which exists today. He dreamed that one university on this planet would give all other universities the global views, inspiration and curricula needed for a peaceful society and right human relations. There is so much prejudice in ourselves. We have constant allegiances and preferences for groups instead of for the total human family. We make absolutes of what should be only relative. It is programed into us, it is "wired in." But bridges and interconnections are being built. We are learning from each other. We are more peaceful than we ever were. We are making constant progress in human relations. We no longer act towards each other like wild, scared animals.

I am convinced that this process of learning will also extend progressively to nations, human groups and institutions. We are entering one of the most fascinating and challenging eras of human evolution. In order to win this great new battle for civilization we must be able to rely upon a vastly increased number of people with a world view. We need world managers and servers in many fields: in the UN and the budding new world institutions, in government, in churches, in world companies, in transnational professional associations. Even if progress at the level of the child may still be distant, owing to the idiosyncrasies of national education, at least at the university level the time has come to make progress and to establish entirely new global curricula aimed at the needs of the new emerging world society.

On the Right Path

I firmly believe that the human race will succeed someday in establishing right human relations and that such a day may not be quite as distant as we think. I come from the border between two countries, France and Germany. I have seen hatred and horrors which I could not have imagined as a child. If someone had told me that peace would someday bless that region and that France and Germany would become friendly towards each other, I would not have believed it. And yet it happened! What was possible between two archenemies like France and Germany can also be possible for the entire world. Humanity has been able to avoid another world war during one of the most dangerous periods ever in its evolution. When I observe the degree of cooperation that already exists at the UN and in the various world agencies, I can only conclude that we are at long last on the right path and that we will find progressively the proper human relations on this planet.

I would even say more: I firmly believe that humanity will be able to elevate human life to unprecedented levels and achieve a happy society on earth. We have this possibility. We have been given by God and evolution the means, the intelligence, the heart and the soul necessary for that. As distinct from other living species, we have the capacity to raise ourselves to higher levels of fulfillment and consciousness. Therefore, in spite of much foolishness, nonsensical armaments and excessive risks of accidents, which ought to be eliminated as quickly as possible, I would unhesitatingly throw down my gauntlet in favor of the success of the human race. The battle of right human relations which started thousands of years ago on this planet will someday be won, and I think rather soon.

3

A Copernican View of World Cooperation

An event which greatly helped me to understand better our global world was a meeting of the American Association of Systems Analysts held in New York City in the 1970s. The organizers had requested that the United Nations send them a speaker on the subject "Can the United Nations become a functional system of world order?"

I was intrigued by the question. What was meant by "functional system of world order"? Who were these men who called themselves "systems analysts"? What was this new science? I was unable to find a speaker among our UN experts, for we simply did not have any systems analysts. Remembering the severe words of H. G. Wells directed at the League of Nations,[1] I decided to go and speak to the congress myself. I attended the meeting during a weekend, which gave me an opportunity to listen to the other speakers and to get acquainted with them. They were very remarkable people— philosophers, sociologists, biologists, mathematicians—who were trying to devise a new world order from the immensely complex relations which bind everything together on our earth. They were the new scientists of interdependence. I was at a loss, however, as to what I could say to them. Their science was too complex, too math-

[1] "Does this League of Nations contain within it the germ of any permanent federation of human effort? Will it grow into something for which men will be ready to work whole-heartedly and, if necessary, fight—as hitherto they have been willing to fight for their country and their own people? There are few intimations of any such enthusiasm for the League at the present time. The League does not even seem to know how to talk to the common men. It has gone into official buildings and comparatively few people in the world understand or care what it is doing there." Wells, *Outline of History* (London: The Macmillan Company, 1920), Vol. II, Book IX, pp. 583–84.

ematical for me. I did not know the first rudiments of it. To pretend
the contrary would have been foolish. Nevertheless, I had to answer
as well as possible a very simple question. "Does the United Nations
perform functions which contribute to the peace, order, justice, well-
being and happiness of humans on this planet?"

Since the listeners were experts in "systems," the least I could do
was to present the UN's work in a "systematic" way. I tried to conceive the most general framework possible. I visualized therefore our
globe hanging in the universe and saw it first in its relations with
the sun. I viewed it then as an orange cut in half and saw its atmosphere, its crust and its thin layer of life or biosphere. Within the
biosphere, I saw the seas, the oceans, the polar caps, the continents,
the mountains, the rivers, the lakes, the soils, the deserts, the animals, the plants and the humans. Within the crust of the earth I
saw the depths of the oceans, the continental plates, the underground reservoirs of water, oil, minerals and heat. Within the mass
of several billion people, I saw the nations, races, religions, cultures,
languages, cities, industries, farms, professions, corporations, institutions, armies, families, down to that incredible cosmos, the human
being. In the human person, I saw the rich, miraculous system of
body, mind, heart and spirit linked through senses with the heavens
and the earth. I visualized that person from conception to death. I
saw the sixty trillion cells of his body, the infinitely small, the atom,
microbial life, the incredible world of genes, which embody and
transmit the patterns of life. And all along this Copernican path, at
each step, I asked myself the question: "Are humans cooperating on
this subject? Are they trying to understand it, to appraise it, to see it
in relation to everything else and to determine what is good or bad
for humans, what should be changed or not? Was the subject before
the United Nations or one of its agencies? Was the United Nations
'system' dealing with it?" And the answer was usually yes.

Yes, the UN is dealing with the relations between our planet and
its sun: in 1954 UNESCO convened a first colloquium on solar energy; in 1961 the UN convened a world conference on new forms of
energy and produced three volumes on solar energy; in 1973,
UNESCO sponsored an international conference on "The Sun in
the Service of Mankind" which reviewed all relations between our
star and ourselves—energy, food, climate, life and habitat. And in
1981 the UN held a second world conference on new and renewable
sources of energy, including the sun.

Yes, the UN is dealing with outer space: a treaty on outer space was concluded in 1967 and a world conference was held on this new frontier in 1968; outer space has been declared a common heritage of humankind, free of all weapons; objects launched into space are registered with the UN; astronauts are envoys of humanity; damages caused by objects falling from space are regulated by a UN convention; a treaty on the moon and other celestial bodies has been adopted; the International Telecommunication Union allocates frequency bands for satellite telecommunications; the World Meteorological Organization receives world-wide weather and climate data from satellites; the International Maritime Organization has an international satellite which serves all ships and navigators around the world; the Food and Agriculture Organization receives outer space information on weather, crop outlooks, floods and plant epidemics; UNESCO is testing educational systems by means of satellites, and the UN held another outer space conference in 1982.

Yes, the UN is dealing with the gaseous layer surrounding our globe, the atmosphere with its components, the troposphere, stratosphere and ionosphere. Under the auspices of the World Meteorological Organization, governments are cooperating in a Global Atmospheric Research Program. The United Nations Environment Program (UNEP) is keeping a check on the state and the quality of the atmosphere and the ionosphere. It convened in 1978 a world conference on the ozonosphere. The International Civil Aviation Organization is dealing with air safety, international air traffic and a legal order for world air transport.

Yes, the UN is concerned with our globe's climate, including the possible recurrence of ice ages: the World Meteorological Organization held a first world climate conference in 1979.

Yes, the UN is concerned with the total biosphere through project Earthwatch, the Global Environment Program of UNEP and UNESCO's program, "Man and the Biosphere."

Yes, the UN is dealing with our planet's seas and oceans through the Law of the Sea Conference, UNESCO's Intergovernmental Oceanographic Commission, FAO's work on world fisheries, IMCO's concern with maritime transport, UNEP's work and treaties on the sea environment, etc.

Yes, the UN is dealing with the world's deserts through FAO, UNESCO and UNEP. A world conference on desertification was held in 1977.

Yes, the UN is dealing with the world's water resources and cycles: UNESCO has a World Hydrological Decade, the UN held a world water conference in 1978 and established a map of our globe's underground water resources.

Yes, the UN is dealing with the continental plates, international rivers, underdeveloped nations, the cultures, races, religions, languages, cities, infants, adolescents, women, malnourished, workers, farmers, professionals, corporations and almost any other conceivable group or global problem of this planet.

Yes, the UN is dealing with the human person, that alpha and omega of our efforts, the basic unit of all this gigantic Copernican tapestry. The person's basic rights, justice, health, progress and peace are being dealt with from the fetus to the time of death.

Yes, the UN is dealing with the atom in the International Atomic Energy Agency, and with microbiology and genetics in UNESCO, the World Health Organization and FAO.

Yes, the UN is dealing with art, folklore, nature, the preservation of species, germ banks, labor, handicrafts, literature, industry, trade, tourism, energy, finance, birth defects, sicknesses, pollution, politics, the prevention of accidents, of war and conflicts, the building of peace, the eradication of armaments, atomic radiation, the settlement of disputes, the development of world-wide cooperation, the aspirations of East and West, North and South, black and white, rich and poor, etc.

I went on like this for more than an hour. When I finished, I still had a bagful to say, but I was exhausted by my exaltation at the vastness of the cooperation I had seen develop over my thirty years of service in the United Nations.[2] It was now very clear to me: there was a pattern in all this; it was a response to a prodigious evolutionary march by the human species towards total consciousness, an attempt by man to become the all-understanding, all-enlightened, all-embracing master of his planet and of his being. Something gigantic was going on, a real turning point in evolution, the beginning of an entirely new era of which international cooperation at the UN was only a first outward reflection. I had not seen it so far, because it had come in a haphazard way, in response to specific events, needs, crises and perceptions by governments and individuals all over the planet. But the result was now clearly here, glorious and beautiful

[2] See Appendix at end of chapter.

like Aphrodite emerging from the sea. This was the beginning of a new age, a gigantic step forward in evolution. It was unprecedented and full of immense hope for humanity's future on this planet. Perhaps after all we would be able to achieve peace and harmony on earth. This time, humankind would be forced to think out absolutely everything and to measure the totality of our planet's conditions and evolution in our solar system and in time. The games of glory, aggrandizement and domination by specific groups would soon come to an end. The great hour of truth had arrived for the human race.

I saw it all coming ever more forcefully, despite the disbeliefs and grins of the cynics. What was the sense of it all? It was simply to achieve peace, justice, order and progress for everybody. And what was behind peace, justice, order and progress? The attainment of happiness and of an unprecedented consciousness and fulfillment of all guests admitted to the miracle of life!

When I finished, there was a long silence in the audience. No one applauded for a while. What I had said was probably too farfetched, too exalted, too beautiful to be true. Or perhaps each listener was absorbed in his own thoughts and perceptions of the incredible human adventure on our fabulous little planet spinning in the universe. At last one of the panel members, a biologist, Edgar Taschdjian, broke the silence and said:

"Friends, I had heard several proposals for world systems during our Congress. Their authors thought that they had embraced the entire world. But I had told you that the most daring of them did not reach the heel of what existed already in the United Nations. I am sure that Mr. Muller would be at a loss to provide us with a complete chart of all the agencies, programs, organs, suborgans, centers, groups, meetings, arrangements and consortia which compose today the United Nations system. Anyway, this system is changing so fast that a static presentation of it would be of little value. Yes, my friends, we are far behind the actual, political world. We must awaken to this fact and raise our sight to the height already attained by the United Nations system. . . ."

I was thinking at high speed during that time: in my Copernican overview I had found several gaps; there was no world-wide cooperation for the globe's cold zones, the mountains, our topsoil, standardization, world safety, prevention, the family, morality, spirituality, world psychology and sociology, the world of the senses, the inner realm of the individual, his needs, values, perceptions, love and happiness. Cooperation was insufficient on consumer protection,[3] on the world's 450 million handicapped, on the world's elderly,[4] on world law, on the ultimate meaning of human life and its objectives. And political men were still dragging their feet in antiquated, obsolete quarrels which prevented them from seeing the vast new universal scheme of evolution which was dawning upon the world.

Or was I dreaming and living in a sphere of fantasy and wishful thinking, like Teilhard de Chardin, H. G. Wells, Albert Schweitzer, Sri Aurobindo, Sri Chinmoy and a growing number of others? They too saw the world from the outside, as it hangs and twirls in the universe, and had visualized the grand journey of humanity towards oneness, convergence and unprecedented happiness. Were they all wrong? Was I wrong too? No. Everything I had learned, lived and observed pragmatically day by day for thirty years in the UN realistically pointed to it. We were approaching Teilhard's point of convergence, Wells's last chapter of *The Outline of History*, Schweitzer's reverence for life, Sri Aurobindo's total consciousness, Sri Chinmoy's world oneness. It was coming as a political reality and much faster than anyone could dare to hope. For the first time in human evolution, it came as a world-wide wave, above and beyond all disciplines and groups, born from our knowledge of the wonders and limits of our planet. And it was only the mere beginning of the apotheosis of human life on earth. Still there was missing a great core of political humanists, thinkers, prophets, poets and leaders of people who would concern themselves with the deeper objectives and reasons of human life, its uniqueness, its miraculous character, our full potentials, our perceptions, sentiments and inner lives. But they would come soon. What a prodigious time we are about to live!

Suddenly an image came to my mind. It was the good person of U Thant. He too had foreseen a serene, enlightened world, a world of peace and understanding enriched by ethics, morality, love, spirituality and philosophy. I remembered the scene at a reception he had offered to the U.S. astronauts after the first moon landing. I was talking in a corner with one of the astronauts. The Secretary-

---

[3] This subject has now been taken up by the Economic and Social Council.
[4] This has been corrected: 1981 has been proclaimed International Year of Disabled Persons, and a world conference on aging was held in 1982.

General came near us and inquired what we were talking about. The astronaut answered:

"Your colleague is asking me what I thought when I saw for the first time the entire earth from outer space."

"Oh, I see!" said U Thant. "I am not surprised by his question. But I am afraid he is not expecting anything new from you. He just wants a confirmation, for he has been living on the moon long before you, looking down on earth with his global eyes, trying to figure out what the human destiny will be."

Vanity of vanities! U Thant was reminding me to take all this with a grain of salt and to return to earth! My Copernican scheme receded for a moment from my mind and there remained only his enigmatic and kind smile, while the systems analysts were pursuing a discussion which became more and more incomprehensible to me. . . .

APPENDIX

The mere list of the eighteen United Nations specialized agencies and fourteen world programs which compose the UN system illustrates the vastness of today's international cooperation. No other living species has ever so equipped itself with global instruments designed to study, observe, monitor and preserve its habitat. In innumerable organs, meetings and conferences, through thousands of experts and delegates, backed by forty thousand world servants, humankind is today probing its entire biosphere and condition, trying to augment peace, to reduce conflicts and tensions, to build bridges and to seek ways for a greater fulfillment of human life to an extent which no philosopher, prophet or social reformer would have ever dreamed possible.

Here is a quick overview of this incipient world system: The eighteen *specialized agencies*: International Atomic Energy Agency (IAEA); International Labor Organization (ILO); Food and Agriculture Organization (FAO); United Nations Educational, Scientific and Cultural Organization (UNESCO); World Health Organization (WHO); International Bank for Reconstruction and Development (IBRD); International Development Association (IDA); International Finance Corporation (IFC); International Monetary Fund (IMF); International Civil Aviation Organization (ICAO); Universal Postal Union (UPU); International Telecommunication Union

(ITU); World Meteorological Organization (WMO); International Maritime Organization (IMO); General Agreement on Tariffs and Trade (GATT); World Intellectual Property Organization (WIPO); International Fund for Agricultural Development (IFAD); World Tourism Organization (WTO), linked with the UN under a novel type of agreement.

The fourteen *special programs:* United Nations Children's Fund (UNICEF); United Nations Conference on Trade and Development (UNCTAD); United Nations Development Program (UNDP); Office of UN Disaster Relief Co-ordinator (UNDRO); United Nations Environment Program (UNEP); United Nations Fund for Drug Abuse Control (UNFDAC); Office of the United Nations High Commissioner for Refugees (UNHCR); United Nations Industrial Development Organization (UNIDO); United Nations Institute for Training and Research (UNITAR); United Nations Fund for Population Activities (UNFPA); United Nations Relief and Works Agency (UNRWA); United Nations University (UNU); United Nations Volunteers (UNV); World Food Program (WFP).

The UN itself is concerned with a multitude of global problems, such as peace, disarmament, outer space, the seas and oceans, natural resources, human rights, racial equality, women, multinational corporations, criminality, etc.

There also exists a first world ministerial council: the World Food Council. Hopefully, similar councils will be established in other crucial fields, energy in particular.

4

Towards a New Spiritual Ideology

It strikes us vividly that the very life and perceptions of the human race are deeply entrenched in our terrestrial environment. We are living beings born, developing and seeking fulfillment in specific planetary conditions: a given atmosphere, a given crust to stand on, a given warmth due to our distance from the sun, a given absorption of the sun's energy by plants and animals. In the entire universe there is probably no other planet offering the same conditions and evolution.

One of the first fundamental elements of that environment which must have struck early humans indelibly is the result of the rotation and orbit of the earth, that is, the succession of day and night, light and darkness, warmth and cold, the change in seasons, the birth and death of nature. Human life on our planet was therefore basically influenced from the beginning by a duality, a constant switch on and off, back and forth, a view of everything from a light or dark side, a mood of optimism or pessimism, hope or despair, life affirmation or fear of death, faith or abandonment.

This dual mechanism "wired into" us by our planet's rotation was reinforced by the life process itself. The learning of life by each newborn individual is indeed a road of trial and error, of finding what is "right" and "wrong," be it in movements, foods, actions, thoughts, beliefs or sentiments. The history of our civilization is the sum total of this learning process by peoples all over the planet, through trials and errors, transmitted from generation to generation in oral and recorded ways. What was found to be good for human life was retained and what was bad was rejected. Since humans were scattered over the earth and were living in different natural environments without much communication with each other, different cultures and civilizations developed which have both common and distinctive characteristics: we all eat, drink, talk, love, create and believe; but we eat a vast variety of foods, use five thousand languages, have many different forms of art and believe in many different faiths and social systems.

One of the most fundamental events of our own time is the convergence of all these life experiences and civilizations and the extraction therefrom of common denominators of what is good or bad for the entire human race. It is the great question of unity in diversity, complicated by the natural tendency of each group, culture, language, way of life, religion and social system to believe that it is the best in the world and that others would be well advised to follow it. Some of them might be very aggressive and expansionist, while others are simply on the defensive in order to survive and escape destruction. This is what causes the immense complexity of today's political, social, religious and cultural scene. Humanity is torn between diverse identities on the one hand and strong currents towards greater unity on the other, and we are only at the beginning of finding out what is "good" or "bad" for humankind as a whole.

There is another reason why the problem of good or bad is so complicated today. During the past few hundred years, and especially since the last world war, we have extended tremendously our physical and mental awareness of our planet by means of science and technology. As a result, we have uncovered an immensely complex reality, which always existed around us but most of which had remained hidden to our senses. Hence the bewildering number of new problems unlocked by our own discoveries and physical transformations of the planet. For example, are the thousands of new chemicals invented and produced every year good or bad for the intake of our bodies? Are new ideas, beliefs, writings, media, communications and advertising good or bad for the intake of our minds? Are faster methods of transportation good or bad? And so forth. We have steadfastly believed for centuries in new discoveries, in changing our conditions, in new industries and economic development, and suddenly there appear serious question marks: should we continue to change our planet at all? If we change it at the present rate, what will it look like and how will human life fare in a future which astrophysicists estimate to be between six and eight billion years?

So, while there is immense progress at the present time in extending human knowledge and mastery in every conceivable direction, there are also vast interrogations, accompanied by deep anxiety. What must we do under these circumstances? First and foremost we must emerge successfully from the shock of the bewildering complexities engendered by scientific discovery and growing human activity: we must put order in our knowledge and derive therefrom a correct image of our place in the universe and in time. As on the eve of the French Revolution, we need a right encyclopedia. Secondly, we must now deliberately take full cognizance of our given planetary environment and realize that we are living in one self-contained, interdependent, highly complex and fragile planetary system. Thirdly, we must outgrow the increasingly erroneous notion of good and bad as seen by a particular group, be it a race, a nation, a faith, an ideology or a business, and define new concepts of what is good or bad for the entire human family. This is absolutely essential. The recent discovery of the interdependent wholeness of our planet must be accompanied by the recognition of the interdependent wholeness of humanity.

For the first time in history, the question of the survival of the entire human family, rather than that of any particular nation or group, has been squarely posed. Many scientists who deal with the long run do not give us much chance of survival. Some do not think that the human species will survive for another ten thousand years, a mere speck in time. They believe that human intelligence, which was a compensation for our species' lack of physical strength, will now lead to our self-destruction. Others, on the contrary, believe that humanity is undergoing a deep evolutionary change and will develop new means and perceptions which will help it survive and find a harmonious relation with its planet and with its own individuals. Having seen the birth of several world-wide organs of diagnosis, monitoring, warning and collective action in the United Nations, I place myself unhesitatingly in that second group.

Finally, in the prodigious process which lies ahead of us, we must restore optimism and continue to sharpen our inborn instincts for life, for the positive, for self-preservation, for survival and human fulfillment at ever higher levels of consciousness. We must conquer the duality, the somber, the bad, the negative, the suicidal. These all contain dangerous self-feeding processes of destruction. We must turn instead to the mysterious self-generating powers of hope, creative thinking, love, life affirmation and faith as they were taught to us by Christ and by all great religious leaders.

The cosmos of the human family is not very different from the individual human person. Each of us is an immensely complex unit, and within each of us every little cell is an immensely complex cosmos of its own. The trillions of cells and many automatic processes of our being are held together and made to function harmoniously through the guiding principle of life itself: if we are optimistic, positive, hopeful, happy to be alive, all is well—the myriads of little factories will all work together in harmony, spurned by higher, elevating forces. If, on the contrary, we give up, let go, despair, then sickness, malfunctioning and often death will occur. It cannot be otherwise. In all living beings there must be foremost a will for life. The greatest freedom of the human being is his choice to believe in life and in himself and thus to be fully part of the eternal stream of creation and evolution. We do not always pay sufficient attention to this fundamental two-way mechanism in the human person and in social bodies, this "night and day" complex inherent in our planetary conditions.

It is the fundamental task of education to teach all new members of the human family to give optimistic guidance to their miraculous bodies, minds, hearts and souls in the complexity of our stupendous reality. Such self-awakening must take place within a peaceful, total human society also guided by belief in our miraculous, luminous journey on an incredible planet in the unfathomable universe. All major religions have understood that when they speak of the "miracle of faith."

It is not the first time that humans have been confronted with a bewildering complexity. For primitive man the surrounding awesome and hostile world—the sky, the stars, the sun, lightning, thunder and winter—was at least as frightening as the complexities of today. The human eye receives at every moment more than one hundred million bits of information and yet the optical ganglia, the brain and the heart reduce this baffling complexity to simple notions and objects, to feelings of bad or good, useful or harmful, ugly or beautiful. Humans will always find new simple means and syntheses to help them surmount any conceivable complexity, including the current one. The most urgent need today is to restore the magic powers of love, confidence and belief in the further ascent and perfectibility of humankind.

For the first time in evolution, the human species has assumed a collective responsibility for the success of planet Earth in the universe. Interdependence, globality and a total view of our planet and the environment are now facts of life. But much more is needed: we humans are also entrenched in a universal environment, the cosmos, the total creation and flow of time. We must feel part of all space and time, of the greatness and wonders of the universe. You know and love your home, don't you? Well, you must also know and love your planetary home as well as your universal home, from the infinitely large to the infinitely small. We must stand in awe before the beauty and miracle of creation. Perhaps this will be the new spiritual ideology which will bind the human race. We must lift again our spirits and hearts into the infinite bliss and mystery of the universe. We are too heavy, too earthbound. We must elevate ourselves again as light, cosmic beings in deep communion with the universe and eternity. We must re-establish the unity of our planet and of our beings with the universe and divinity. We must have our roots in the earth and our hearts in heaven. We must see our planet and ourselves as cells of a universe which is becoming increasingly conscious of itself in us. That is our royal road out of the present bewilderment.

5

A Cosmic-Spiritual View

I have been privileged to work for the United Nations almost since its beginning. As I saw the world organization grow and change over the years, I often wondered what the ultimate destination, the end of the journey, would be. Since its birth the United Nations has grown tremendously in scope and in complexity. It encompasses today virtually all nations, thus fulfilling the dream for human universality of many enlightened philosophers, prophets and thinkers. It has branched out into a variety of specialized agencies and world programs concerned with almost every conceivable facet of our planet and of humanity. The process never ends.

I try very hard to understand what this all means in the total stream of time. Are we carried forward, half knowingly, half instinctively, by the will of God or of other forces towards some ultimate objective? What is that objective? What will the image of the world and of its organization be in a hundred, in a thousand years? In my particular function, whence I can see the totality of the world's problems, I could easily drown in an ocean of complexity and despair if I did not detect a logic, a necessity, a sense, an order in all that is happening. Humans were always faced with a very complex reality: our planet is the most complex one in our solar system and we are the most complex species on it. How could our marriage therefore be anything but complex? For our cave-inhabiting forefathers, nature and life were at least as mysterious and complex as they are for us today, but certain great simplifying means were given to us in order to survive and thrive in the maze. The heroic, astounding notions of God, love, peace, beauty, good, happiness and faith came to our rescue and helped us believe and enjoy the great gift of life on our miraculous planet in the immense, mysterious universe.

Today, the known, uncovered reality is a billion times more complex than it was for our forebears. We know so much more about the universe, the infinitely large and outer space, and we have penetrated ever deeper into the infinitely small, the atom and its particles. For example, scientists are wondering these days how nature is able to "package" into a few microns genetic codes, the formulas of which are several feet long! Complete universes and living factories of immense complexity are unceasingly created by nature within astoundingly small spaces. The totality of scientific knowledge is today so minute, so vast and so staggering that many people give up the effort to understand. All this knowledge culminates in the United Nations, nowadays the most complex organization on earth.

And this is far from all: in addition to scientific complexity, we are also the receptacle of all social, man-made and cultural complexities: problems between the North and the South, the East and the West, the rich and the poor, regions, races, sexes, nations, occupations, languages, institutions, firms, etc. No wonder then that the UN has become the social laboratory of our earth, the vastest anthropological institute and political crucible there ever was. It has come to a point where it is well-nigh impossible to draw a complete accurate chart of the whole United Nations system and of its innumerable organs. Strangely enough, such a chart would begin to look like a brain—the brain of the human species.

There must be a sense in all this, a clarity, a heart, a bloodstream, a great human aspiration and creative motion. It is not by accident that all this is happening. There must be a law, a will, a structure in it. It is part of destiny, of our perennial forward march towards fuller, happier and godlier lives for all. It is part of our progressive settling down in our planetary home in the universe. It is part of the fulfillment of increasingly apparent cosmic laws.

I tried to find a scheme, an outline, a table of contents for this fabulous human saga which had to fit in one way or another into my mind.

First, I adopted a classification of all our knowledge from the infinitely large to the infinitely small as it had revealed itself to me during my work at the United Nations: the universe, astrophysics, the solar system, the earth's relations with our sun, outer space, the atmosphere, the biosphere, the continents, the seas and oceans, the mountains, the rivers, the poles, the tropics and equator, the deserts, the earth's crust, the fauna, the flora, the underground sources of water, heat and minerals, down to the microbial world, the genes and the atom. To that cosmic picture of the physical world I added the view of our social cosmos with its innumerable groups, institutions and associations down to the natural family and the individual. For each of these layers of the total physical and human reality I had observed a form of international cooperation somewhere in the United Nations. World cooperation suddenly appeared to me as a prodigious, all-embracing global effort at understanding total reality! What was happening was indeed a progressive falling into place of all scattered, dispersed, uncoordinated human knowledge and efforts all over the planet and over eons of time! As a matter of fact, it is from the United Nations' living world cooperation that my thirst for logic and light was able to discern the cosmic scheme of realities which now presses itself more and more clearly upon us. This was the first facet of the United Nations' cosmic vision.

I had also noticed that humanity was moving increasingly and simultaneously towards a better understanding of our place in time. More and more I saw the United Nations and its agencies concerned with the past: preservation of our elements, of our natural and cultural heritage, of endangered fauna and flora, of genetic material, of antiquities, great landmarks, languages, legends, customs, traditions. Our planet's past evolution and history became ever more precious, as if the human species knew that some losses might impoverish it forever. Simultaneously our concern with the future increased tremendously: there is not a single United Nations agency or program today that does not have at least the year 2000 as its yardstick.

From the infinitely large to the infinitely small, and from the distant past to the unfathomable future, these are the two poles of infinites along which human progress unfolds right under our eyes! It all makes good sense. At our point of evolution, after having groped, tried, erred and learned so much, it is normal that our knowledge should suddenly accelerate and fall into perfect space and time dimensions which always existed and are now becoming increasingly clear to us.

Of course, this mushrooming of knowledge into the four infinites happens to be one of the main causes of our current anxiety. How can we make sense of it? Whom should we believe? What is relevant and useful in all this knowledge? What will our future be? How should we behave? What does life mean in such a universe? What is in it for the individual?

It was U Thant who gave me the key to it. As a Buddhist he believed that humans would never be able to comprehend the total creation and would forever be condemned to live in mystery and "darkness." But he placed the human person at the center of all pre-occupations, the ultimate question being the proper relation between the individual and the surrounding world and universe. Starting, consequently, from the individual, he persistently used and never retreated from a classification of basic human characteristics and needs into physical, intellectual, moral and spiritual. What I had observed at the United Nations bore him out and again made good sense: the paramount importance attached to individual human rights, better nourishment, health, shelter, education, peace, non-violence, compassion, help, cooperation, the many programs in these fields—all this was the story of the physical, mental and moral fulfillment of individual human life. And this effort was now world-wide, with priority attached to the largest discrepancies and most crying injustices. The Universal Declaration of Human Rights was a new magnificent consecration of the individual, and the United Nations Charter was a first code of behavior for nations.

But there was an element missing and it happened to be the one to which U Thant attached the greatest importance: spirituality. He kept repeating that this was the highest and ultimate fulfillment of the human person. How did he define spirituality? For him it was the harmony between the innermost life and the outer life, or the life of the world and the universe. It was a serene comprehension of life in time and in space, the tuning of the inner person with the great mysteries and secrets around him. It was a belief in the goodness of life and the possibility for each human person to con-tribute his goodness to it. It was the belief in life as part of the eter-nal stream of time, that each of us came from somewhere and was destined to somewhere, that without such belief there could be no prayer, no meditation, no peace, no happiness. His belief in the long-term improvement of humanity through right individual behav-ior gave me the last missing piece of the puzzle. Now the universe, our earth and the individual's place in time and in space made sense. What lessons I had received from the United Nations!

Of course I could not fail to notice that this outcome resembled strangely the visions of all great religions. Even without knowing that the world was round, the great prophets and founders of religions had visions which reached from the infinitely small to the infinitely large and from creation to the apocalypse. The Hindu view of the world and trinity, for example, is fully borne out today by the findings of astrophysicists regarding the birth, the stability and the death of a star or solar system. Each religion again saw the fundamental place of the individual human person in the total reality and considered him as a miraculous entity of divine origin, made of physical, mental, moral and spiritual aspirations. Human fulfillment was never limited to purely material and mental progress as it is so often today. Life was to be also a moral achievement and above all a spiritual transcendence. Religions never shied away from the ultimate, fundamental questions: What is life? Why am I on this earth? What is this strange miracle? What is the sense and purpose of it all? What exactly was I given when I was born and admitted to being, to existing? For what and to whom must I be grateful? What should I do, think, feel and hope for? What does my short-lived but so magnificent spark of consciousness mean in the universe?

Spirituality starts with these questions. This is why U Thant gave it the highest value: it represented in his eyes the deepest questions. The answers, of course, have varied greatly during human history: thousands of religions, (with or without God or gods, e.g., Buddhism, Jainism and Sikhism), philosophies and spiritual practices have offered humans their manifold insights and beliefs. Most of them thought that they had the ultimate, total truth or universal principle, and they were all too often prone to fight each other to assert their belief.

So we find that the United Nations is repeating the same old, all-encompassing story. It is forced to it by the nature of things. Year after year, governments increase the scope of the United Nations' work and improve through it their perception of the total reality. This is one of the most prodigious and amazing stories the earth has ever seen. Alas, it is understood by only a very few. But there are two fundamental differences with the past: first, the UN and every nation must integrate the achievements of science and technology within a broader moral and spiritual dimension; and second, while most religions were born in localized, different regions and cultures, this time the story comes from a center, from the place of convergence of all human problems, dreams, aspirations and exertions. The United Nations is the school where they all learn from each other, listen to each other, try to find solutions and define what is good and bad for the whole human race. It is the place of a thousand bridges, the cradle of future world destiny, a lighthouse from which one global signal after the other is emitted to humans all over the globe. It is the birthplace of unique world efforts which help humanity to know itself better and guide its behavior in our planetary home. As Martin Luther King said, "The UN is a gesture in the direction of non-violence on a world scale."

But the religions and the prophets, the poets and the artists did not need a United Nations, a world organization, conferences or experts to help them discover the truth. They saw it straight with their hearts, with an internal vision, with an instinct that went right to the core without getting lost in the convolutions of the mind. They all gave us generally correct codes of conduct, codes of internal serenity, codes of happiness, codes for the highest fulfillment of the miracle of life.

This is why we must listen attentively with all our minds, hearts and souls to what the great religions and spiritual leaders have to say. They have a long experience of human life and often their perceptions are still the quickest and most accurate. This is why we must also be grateful to anyone who gives the work of the United Nations a spiritual interpretation, thus following the examples of Dag Hammarskjöld and U Thant, who saw in the United Nations the renewed story of the total dimension of human life. Their message was one of love, compassion, understanding and human fraternity. That message, after many vicissitudes throughout world history, is re-emerging as forcefully as ever, but now on a universal scale. It is a fascinating story and we are probably the first species ever able to comprehend it. I have always been an optimist, deeply in love with humanity, precisely because of its capacity to elevate and transcend itself into constantly higher levels of physical, intellectual, moral and spiritual fulfillment. The march towards that transcendence has now started on a planetary scale, and we are privileged to be among its first witnesses and workers. We must cater to it, nurture it, love it, help it grow in beauty and in strength, so as to fulfill the prophecies of all great spiritual leaders. In particular I would agree with the prophecy of that spiritual believer in the United Nations, Sri Chinmoy, when he said:

"At the end of its voyage, there is every possibility that the United Nations will be the last word in human perfection. And then the United Nations can easily bloom in excellence and stand as the pinnacle of divine enlightenment."[1]

[1] Sri Chinmoy, "The Inner Message of the United Nations," Dag Hammarskjöld Lecture Series, January 1973.

6

Prayer and Meditation at the United Nations

Prayer, meditation and spirituality at the UN are fascinating subjects. All major world religions are accredited to the United Nations as non-governmental organizations. For example, no less than twenty-four Catholic organizations are represented at the UN. Several of the world's religious leaders have visited the international organization. Most memorable were the visits of His Holiness Pope Paul VI during the General Assembly in 1965 and of Pope John Paul II in 1979. Many religions have special invocations, prayers, hymns and services for the United Nations. The most important examples are those of the Catholic, the Unitarian-Universalist, the Baptist and the Bahai faiths. It is a common practice of the Unitarian-Universalists to display the United Nations flag in their houses of worship. So does the Holy Family Church, the parish church of the UN, with its international reliquary and its many religious services and activities catering to world peace and to the international community.

When it comes to the United Nations proper, one can obviously not say that it is a spiritual organization. How could it be otherwise? For the UN is the creation and mirror of governments, most of whom have "secularized" themselves, i.e., separated spirituality from their daily lives and preoccupations. Nevertheless, prayer and spirituality play an important role in the United Nations. It is a moving experience, for example, to witness the minute of silence for prayer or meditation at the opening of the yearly General Assembly, when men and women from all nations center their minds and souls on the job to be done and when at the end of the Assembly a similar minute of silence permits them to reflect on their achievements and failures.[1] Thus, the world's first universal gatherings of nations are placed under the symbol of prayer or meditation. Also, there are many delegates and world servants whose cultures do not make any distinction between spirituality and public service. Then there are those who are deeply attached to their faiths or for whom the United Nations is a new form of spirituality and ethics, while they remain faithful to their respective religions. Some delegates are known to meditate in a place of worship before speaking in a UN assembly. One of the greatest orators ever at the United Nations, Professor Belaunde from Peru, meditated on his speeches in St. Patrick Cathedral. Then we have the UN Meditation Room, which is visited by hundreds of thousands of visitors each year.[2] We have also a UN Meditation Group led by an Indian mystic. One could tell several moving stories of the spiritual transformation the UN has caused, to the point that this little speck on earth is becoming a holy ground. For example, the rational, intellectual economist Dag Hammarskjöld found God at the United Nations and inspiration for his work as a world servant in the mystics of the Middle Ages. Towards the end, his *Markings* overflow with spirituality and mysticism.

Then there was U Thant, the man from the Orient, who saw no difference between life and religion, who held that spirituality was the highest of all human needs and virtues. The Western distinction between secular and spiritual lives was totally incomprehensible to him. He found in such cleavage one of the principal causes of the world's conflicts, tensions, injustices and disarray. For him, every single moment of life called for prayer, virtue, reverence, gratitude and total communion with humankind and the universe. He was of Buddhist faith, a religion which does not believe in God, and yet he was one of the most spiritual persons I have ever known.

There are many also in the United Nations for whom the cooperation of all nations towards common goals and values is a kind of

[1] Rule 62 of the *Rules of Procedure of the General Assembly* provides: "Immediately after the opening of the first plenary meeting and immediately preceding the closing of the final plenary meeting of each session of the General Assembly, the President shall invite the representatives to observe one minute of silence dedicated to prayer or meditation."

[2] It is symbolic that the new Secretary-General, Mr. Javier Perez de Cuellar, on the first day of his term in January, 1982, visited the UN Meditation Room before proceeding to his office.

new religion, a supreme path or way. They see in the UN the same perennial human dream which has obsessed all great religions and philosophies, namely, the establishment of a peaceful, just, happy, harmonious world society. But there is one difference: while in the past all religions and philosophies were born within specific local, cultural contexts, today we are witnessing the birth of a new philosophy, ideology or ethics which originates from a central place of synthesis where all dreams, aspirations, claims and values of humankind converge. This is new. It constitutes one of the greatest and most exciting attempts at total human fulfillment in the entire evolution of the human race. There has never been anything like it. It is a magnificent story, the beginning of a profound world-wide transformation and transcendence of the human society, a new paradigm of the coming age. True enough, it is as yet a fragile and incomplete story, for the UN largely reflects the priorities and dominant values of our time. For the poorer countries these are food, health, shelter and education, without which there can be no decent life. First one must live, then one can philosophize. In the Western countries too, material, scientific, technological and intellectual achievements generally still occupy the highest priority. They live in an age of rationalism which believes that everything can be explained by scientific, rational means, and this is reflected in the United Nations. But increasingly there are voices which point to other values. U Thant, in particular, was the first great prophet who reminded us of the moral and spiritual dimensions of life and who firmly advocated the development of our moral and spiritual values in order to catch up with rapid technological and scientific advances. For him, the solution of many of our individual, national and international problems rested in the practice of truthfulness, integrity, tolerance, love and brotherhood. And beyond these moral virtues he felt that each individual carried in himself a fundamental question regarding our relationship with the universe and eternity. Hence the paramount place he accorded to spirituality. In his memoirs he wanted to show how spirituality and philosophy should lead, inspire and guide politics.

This point has not yet been reached in the United Nations, but year after year one can observe how moral and ethical issues are being brought to the world organization. A host of codes of ethics and conduct are being elaborated at the UN. The Charter itself is one of the boldest codes of ethics ever drafted for the behavior of very powerful institutions: armed nations. Although its rules are all too often broken by its members, it nurtures progressively a better behavior, a greater understanding and an improved general moral political atmosphere. Our scientific and industrial age has yielded incredible progress to the human race and we should be immensely grateful for it. But this success perhaps led us to believe that material achievement and intelligence were the apex of civilization. There no longer seemed to be any need for ethics, purity, morality, compassion, love and spirituality. This unnecessary poverty of our age is now being increasingly recognized. Humanity needs also to probe the immense possibilities of its heart and of its soul. This is the great new challenge which has been raised very forcefully by a younger generation tired of war, hatred, hypocrisy and injustices.

I have a Christ in my office. My colleague next door has a statue of Shiva. U Thant had a Buddha in his room. Each of us, be he from North or from South, from East or from West, has his own way of expressing faith in the human race and destiny. When a conflict breaks out any place on the globe, we are all in agreement that it must be stopped, that people cannot be allowed to kill each other, that life must be revered everywhere, that the human person is the supreme care of all our efforts. So, despite its imperfections, the UN is becoming one of the greatest and most beautiful sagas of modern times. King Paul of Greece saw it as a "cathedral where we can worship what is best in each other." Pope John Paul II said that we were the stonecutters and artisans of a cathedral which we might never see in its finished beauty. I would not have dreamed that when I joined the United Nations a third of a century ago. The scope of the UN has widened in every direction, owing to the imperatives of a new global, interdependent world. But people do not really know how vast and vital its activities are. The tapestry of its work encompasses the total condition of humankind on this planet. All this is part of one of the most prodigious pages of evolution. It will require the detachment and objectivity of future historians to appraise fully what happened in the last third of our century and to understand what the real significance of the United Nations was.

Meditation, prayer, dream, hope, vision, faith, guidance, foresight and planning all go hand in hand in so many ways. The tall Secretariat building of the UN is an edifice of human hope and dream jutting into the universe and receiving from that universe increasingly clearer messages. Perhaps the time has come when we will understand the full significance of our cosmic evolution. Year round people from all creeds and cultures gather at the UN to design a better future for the world. And they will succeed. Our children will know a better future, a more peaceful world, an unprecedented fulfillment of individual human life and consciousness.

Little by little, a planetary prayer book is thus being composed by an increasingly united humanity seeking its oneness, its happiness, its consciousness, its peace, its justice and its full participation in the continuous process of creation and miracle of life. Once again, but this time on a universal scale, humankind is seeking no less than its reunion with the "divine," its transcendence into ever higher forms of life. Hindus call our earth Brahma, or God, for they rightly see no difference between our earth and the divine. This ancient simple truth is slowly dawning again upon humanity. Its full flowering will be the real, great new story of humanity, as we are about to enter our cosmic age and to become what we were always meant to be: the planet of God.

7

The Four Cries of Humanity

U Thant was a great man because he was able to distill from the immense complexity of the surrounding world and from his observations of life a vision, a few basic, deeply felt principles. These were always the same: that every human being had physical, mental, moral and spiritual qualities and needs. He established a hierarchy among them, for in his view the final objective of human evolution was spiritual fulfillment. This inspired his entire life and work.

I knew U Thant well and I have read assiduously much of what he has said and written. And everywhere I can find the expression of the influence of this simple but so fundamental classification of human attributes and needs. Therein lie the fourfold cries of humanity or basic stages of evolution: for optimum physical life, mental life, moral life and spiritual life.

The Cry for Physical Life

U Thant was very outspoken when he expressed his belief in the sanctity of life, non-violence and the non-harming of human beings. For example, in a speech on education in 1967, he said:

"I have been trained all my life to regard human life as sacred. I abhor violence and violent death. I do not particularly worry much about my own life, but I do worry a great deal about the children of today. How they should be taught, how they should be brought up, what kind of life they should live and what values they should cherish. I do not particularly distinguish between the lives of my own children and the lives of the children of other people. Nor do I distinguish between Burmese lives and American lives and Russian lives and Chinese lives. It is life itself that is threatened."

U Thant always took an unequivocal stand for the sovereignty of life. He condemned war and violence in all their forms. His speeches abound in beautiful statements on non-violence and on the universal law of love, reverence and respect for all living beings. He was against war, against nuclear weapons and all armaments, against poverty and all human suffering. He never hesitated one moment to express his full commitment to life and non-violence, often to the great annoyance of the powerful, armed and wealthy.

The Cry for Mental Fulfillment

U Thant was a teacher. Although he usually didn't resort to such extreme language, he began the above speech as follows: "I am going to speak with a feeling of trepidation because I am going to speak about something which is very close to my heart: education." What he saw foremost in education was the fulfillment of the human mind. There can be no conscious life if a human being does not receive a proper education. Otherwise, how can he understand and enjoy the beauty of life? He pleaded constantly for the education of the children of the poor and for the work of UNESCO. But for him education was even more: it was a preparation for life as a member of a universal, human family. Therefrom arose his great love and support for the international schools and his proposal for a United Nations University. He believed that only through proper education would we be able to build the world of peace and kindness humanity has always dreamed of. It was one of his staunchest beliefs.

The Cry for Morality

Here U Thant had a long list of cravings: e.g., his wish for truthfulness between nations. He wanted nations to be true to each other, not to lie, not to exaggerate, not to cheat, not to start from those falsehoods called "bargaining positions" which so often mar international diplomacy.

He craved for understanding between nations, non-violence, generosity, live and let live. He believed in the magic of love and compassion in international relations. All this is reflected in his statements on apartheid, racism, colonialism, violations of human rights and whatever else is reprehensible on this planet. He was not just repeating the political slogans of the day, he was speaking from a sound, all-out commitment to human life. U Thant's great strength, the alpha and omega of all his action and thinking, were the supremacy and centrality of the human person. In his farewell speech to Planetary Citizens on December 17, 1971, he said:

"What was my basic approach to all problems? What was the 'system' I employed? I would describe it as the human approach or the central importance of the human element in all problems: political, economic, social, colonial, racial, etc. And when I say the human approach, some of you are aware of my philosophy, of my basic concept regarding the human community and the human situation."

And once again he repeated his four categories:

"There are certain variations and priorities in values. In my view, an ideal man or an ideal woman is endowed with four virtues, four qualities: physical qualities, mental qualities, moral qualities, and above all, spiritual qualities."

The Cry for Spirituality

The world U Thant saw around him, the system of Western values culminating in the UN, was far from being the spiritual garden he was dreaming of. The UN was doing much for the physical and mental well-being of humanity, and it was also fostering the birth of world morality in many fields. But the world organization did not possess the all-encompassing spirituality he found so necessary. And yet he firmly believed that spirituality would be the next stage of evolution, transcending our earlier periods of material and intellectual progress. He believed that only spirituality and not balance of power, interests or reason would bring about peace and justice on earth. For him, spirituality was the ultimate harmony, the individual's and society's right perception of the cosmos, of our planet and of all human relations. This was for him the highest stage of development humanity could reach, the ultimate, fullest realization of human destiny in the universe. Once you find your right, harmonious place in the total order of things, then love, compassion, understanding, good behavior, reverence for life and peaceful relations with others automatically ensue. Then you have reached enlightenment and you feel in yourself the plenitude of the miracle of life. Then you are a peaceful, happy, serene, fulfilled, untroubled, harmonious, well-functioning cosmos which knows its place amid the myriads of cosmoses of the universe. U Thant's view of harmony resembled very much that of Confucius, who saw in government the art of achieving ultimate human harmony on earth and with the universe. It is revealing that the word "government" in Chinese means: to put things in the right place, to achieve harmony.

Unfortunately we are still far from this stage of evolution. The Western world has succeeded tremendously in the physical, intellectual and scientific spheres, but it has not yet perceived the virtues of harmony and the fathomless treasures of moral and spiritual fulfillment. Power, glory and wealth are still the dominant cravings. The heart and soul of Western man have not followed the development of his mind. As U Thant said in his speech to Planetary Citizens:

> "I am in no sense anti-intellectual, but the stress of education in the schools of highly developed societies, as I have stated on many previous occasions, is primarily on the development of the intellect or in physical excellence. To me, moral and spiritual aspects of life are far more important than the physical and intellectual aspects of life."

In his kind and unobtrusive way, U Thant was far ahead of our time. He saw for the entire world what he had discovered for himself, namely, that thought, meditation, prayer, contemplation, inner search and interrogation are the links between the miracle of human life and the universe. Good physical lives—respect for one's body; good mental lives—the acquisition of knowledge; good moral lives— the practice of love; and good spiritual lives—the practice of prayer and meditation, merge individual life with divinity, the universe, infinity, and lead to a wondrous respect for all creation and a deep gratitude for the miraculous gift of life in a vast, mysterious universe. This is the royal path to world peace and happiness, not the path of power, wealth and vainglory, which belong to an earlier, more primitive period of evolution.

Humanity is finding its right way, slowly but surely. Much has been achieved for the physical and mental improvement of human lives, but it has not yet reached the entire world since so many of our brethren and sisters are still living in poverty, sickness and ignorance. But in a great part of the world life now is generally long, good and healthy, and a school child knows more than any earlier king or emperor in all of human history. Good bodies and good minds bring us nearer to divinity and to a full consciousness of our place in the universe. The same is true of morality and spirituality: they are fundamental parts of human ascent. But here we have still great progress to achieve. There is much corruption and immorality in today's world. Mammon and not the God of the universe is on the altars of our societies. How small we have become, how unnecessarily our vision has shrunk, how limited our ambitions are amid our material and intellectual achievements!

There is need for a vast moral and spiritual renaissance to set our conquests at their right place within the magnificent order of things in the universe. The people are crying for moral and spiritual values. They are tired of wars, immorality and lack of meaning of the mystery of life. They know that the absence of moral and spiritual order means lack of civilization, that without such order a society is on the brink of decadence.

In our human garden, there are many flowers, many beliefs, many religions, there are even plants without flowers and faiths without God. For many God is the symbol of perfection, of that fullest life, knowledge, love, soul-consciousness and supreme happiness humans have been seeking since the beginnings of time.

U Thant often spoke of the law of *karma*, the principle that every action has a reaction, good or evil. I am grateful to him for having taught me this law. I hope that his message will continue to spread, that the law of a good *karma* will operate throughout the world and that more and more people will understand that the key to the future rests in their own garden, in their potential four and a half billion commitments to peace, love, kindness and human fraternity. To the concept of the noosphere, or sphere of the mind encompassing all humans, we would be well advised to add those of a karma-sphere, or sphere of good actions, mettasphere,[1] or sphere of love, animasphere,[2] or sphere of the universal soul. Then humanity could progress and lift itself upwards towards a total communion with God, the universe and eternity.

[1] From the Buddhist concept of *metta*, or love and kindness towards all living beings.
[2] From the Latin *anima*, soul.

PART II

The Global Transcendence
of Human Values

8

An Education Through Love

Humanity has discovered of late a great number of interdependencies which encompass our entire planet. The UN Stockholm Conference on the Environment brought to light the concept of the biosphere: a little sphere only a few miles thick enrobing the globe and containing all life of our solar system. The interdependencies of our environment, of our water, of our seas and oceans, of our air, of our energy and resources have revealed that we are all part of an extremely complex, marvelous fabric of life, of a unique, astonishing living body in the universe, which must be the object of our utmost care. Also, during the last century, humanity has added its own list of teeming man-made interdependencies through science, trade, business, transportation, communications, international exchanges, travel and tourism. Finally, we have discovered our indissoluble interdependence with the past and with the future. Our planet and its precious cargo of life advance in time as a huge, complex, miraculous, evolving intergalactic body.

In this vast list of global interdependencies, there is one which is particularly vital: *our children*. Humanity's children form the most precious network of human interdependence, the link between past and future without which all other interdependencies would cease to be relevant, for without the children humanity would soon cease to be.

When I think of the family, I always remember the beginning of Rousseau's *Contrat social*, in which he says that the only natural society is the family. The family is indeed the most highly interdependent society, perfected over millions of years of evolution. In it, grandparents, father, mother and children normally adapt to each other in many mysterious and marvelous ways, among which the most important one, insufficiently studied by humankind, is love. The first education that the little baby receives is entirely through love, particularly the mother's love. This great unexplored concept has been vastly underestimated as a means of increasing the knowledge, peace, understanding and interdependence of humanity and the general functioning of our planet. It is rarely used as an instrument of international relations. Political personalities, experts, scientists and diplomats, in our age of dry reason, rarely use the word "love," neglecting its cardinal value to achieve a more harmonious, well-functioning, happy human society and planetary habitat. And yet, to conduct our mysterious and miraculous journey in the universe we need above all faith, hope and love. And of the three, as so many saints and prophets have proclaimed, the most effective is love.

The greatest group of people to which we must henceforth direct our attention is the *human family*. Again, the Buddha, Christ and all great visionaries, philosophers and prophets saw the fundamental unity of humankind even though they lived in small separated societies scattered over the globe. Today, it is a completely different story. Today our world society of more than four billion people knows very well what is happening across the waters on the other side of the world. It is the transformation of this last-born and greatest society of all *into a family* which is the fundamental task of our time. How can we bring about this larger community? How can we find the natural, optimum, harmonious adaptation, relations and understanding between nations, races, religions, languages, institutions, enterprises, ideologies and professions? The search for a peaceful, reciprocal enrichment of all these diverse groups within one perfect human family is our next fundamental task on our evolutionary path. So far in history, humanity itself has been the great neglected orphan.

Our future family will be that of our children. If we give the right education to the fifteen thousand children born every hour and make them feel part of the beautiful human family and its mysterious physical, mental, moral and spiritual interdependencies, then we will obtain a better world. We must give a global education to all the world's children, teach them about the miracle and sanctity of life, the necessity of love for our planet, for our great human family, for the heavens and for the Creator of all these marvels. We must teach them rules of good behavior towards our global home and all our human sisters and brothers, so as to ensure peace, justice and happiness for all, and make our planet a showcase in the universe, as God wants it to be. This is the true, ultimate purpose of our evolution and of our efforts.

If we can teach right from the primary school the type of interdependent society into which children are born, then we will progress towards a truly good human family on a unique and well-run planet. Our minds must be directed towards these newcomers, towards the new human society being formed hour after hour under our very eyes by the arrival of new children. Through the education of all the children of the world and the right education about their world, we will prepare the novel planetary society which is in the making and which begins to be visible in the United Nations.

Recent history has shown that the old ways of taking the world by force, conquering and dividing, fragmenting, hating, fearing, arming, subverting, ruling and destroying no longer work in the interdependent circumstances of our planet. We must now try other ways which should be thoroughly studied by the best minds and applied by the political leaders of our planet: the ways of love, understanding, cooperation, altruism, justice and harmony, the superiority of which has been proved so irrefutably by the oldest, most advanced and most natural of all societies, *the family.*

9

Of Science and Love

One day at the UN I received in the mail a big volume written by a religious scholar on the history of the philosophy of science. The book was accompanied by a letter in which the author expressed the wish to see me after I had read his book.

I began to read it and I was deeply enthralled by it. The UN was about to hold a major conference on science and technology, and such a work on the deeper, philosophical meanings of science and technology was very timely.

Alas, in an active position like mine there is very little time to read more than a dozen printed pages a day. But I set my mind on it, determined to gain valuable knowledge. Unfortunately, the book was so hard to read, so dense with philosophy and theories, that each time I resumed my reading I had to start from the beginning. I knew it was hopeless and that I would never be able to finish it. I looked in vain for a conclusion or summary in which the author would have listed his main findings. But there was none. It was a book meant to be read from beginning to end. There was no escape from it.

So I put it aside, together with piles of other books sent to me by authors, awaiting the hypothetical time when I would have sufficient leisure to catch up with my reading.

A couple of weeks later the author called me and asked for an appointment. In the meantime a diplomat had told me that he was a very fine scholar, perhaps a little too much in love with matters of the mind and not enough in touch with reality. He asked me to guide him towards the practical problems encountered in the UN.

So the author showed up in my office one day. He was a middle-aged, tall, distinguished, well-bred, extremely good-looking gentleman. I greeted him, congratulated him on his fine book, seized the volume from a shelf and said:

"Alas, as much as I regret it, I have not been able to read your work, except for a few dozen pages. It is a scholarly book, very hard to read for a busy person like me. I have tried my best, but every time I had to start all over again. Finally I gave it up and I am afraid I will never finish it. I am sorry, but this happens frequently to people in my position."

I asked him if he didn't have a summary or conclusions of his book.

He dryly answered no.

I asked him if he could not prepare one:

"Your work and conclusions could be of immense value to the UN, especially to my colleagues in charge of the Conference on Science and Technology. I often regret that we do not have any philosophers at the UN. You have spent a lifetime on this momentous subject. Couldn't you summarize your findings for the Secretary-General and other concerned officials? I could advise you to send them copies of your book, but I know all too well that they do not have the time either. Secretary-General Waldheim has warned us all in this house: he will not read any text that is more than a page long. It is hard for us to comply, for it is much more difficult to write one page than twenty."

But he remained adamant and said wryly:

"My book cannot be summarized. It is the story of humanity's efforts in science and technology. It must be read from beginning to end."

"Couldn't you give us at least your conclusions, the philosophical considerations you think the delegates to the UN Conference on Science and Technology should have high on their minds?"

He remained silent.

To break the ice and pursue the conversation, I asked him abruptly:

"Do you treat the subject of love in your book?"

His superb impassivity left him all at once. He looked utterly astonished, examined me from top to bottom, then looked around my office as if wondering what kind of a crazy man the UN had in its service. I was glad that a large Crucifix was hanging behind my desk, protecting me from his total contempt.

He finally uttered these words, which fell condescendingly from his lips, as if he wanted to distance himself entirely from the nonsense I had said:

"Love! Love! What on earth has love to do with science?"

The moment had come to stick a banderilla into his intellectualism. I answered:

"Yes. Perfectly. I mean love. It has always struck me that love is one of the mightiest and most effective scientific concepts there is in this world. In my case, it is primarily through love that I see my relationships with the total earth, its people, my colleagues, my work, the universe, infinity and God. But to give you a more immediate and down-to-earth example: when a young man and a girl fall in love with each other, what happens at that moment? Isn't it a prodigious synthetic, unitary answer to a multitude of scientific questions? Two extremely complicated cosmoses made up of trillions of cells and immemorial genetic experiences decide to unite and to continue the chain of life! What a prodigious and momentous decision! Science could never give a satisfactory answer to such a colossal biological problem. And yet love does it in the most mysterious, simple, effective, pleasurable and miraculous way. Hence love is in your domain as it is in mine. I would even go so far as to say that love for life, passion for life, fascination with life is the prime motive of true scientific investigation. Human love for knowing and piercing the amazing creation is part of the spiritual process."

He had listened very carefully to me and when I finished his entire behavior changed forthwith. His face lit up, became warm and more human, he got up on his feet, paced my office up and down, thinking, smiling and rubbing his hands. Suddenly he stopped abruptly in front of me and asked:

"Do you have a Bible?"

"Yes."

"Could you give it to me?"

I handed him a venerable leather-bound volume whose pages he turned rapidly. He finally found the passage he had been looking for and pointed at a text which he asked me to read. It was from the Proverbs and it said:

"There are three things, nay, four, which are too wonderful for me to understand: the way of an eagle in the air; the way of a serpent on a rock; the way of a ship on the seas; and the way of a man with a maiden."

He then relaxed into a warm, friendly attitude and said to me in a humble way:

"You have taught me a lesson and reminded me of a very basic truth. I will not forget it."

The time had now come to fulfill my promise to my friend the diplomat:

"You see, the UN Conference on Science and Technology is also in the end a question of love. Reason and interest alone will not do it. Only love for our brethren and sisters in the poorer parts of the world, and love for our entire beautiful planet, will allow us to find the answers to that great conference."

And I was able then to give him the pertinent information on that lastest UN venture in which at first he had shown little interest.

Ever since then we have been great friends. He took an active part in the conference and wrote several excellent short, action-oriented, down-to-earth papers.

And each time when I receive some of his writings, I look up at my Crucifix and I see a little, delighted smile of complicity on the loving lips of Jesus.

* * *

I have one further story on that subject:

One day Professor M. from the Institute of Life in Paris visited me to see if his organization could be of help to the United Nations in some of the matters of current concern, in particular the International Year of the Child, the UN Conference on Science and Technology and the World Assembly on Aging. We discussed several possibilities, for I had high regard for this association of some of the world's greatest scientists dealing with human life. I always derive much knowledge and advance perceptions of new global problems from their congresses and communications.

At one stage of our conversation I asked him point-blank:

"Why don't you deal with the subject of love in your institution?"

Like the religious scholar, he could not hide his disbelief at what I had said.

He mumbled grudgingly: "Love, love? What has love to do with the science of life?"

I commented:

"Isn't the love of a mother for her child a great mysterious reality which should be the subject of scientific investigation? Isn't humanity's love for its children the alpha and omega of the International Year of the Child? Isn't love for our older people the key to the World Assembly on Aging? Shouldn't your institute study and foster the concept of love for the improvement of the human condition on our planet?"

He thought for a moment and came up with an answer:

"We are dealing with it, but in a different, more scientific way. It has been proven recently that the physical and mental development of a child depends in a very large degree on his affective environment, especially the mother and the family. This has become a major subject of research among pediatricians and specialists of children."

I looked at my Crucifix and wondered once more in my life why scientists had always to resort to a special jargon, instead of using the beautiful words inherited from millennia of evolution. Love is scoffed at as being non-scientific. Then the word "environment" becomes fashionable and love reappears under the term "affective environment"! What a complicated, devious world! What a lack of courage to be simple, straightforward and to speak from the heart understandably to all peoples. What is wrong, I ask you, with the word "love"?

After he left my office I made a number of telephone calls to my colleagues and said to them:

"Henceforth I would advise you to use generously the words 'affective environment': for the child, for youth, for the handicapped, for older people, for relations between nations, for our planet and for the entire human family. Love doesn't sell as yet, but quality of life and affective environment are now respectable scientific notions. Let us therefore use them up to the brim."

But in the evening when I came home and looked at my wife and children, I thought that affective environment was a very poor substitute for what I felt for them. O humanity! When will you decide to restore the great, simple, noble, tested, down-to-earth common-sense values which from time immemorial have been the foundations of our civilization and happiness? Why do the scientists dislike so much the words "love, beauty, faith, joy, happiness, kindness, goodness, fascination, ecstasy, God," etc.? Why? Why don't we all revolt against the heartless scientific jargon and state our right to an understandable, inspired, heartfelt language?

10

The Issue of Human Rights

I have learned during my many years at the United Nations that the nobler an objective the more difficult it is to achieve. The four most difficult issues in world affairs still remain disarmament—i.e., a planet devoid of arms, especially nuclear arms—the development of the poor countries, human rights, and world democracy, or the participation of people in designing their own fate and future on this planet. Of the four, perhaps human rights has fared best. Where do we stand on this crucial issue today?

There are two basic aspects to human rights. On the one hand, there is the formulation of what the rights of the human being should be, and secondly, there is the implementation of the philosophy. As regards the concepts of human rights, undoubtedly since the adoption of the Charter of the United Nations immense progress has been achieved. Truly, I would never have expected, coming out of the Second World War, that humanity would be able to draft a philosophy of life through intergovernmental committees. We have today, after these several years, a Universal Declaration of Human Rights complemented by detailed Covenants on political and civil rights, economic, cultural and social rights. If you take these texts together you have a beautiful, unique charter of what human life should be for each individual on this planet. I cannot emphasize enough that this is one of the great achievements of the human race in recent years: it has been able to define a collective philosophy of what human rights should be. There is often great beauty in these texts. I wish that the Universal Declaration of Human Rights would be taught in every school on earth. Beyond this universal text, over the last decades, a systematic effort has been made to look at human rights from every possible aspect. There are not only the rights of the human person as such, but humans have also a race, a sex, physical and mental capacities or incapacities, and an age. Over the years, the Universal Declaration and the Covenants have been complemented by a series of special declarations for these various groups. There is little doubt that regarding racial equality the world has changed profoundly since 1945. Despite a few last pockets of resistance, immense progress has been accomplished in world-wide recognition of the equality of races. There is further the example of the Declaration of the Rights of the Child the twentieth anniversary of which was celebrated during the International Year of the Child. Much misery still affects the children of this world: ten per cent of the newly born die before one year is over and another four per cent die before five years have passed; several hundred million children go hungry; one hundred eighty million children still do not go to school; fifteen million children under the age of fifteen are working despite the provisions of that Declaration.

The world has also looked at the rights of women. This is one of the earliest works of the United Nations. It culminated in a World Women's Conference, held in Mexico in 1975, and another conference in 1980 in Denmark to see what progress has been achieved world-wide in implementing the equality of the sexes.

Another problem has strongly come to the fore. It concerns the physical and mental characteristics of people. We have, unfortunately, four hundred fifty million handicapped persons on this planet. They need special protection. That protection has been laid down in the Declaration of the Rights of the Mentally Retarded of 1971, in the Declaration of the Rights of the Handicapped of 1975, and in the Declaration of the Rights of the Blind of 1980.

We see therefore the Universal Declaration of Human Rights being refined and complemented year after year. The United Nations first World Assembly on Aging is expected to consider a declaration of the rights of the hundreds of millions of elderly persons on our planet.

These conceptual frameworks of human rights will probably never be complete because our concept of life is changing with time. New unprecedented preoccupations do appear and make claims for new types of human rights. For example, of late there has been a great preoccupation with the rights of the individual to be protected from incursions in his private life—for example computerization, and scientific, genetic and technological tampering with life. The whole question of human rights, from the development of the child in the womb of the mother to the moment of death, has been examined by the World Health Organization. In the not too distant future another problem will come up in the United Nations, namely, the right to a certain quality of life. A good environment is beginning to be perceived as a basic human right. As the years pass we will also hear of a Declaration of the Right Not to Kill and Not to Be Killed, not even in the name of a nation. It is very interesting that the provisions on human rights of the UN Charter speak of the realization of human rights and fundamental freedoms for all without distinction as to race, sex, language or religion. But the word "nation" has been carefully omitted. Today, you can still "rightfully" be asked to kill another human being in the name of a nation. Conscientious objectors have brought this problem to the United Nations and the time will come when a human being will be given the right not to kill and not to be killed.

Someday there will also be the right to live on a planet devoid of armaments, in particular nuclear armaments. This should be a basic right of each human being. Life on this planet requires a certain number of fundamental obligations of states. One of these is not to endanger life and the planet with cataclysmic anti-human armaments. The whole concept of human rights must evolve with the problem of nationhood. You are well protected as a member of a state or nation but not as a member of the human race. From the moment you become a refugee, you no longer have any rights left. There are today on this planet more than twelve million refugees, half of them children. They have very few legal rights. They are living in camps set up by the United Nations. Eventually they will be given new rights, but it takes such a long time to find a country of "asylum." Human rights are recommended internationally but they are granted by national jurisdictions. This is not just. The human person and planetary citizenship must be given absolute priority over national citizenship. It cannot be otherwise.

The second aspect of human rights concerns implementation. We now possess very beautiful texts and norms. We have a body of world directives—not legislation—which command admiration and respect. But the question of implementation is quite another story.

Implementation of human rights can take place at the national level, at the regional level and at the world level.

At the national level it is the duty of states which have adhered to the Conventions to implement their provisions. National legislation can full well protect human rights and one could envisage a world in which each nation would protect them adequately. But here we run into difficulties. Many nations do not believe that they are in the service of human beings. They claim that citizens owe allegiance to the state, a religion, a way of life or a philosophical concept. There are on this planet a number of states which require highest allegiance to a religion. In some of them the constitution is a religious text. These states may require that you be of a certain religion to be a citizen! It is quite a problem, for example, to see how human rights of women are implemented in countries which function under ancient religious codes. In these countries the law of a religious book is the supreme law, not the recommendations of the United Nations. In other nations the state or an ideology has supreme priority. As a result the individual has to submit to the priority requirements of the state or ideology, with the possible loss of personal rights. In other countries primacy is given to a philosophical concept, for example, the philosophy and practice of liberty: freedom of expression, freedom of activity, freedom to accumulate wealth. But this too can lead to much excess, monopoly and injustice. In the poorer countries, the most important preoccupations are survival, food, health, education, employment and dignity. We still live in a very imperfect, checkered world, a world of dazzling inequality and diversity of conditions, endowments, aspirations and dreams. Nevertheless, the world community is asking states to accept at least those common denominators of the rights of the human being which have been agreed to in the United Nations. Even that implementation is far from being satisfactory.

There are only two continents where human rights are protected by regional conventions and institutions. Western Europe has had a European Convention of Human Rights for more than twenty-five years. It has a Court of Human Rights. An individual, a non-governmental organization, or a state can introduce a complaint of violations of human rights to that court. When the court has taken a decision the state has to implement it, either by paying indemnities or redressing the injustice. This is the only place on the planet where an individual has effective recourse against national mistreatment in a court with international jurisdiction. Recently, progress has been made in Latin America: the first Latin American Court of Human Rights has been established in Costa Rica, but only a state and not an individual can have recourse to it. How far we are from the day when individuals will be able to seek redress against violations of human rights by states to a world human rights court!

How does the situation look on a world-wide basis? Well, here the situation is not good at all. True enough, we have Covenants. But the first question is: who has ratified those conventions? Out of one hundred and fifty-seven member states of the United Nations not more than a third have ratified them. In other words, many countries of the world do not even consider themselves bound by these texts. And there are some very large countries among them!

When you look more closely at the Covenants, you will find many escape clauses. Some of them contain a protocol which provides that a government accepts that individual petitions may be addressed to the United Nations. But the number of countries which have accepted that protocol is limited to about two dozen. There are thus less than two out of ten countries on this planet that allow an individual or a non-governmental organization to turn to the international community with a complaint under the Covenants! Of course, an individual can send any complaint to the UN. These complaints are handled under procedures which still reflect the reluctance of nations to be internationally probed, criticized and condemned. The first official complaint ever dealt with under the Covenants was a complaint from private citizens of a Latin American country. The government of that country was condemned, but it does not have to abide by the decision or redress the situation if it does not want to. There is no forceful implementation!

This shows the enormous distance still to be covered both conceptually and practically until there is a satisfactory implementation of human rights on this planet. Is it a desperate situation? Not necessarily. It has taken humanity hundreds of years to get rid of slavery and it has done so. Human ascent requires that we work at such issues relentlessly. We have at least a Universal Declaration of Human Rights. It was adopted at a time when there were only fifty-one nations in the world organization. Today the United Nations is as universal as its Declaration. For the first time in the entire evolution of humankind the dream of all the great prophets and visionaries has been fulfilled: now on this planet we have a universal organization. This will progressively force governments to abide by the new ethical concepts which are being forged in humanity's collective institutions. The chances for progress are immensely fostered by the mere existence of this universal organization. This is why I appeal to all men and women of this planet to give their fullest support to their universal organization, because the better, the stronger and more respected it is, the greater our chances will be to see our individual human rights finally implemented by the states to which we "belong." It is not only in the interest of nations to have the United Nations. It is of even far greater interest for individuals to have the United Nations, so that we will finally obtain from our states, governments, institutions, legislators and executives respectful behavior towards the individual. A state and an institution have no life. Only people are endowed with the miracle of life. They should have priority over states and institutions. Without people states and institutions would be empty shells. They should never forget it. Laws, governments, institutions, religions, associations, corporations and the United Nations have been created by "we, the people," for the improvement of the life of human beings, for the physical, mental, moral and spiritual fulfillment of the individual. The story of humanity is the story of the flowering of life of individuals who alone can live, love, be happy and procreate.

We must thank God and those who have perished in the Second World War that the Charter has not forgotten this and that it has included the issue of human rights as one of its most fundamental preoccupations. But we must help accelerate the process, which is far too slow, for after the rights of the human person have been taken care of there remain other rights to consider, in particular the rights of the planet itself and the rights of future generations.[1]

I have worked in this organization for an entire adult's lifetime. I saw in the Second World War two very civilized countries, Germany and France, lash out at each other like savages. I was born on their common border. I could see the other country across the river from my window. I was told during my youth that France was the greatest country on earth and then the Germans came and told us that they were the greatest. Both sides gave us guns to shoot at peo-

---

[1] A Draft Charter for Nature has been submitted by the government of Zaire to the General Assembly. The Jacques Cousteau Society for its part has prepared a Draft Declaration of Rights of Future Generations which it wants to see adopted by the United Nations.

ple who were human brethren, who had the same names—who spoke the same language; who had the same faces; and who were our blood relatives. Nevertheless, in the name of a nation, we were clothed in different "uniforms" and asked to kill each other. This is no longer tolerable at the present stage of evolution. This planet was not created for international mass murders. It was not born cut up in borders, nations and groups. It is and has always been an interdependent planet, a complete biosphere, a sphere of life in which all human beings are sacred irrespective of their group affiliations. It might be some time before the political world catches up with this reality. But I have seen enough progress during my lifetime to believe in the success of the human race on our miraculous little planet in the universe. We should all remember these good words by Edmund Burke:

All that is necessary for evil to flourish is that good people do nothing.

11

The Right Not to Kill

In every epoch of history there are a few exceptional human beings who are blessed with a correct vision of the place of the human person on earth and in the universe. This vision is always basically the same:

— it recognizes the oneness and supremacy of the human family, irrespective of color, sex, creed, nation or any other distinctive characteristics;

— it recognizes each individual human being as a unique miracle of divine origin, a cosmos of his own, never to be repeated again in all eternity;

— it rejects all violence as being contrary to the sanctity and uniqueness of life, and advocates love, tolerance, truth, cooperation and reverence for life as the only civilized means of achieving a peaceful and happy society;

— it preaches love and care for our beautiful and so diverse planet in the fathomless universe;

— it sees each human life and society as part of an eternal stream of time and ever ascending evolution;

— it recognizes that the ultimate mysteries of life, time and the universe will forever escape the human mind and therefore bends in awe and humility before these mysteries and God;

— it advocates gratitude and joy for the privilege of being admitted to the banquet of life;

— it preaches hope, faith, optimism and a deep commitment to the moral and ethical virtues of peace and justice distilled over eons of time as the foundations for further human ascent.

Only people with this simple vision, unmarred by political and personal interests, do ultimately survive in the memory of humankind. They are the great religious leaders, saints, philosophers, artists and humanists of all times. They sing a breath-taking hymn to life, to our planet and to the universe. They deal with the fundamental truths.

Our time has been fortunate to count several such great people, whose number might well be on the increase. We were blessed with a Gandhi, an Albert Schweitzer, a Sri Aurobindo, an H. G. Wells, a Teilhard de Chardin, a Toynbee and, nearer to us, Dag Hammarskjöld, U Thant, Pablo Casals and Mother Teresa. Last but not least, it was the turn of the American soil to produce such a great human being, Martin Luther King. It did it in the true American way: Martin Luther King had his roots in Africa, bore the name of a European and professed a Christian faith born in the Middle East. His life and work overflowed with the unmistakable accents of true vision. One could quote endless thoughts and words of his which make one's heart vibrate, which inspire, which elevate, which make us feel better, greater and proud to be human. Everything he did and said bore the stamp of that same great human dream which is also being sought under the cupola of the UN. This is why he was described as a first citizen of the world, a man of all ages and of all continents. We find in him the same ultimate message left to us by Dag Hammarskjöld and U Thant, namely, that love is the secret of secrets, the great transcending force which alone can break the nemesis of war and violence. These were his words in this regard.

To the crowd gathered outside his bombed home in Montgomery: "We must love our white brothers no matter what they do to us. We must make them know that we love them." In an address to a huge gathering in Washington in 1957: "We must never be bitter— if we indulge in hate, the new order will only be the old order. We must meet hate with love, physical force with soul force." After being jailed in Montgomery: "Blood may flow in the streets of Montgomery before we receive our freedom, but it must be our blood that flows and not that of the white man. We must not harm a single hair on the head of our white brothers." In the sermon "Loving Your Enemies": "To our most bitter opponents we say: Do to us what you will, and we shall continue to love you. Throw us in jail, and we shall still love you. Bomb our homes and threaten our children, and we shall still love you."

Martin Luther King and Pablo Casals were foremost in reminding us of a fundamental human right which is not often heard of in UN debates: the right not to kill and not to be killed, not even in the name of a nation.

Many facets of human rights have indeed been studied, defined and codified over the years, but that one has remained surrounded by a strange silence!

During our human evolution and especially during the last few decades it has become increasingly clear that each individual human life is an astounding miracle. Scientists stand in wonder before their genetic discoveries and the functioning of the human being. The more they discover, the more each human appears as an incredible cosmos which has never existed before and will never exist again in the same form in all eternity. All great visionaries, religious leaders, prophets, philosophers and ethical luminaries knew that by intuition thousands of years ago. Great artists, poets and writers have proclaimed it throughout the course of human history. Pablo Casals and Martin Luther King were two of the latest to proclaim it in the most moving terms and in visible action. Now science is confirming it in its own astonishing ways. There is no doubt that, of all life forms on our planet, humanity is the only one that can elevate itself above its condition, uncover a reality which was closed to its senses, comprehend outer space, inner space and ever larger and smaller infinites, conceive God and transcend itself continuously above its earthly abode. This is why, the more we advance, the more we stand in awe before this miraculous, mysterious, incomprehensible, mind-boggling cosmos called a human person.

What conclusion must we draw from this? Pablo Casals had the artist's straight answer when he said: "If I am a miracle that God or nature has made, how could I kill? No, I can't. Or another human being who is a miracle like me, can he kill someone?" He was thus restating a fundamental truth which has been advocated by all great religions and moral codes: "Thou shalt not kill." This law of civilized society is as true today as it was throughout our past history. To break it in any way is to break the fundamental law of civilization. Therefore, at a moment when the entire question of human rights is being so forcefully debated, we must have the courage to place the right of each human person not to kill and not to be killed at the top of the list. This should be the most sacred law of humanity. As one of the most urgent topics for world ecumenism, I would suggest a meeting of the world's religions to agree and proclaim that no human being shall be required to kill in the name of a nation, a religion or any other group.

The time has come to start a new history in this respect. We must establish reverence for life as the cornerstone of civilization: reverence for life not only by individuals, but also by institutions, foremost among them nations. Institutions were created originally for the good and survival of the people. This is their main justification and merit. They have no right to kill or to develop and stockpile incredible arsenals of weapons meant to kill millions of people, possibly all humanity. And the same nations come to the UN and dare to speak about human rights! Do these include the right to life and the right not to kill? Perhaps if we approach the question of disarmament from the fundamental principle of reverence for life, we might achieve better progress. As a humanist and as a member of the human race who has seen so many killings and violations of human rights during his lifetime, I just cannot conceive and accept the idea of a peaceful and orderly planet of armed nations. As we approach the new global age of humanity, we must unequivocally proclaim and enforce this fundamental, sacred and inalienable right and obligation of all human beings on our planet:

THOU SHALT NOT KILL, NOT EVEN IN THE NAME OF A NATION.

12

The Need for World Gratitude

When the bells, muezzins and gongs will ring again

Invited to inaugurate the World Gratitude Center at Thanksgiving Square in Dallas, I reflected deeply and found that, although throughout my life I had been grateful for the gift of life, I had never thought much about the concept itself. I therefore turned to any encyclopedias I could find, including children's encyclopedias, but except for a few words on the celebration of Thanksgiving, I could not find anything.

I was puzzled. I consulted other books and found that the word "gratitude" was well covered only in two: the Bible and my old Latin dictionary. I was not surprised to find it in the Bible, for daily prayer and thanksgiving to God are two main pillars of religion. But the several pages of quotations from Latin authors were a revelation. The Romans had established gratitude—*gratia*—as a profound philosophical concept at the root of their empire and Pax Romana. Gratitude to the gods was a central rule of public Roman life. Then I consulted an old German etymological dictionary inherited from my grandfather, and I found that the words "*Dank*," "thanks," "*tak*" (Danish), "*dank*" (Dutch), etc., came from *denken*, "to think," and meant to remember something agreeable that had happened or had been given to you. At the UN I consulted colleagues from different lands, and I got some fascinating answers: the Greek *eukharistia* means "expressing joy" (*kharis*); the Arabic *shukran* is related to "sweetness" (sugar); Chinese *shie-shie* meant originally "to decline," for it was a Chinese custom to decline three times before accepting a gift or favor. The different cultural perceptions of "gratitude" were so interesting that the UN Linguistics Club decided to collect its etymology and meanings in as many languages as possible.

The concept seems to be deeply entrenched in all cultures, and it is regretful that in our modern world we have almost forsaken it. We must re-establish gratitude at the center of our global civilization. In tomorrow's planetary society, as in yesterday's Roman Empire, it must be a common spirit occupying the hearts of all citizens. We must conceive of a time when all the billions of humans of this planet, upon rising in the morning, will give thanks to God for the gift of life on our beautiful planet. The bells, the muezzins and the gongs must ring again all over the globe and reverberate into the universe our gratitude, our eucharist or expression of joy for the resurrection of life and of another day. We will never grasp the infinity and eternity of God's creation, but we must at least be joyful for seeing and knowing such a vast and marvelous part of it.

When I think of gratitude, the image of Pablo Casals comes again to my mind. I have seldom met anyone who was able so constantly and so deeply to express his thankfulness for life. When he spoke on that subject, he often ended up in tears, lamenting the incapacity of so many people to understand what an incredible miracle life is.

Another master of mine who shared this view unreservedly was U Thant. His religion was quite fundamental to him and in his memoirs he explained which precepts of Buddhism were particularly useful to him as Secretary-General of the United Nations.[1] One of them was the principle of *metta*, or impersonal love or good will which embraces all beings impartially and spontaneously, friends and foes alike. He considered that each human being was a unique manifestation of the miracle of life in the universe and that consequently we should approach all our human brethren and sisters with deep respect, kindness and wonder. He held that one should never harm or diminish another person, not even verbally. Respect, understanding and love were for him the only correct attitudes towards the prodigy of life. He applied this philosophy very strictly, never criticizing or diminishing other people, never doing harm but, on the contrary, rejoicing at the qualities, achievements, prosperity and good fortune of others. When he disapproved of another person, the worst he would do would be to remain silent.

Turning to the thinkers who had an important influence on him,

[1] *View from the U.N.* (New York: Doubleday & Co., Inc., 1978), Chapter Two, "How I Conceived My Role."

he mentioned Albert Schweitzer and Teilhard de Chardin. Of Albert Schweitzer, he wrote:

> In his *Philosophy of Civilization,* Schweitzer first presented the ethic of "reverence for life"—a theme consistently featured in his life and thought, and the central core of most of his speeches and conversations. . . . He stubbornly pressed hard to bring home his point and developed the theme to encompass wider horizons. Man, he said, must not limit life to the affirmation of man alone; man's ethics must not end with man, but should extend to the universe. He must regain the consciousness of the great chain of life from which he cannot be separated. He preached the necessity of "the will to live an ethical life," which should be the primary motivation of man, and he said life should be for a higher value and purpose—not spent in merely selfish or thoughtless actions. What then results for man is not only a deepening of relationships, but a widening of relationships.

U Thant himself left us some very important teachings, in particular his distinction and hierarchy of the four natures and needs of the human person. If we think for a moment of the human body, its incredible complexity, the marvelous functioning of its trillions of cells, miles of vessels, hundreds of automatisms, a miracle such as the human eye and nervous system, we can but stand in awe before this prodigy. The same is true of the brain, a phenomenal natural, organic computer. And what should we say of the heart, capable of love for our children, family, friends, profession and the entire planet, and last but not least, of the soul, hungry to seek the outer limits of the universe and of time, from creation to the apocalypse? When you think that we have been given such attributes, then there can be only one conclusion, namely, that life is indeed a miracle and that to be a human is an incredible privilege in the universe. We must therefore be grateful for it from morning to evening. In the morning when we rise we should look at the sun, as so many of our brothers and sisters still do in countries like India, in the monasteries and in the rural areas of the world. To pray to the rising sun is to perceive the greatness of the universe and of God, and to recognize the resurrection of the day and of ourselves. In the evening, we must pray again and be thankful for all we have received, learned and enjoyed. As Dag Hammarskjöld put it so beautifully:

> *To everything that has been—Thanks.*
> *For everything that will be—Yes.*

There is so much to be grateful for. It is our duty to give thanks at all times for our admittance to the festival of life, especially in those countries where hunger and poverty have been eliminated. In ancient times it was said that God punished the ungrateful. This is no less true today. For the rich to complain is really to tempt God. Nothing is more shocking indeed than the murmurs and dissatisfaction of the healthy and wealthy. Think of the 500 million hungry in this world, of the 600 million jobless, of the 450 million handicapped, and you will realize, you the healthy and rich, how thankful you should be. The least we must expect from the rich is for them to put an end to their lamentations, waste, greed and unhappiness and to come to the help of their less fortunate brethren and sisters at home and abroad. The first great step towards a happier world is for the well-to-do to acknowledge that life has been good to them and to be grateful to God. If not, what is the use of working so hard to bring about a more prosperous world? Humanity would be well advised to take inspiration from our American Indian brothers, the Senecas, for whom every moment of life is gratitude to the Great Spirit and who express it so beautifully in their greetings, their traditions and in their story of creation.[2]

And we must be grateful to all our Promethean artists—musicians like Bach, Mozart and Beethoven, painters and sculptors like Leonardo and Michelangelo, authors like Shakespeare, Dante and Goethe—for having sung the splendor of life and of the universe and making us vibrate in unison with the beautiful, divine, inscrutable forces of the cosmos.

Thanksgiving Square

Thanksgiving Square is a beautiful place situated in the heart of Dallas, amid gigantic skyscrapers. It is dwarfed by the masses of steel, concrete, glass and aluminum that jut into the air all around it. Nevertheless it manages to prove that smallness with a soul can be as great as if not greater than gianthood without one. While the skyscrapers monotonously look alike, the square abounds with individual features, nature, forms and symbols. A chance has been given here to practically every gradient, shape and geometric form conceiv-

[2] See Elizabeth Tooker, ed., *Native North American Spirituality of the Eastern Woodlands* (Classics of Western Spirituality) (Ramsey, N.J.: Paulist Press, 1979).

able. The most interesting and impressive symbol is the chapel built in the form of a spiral. Those who conceived Thanksgiving Square considered many ideas including that of a Tree of Life. The concept finally retained was suggested by a monk, Brother David Steindl-Rast. He proposed the idea of the spiral, a mysterious, thought-provoking symbol of infinity. As you stand inside, outside or under the chapel, you are taken by its spirit. In your mind you continue to draw the spiral and you visualize it expanding endlessly into the infinite, encompassing the entire universe! Such is the nature of a simple spiral. In the Orient, particularly in India, it was given in cosmic significance long before Western mathematicians became intrigued by it. In Dallas it is a symbol of East-West brotherhood on the American soil.

There is another notable symbol: the stained windows of the chapel come from Chartres, where they were made by the descendants of the craftsmen who fashioned the marvelous glass panes of the glorious French cathedral. Another feature is particularly dear to me, for it is a dream of mine that has come true. During my many years in the United States, I have often missed the sound of European church bells. Since childhood I have loved the soul-stirring, crystalline voice of morning bells which seemed to come from heaven at that very special moment when the day is born again. Bells too represent vibrations which from the tiniest human community on earth reach into the infinite, as a spiral does for the eye and the mind. Bells call the people to prayer and gratitude for daily life as it is so beautifully represented in the famous French painting *The Angelus* by Millet. Today three magnificent bells cast in Annecy, France, adorn Thanksgiving Square and try to stir the souls of the people.

There is only one rectangular shape in the square: the altar on which stands a beautiful, massive glass candelabrum from Ireland. The Hall of Thanksgiving under the chapel offers the sight of immaculate white columns representing various civic associations. Behind these columns flows a sky-blue illuminated water. In the center of the hall, right under the nexus of the spiral, stands a permanent exhibit with a plaque from the UN Meditation Group. Thus the United Nations is present in the temple calling for the prayers of the visitors for the world's first universal peace organization.

It is most interesting to observe the visitors. There are many people from Dallas, especially young people who work in the skyscrapers and who come to dream, relax or have their luncheon in the square, sitting on benches or stone walls, under a tree or near a waterfall. Each person interprets the place in his own way, according to his soul, feelings and inclinations. When I said good-by to the chapel a hippy was sitting there immersed in deep meditation, a prayerbook resting on his lap. I asked the attendant who had been the last person registered in her visitor's book. She said:

"It was a little boy who had come a few days ago to pray to God for rain for the farmers. He came back today to thank God for having made it rain yesterday!" And she added that she could tell scores of similar moving stories.

Thanksgiving Square is a place where you can feel the need of the human being to be grateful for the gift of life, that unique, mysterious outcropping from darkness in the void, that flowering of being under sunlight and the stars. Yes, out of a cell, of a seed, as from the center of a spiral or the impact of a sound, we are grown into a cosmos, a universe of our own, sentient, seeing, feeling, thinking, linked with the great chain of being, from the nucleus of the cell to the vast intergalactic universe, capable of loving and encompassing the entire world in our heart, of feeling the divine, and of lifting ourselves to the Godhead on our own will. You can sense this in the square. It is something unique, and I am grateful that the United Nations has been associated with it. I hope that the spirit of thanksgiving for life will someday encompass the entire planet and illumine peace in the hearts of all human beings.

A Prayer to God at Thanksgiving Square

Dear God, I believe that there is an account on which we have failed You utterly—where we have been regressing rather than progressing of late. We have been able to expand tremendously our physical capacities and to transform profoundly this planet. We have been able to widen immensely the reaches of our mind, but we have not even tried to exercise fully the potential of our hearts and of our souls. This we knew to do in the past, but today sentiment, love, morality, understanding, humility and compassion are concepts which are usually derided in political and intellectual circles. The soul too has shrunk. Spirituality has been segregated from most government, public institutions and education. Finally, I am sorry to

say, most of us have forgotten the good habit of saying "thanks" to
You.

When I was a little boy, I remember that we had in our dining
room the reproduction of a beautiful painting which showed a peas-
ant and his wife in a field praying in the morning at sunrise when
the bells were striking. It reminded the children in every home of
France that we had to give thanks to You for all the blessings of this
earth. When French peasants walked by a wheat field, they took off
their caps. Bread was blessed by the father before being broken.
Today, this has disappeared from many homes. I seldom see *The
Angelus* of Millet any more and for years I have not seen anyone
make the sign of the cross on a loaf of bread.

But in this beautiful square in Dallas, a new movement has
begun. The dream of restoring gratitude in the world is becoming
true. It is an idea whose time has come.

You know, dear Creator, again when I remember my youth, another image often comes back to me. At that time cars often stalled
or would slide down the shoulders of the road, and we children were
often called to help push them back onto the road. There came a
point when we got tired and so we would place a stone or a block of
wood behind the wheels. Then we looked proudly back at the distance we had covered. This is what the world must also do. This is
what each individual must do. We must count our blessings. We
must take inventory of what we have achieved. We must look back,
be grateful and then look up at the rest of the road. This is why this
world center was created. It must become a world movement, a spiral of the heart and of the soul outreaching for all leaders, educators,
media, world servers and people, reminding them that above all we
must be grateful to You for what we have received. Each of us in his
own way and all together, we must help achieve an unprecedented
destiny and fulfillment of the miracle of life on our wonderful
planet. To do this, our friends of Thanksgiving Square have com-
mitted their help.

Dear God, I pray that we should be able here in this chapel to report to You each year on further progress of the human family, to
strike out from our liabilities wars, conflicts, injustices, hatred, dis-
honesty and prejudice, and to add to our assets new friendships,
more love, more world cooperation and a greater recognition of the
miracle of life in the incomprehensible, vast universe.

Thank You, O God, for our little planet so rich with life, light,

warmth, beauty, dream, invention, history, diversity and future.
Thank You, O God, for the prodigy of life. My heart is smiling at
the thought of all Your gifts. Thank You, dear God, thank You very
much.

13

To Reach Peace, Teach Peace

Soon after his elevation to the pontificate, an event which took place during the International Year of the Child, Pope John Paul II sent his first message to governments and to heads of international organizations. It was entitled: "To Reach Peace, Teach Peace."

No theme could have been more timely. Indeed, the International Year of the Child obliged us to reflect collectively, nationally and individually about the conditions into which children are born today and the kind of future which is being prepared for them in various regions of the world. Also, it was a year of profound rethinking and activity in the field of world education. From various walks of life and regions of the world, news reaches us of mounting dissatisfaction with the way children are being taught about our planet and its peoples. Many schools and universities are turning to the United Nations for help in improving their curricula. From Peru comes the suggestion for an International Year for Global Education. The methods of teaching and the curricula of the UN international schools are attracting wide attention, and university students are turning their high, almost fascinated hopes towards the United Nations University in Tokyo and the University of Peace in Costa Rica.

Pope John Paul II's message dealt with many aspects of the subject, including linguistics, from which he would like to see eradicated concepts and language perpetuating hatred, conflict, division and war. Two aspects are particularly important to world servers: one is the necessity to convey to the children and peoples the right knowledge about this world; the second is the necessity to teach them the right attitude.

Teaching the Right Knowledge

Each human being is born into this world with given senses, a physiology and a genetic legacy which epitomize the entire past evolution of humankind in our planetary conditions. His life will be the result of the interplay of his aptitudes with his physical and human environment. He is literally "led out of ignorance" (*e-ducare*) by the family, school, religion, higher education and, last but not least, by life itself. Generation after generation, humanity's total growing knowledge is genetically and socially transmitted to a constantly renewed and expanding stream of human life.

One of the most crucial questions facing humanity at the present juncture of its evolution is whether we do convey the right information and knowledge about our planet and its people to the four and a half billion human beings alive, especially to the newcomers, the children. Such knowledge falls basically into three categories: the earth, humanity and the individual human person.

As regards *the earth*, humanity has made incredible progress in knowlege of our globe and its exact place in the universe, our relations with the sun, outer space, our atmosphere, biosphere, our seas and oceans, our land masses, our arable land, the planet's water, its mineral and energy resources, our vegetal and animal world, the inside of the earth's crust, down to the infinitesimally small world of the atom, of particles, of the cell, of genes, of microbiology. Yes, it is a prodigious scientific image which reaches the United Nations through its thirty-two specialized agencies and global programs. As a result we can educate our children as we have never done before about our little but so miraculously rich, life-teeming planet circling in the vast universe. We can show them an astonishingly beautiful, well-ordered tapestry of human knowledge, from the infinitely large to the infinitely small, as no Galileo, no Newton, no Copernicus would ever have dreamed possible.

My only misgiving is that rarely do schools and universities mention the world institutions in which the synthesis of this knowledge converges and in which the great tapestry is being woven. Where are the schools of this world which teach the young about the UN's work and major world conferences on outer space, on the seas and oceans, the world's climate, food, water, the deserts, science and technology, the atom, etc.? Where is the child who could name a few of the world's specialized agencies? Only UNICEF and the UN's Stockholm Conference on the Environment are known to any extent in the schools. We are thus missing a great opportunity to reassure the children and the people that governments are beginning to work together on an unprecedented scale to know, monitor, protect and manage our planetary home better.

Similarly, when it comes to knowledge about *the human family*, we have made great progress: we know how many we are, where we are, how many children, men and women, adults and elderly we are; we know that there are four hundred and fifty million handicapped, five hundred million malnourished and not far from a billion illiterates; we know how long we can expect to live in various parts of the world. No major aspect of the human family has been neglected during these last few decades: we had Economic Development Conferences, a World Population Conference, a Youth Conference, a World Assembly on Aging; UNICEF is looking after the children; the Human Settlements Conference has surveyed our location and migrations; there were two World Women's Conferences; there was an International Year of Disabled Persons; there were vast efforts and a World Conference on Racism, and so on and so forth. But again, not enough is being taught to the children about our knowledge of the exact and often so unjust and disparate conditions of the human family on our planet, or about the objectives humanity seeks to attain.

The situation is even worse when it comes to the groups into which humanity has been divided by history: the group into which a child is born is often presented to him as being superior to the totality. A nation is shown to be greater than humanity, a language greater than human communication, a race better than others, an ideology or political system superior to others, a culture or history more glorious than others, a religious rite more valuable than universal spirituality, a corporation as the greatest, and so forth and so on. It is especially from these struggles among groups that conflicts and wars originate. This is indeed one of the greatest problems of our time, an anthropology or social biology which still remains to be written, studied and resolved: what are the reasons for this phenomenon, why is it that the supreme interests of the entire human family are so difficult to recognize, to organize and to respect, how can the innumerable groups on this planet be made to work together in peace, harmony and common purpose, without arms, waste and risks of endangering the entire life of our globe? These problems have not yet found an answer, and we can therefore not reproach educators for not educating children in the right way. All we can do, for the moment, is to teach that recourse to war and violence must be eliminated from group relations. This is the first preliminary step towards peace and disarmament. And when we look back at the eradication of slavery on this planet, at the progress achieved in racial equality and equality of men and women, there is good hope that we will also solve sooner or later the problems of economic and social injustice, and of peace and war. There can be very little doubt about it.

Thirdly, when it comes to *the human person*, that alpha and omega of all our efforts—endowed with the miracle of life—we should also show the child the good progress achieved and the distance still to be covered. Humanity is expending countless efforts to know better and improve the physical and mental life of the human person, but greater attention must also be given to the moral and spiritual aspects of life. The worlds of morality, of feelings, of introspection and spirituality lag far and unnecessarily behind the colossal advances of science and technology. In the United Nations, humanity has written in common one of the greatest sets of philosophical documents ever: the Declaration and Covenants on Human Rights, including those of disadvantaged groups. Here we have an official, world recognition of the miracle each human life represents in the universe, the care, respect, dignity and treatment it demands. The philosophy of this planet's four and a half billion individual human lives, including the child's right to economic, social, moral and spiritual development, has been largely written in the United Nations. Alas, in how many schools of this earth are these human rights being taught? Would it not be an immense progress towards peace, and justice if each child of this planet were taught about the Universal Declaration of Human Rights? What more beautiful charter could there be for our world social relations than these words:

> All human beings are born free and equal in dignity and rights. They are endowed with reason and conscience and should act towards one another in a spirit of brotherhood.

To complete the general sketch of a right global, planetary education, one would need to add the time dimension, from the eternity of the universe to the infinitesimal life span of an atomic particle, from the four and a half billion years of our past to the six to eight billion years of our future, the three million years of human evolution, our climatic past and future, the histories and futures of languages, cultures, beliefs and human groups, the life span of the human person in all this emerging, grandiose picture of the universe, our being the product of all past and a building block to all future, and the rules and responsibilities deriving therefrom for each of us. The correct time framework of education still leaves much to be desired. We could learn immensely from the religions, which have always seen the human person as part of the universe and of all time, his total physical, mental, moral and spiritual dimension as a unique, unrepeatable convergence of infinity and eternity.

Teaching the Right Attitude

Pope John Paul II starts his message as follows:

> The great cause of peace between the peoples needs all the energies of peace present in man's heart. It was to the releasing and cultivation of these energies—to the training of them—that my predecessor Paul VI decided, shortly before his death, that the 1979 World Day of Peace should be dedicated: "TO REACH PEACE, TEACH PEACE."

This is another fundamental requirement for the peace and further progress of human civilization on our planet. We must want and work with all our hearts and strength for peace and the fulfillment of the miracle of life for all. Without such will we shall fail; with it, we will succeed. There is a mysterious yet unexplained choice in individual as well as in collective life: we can abandon, be pessimistic and give in to despair, thus setting the stage for our own defeat and downfall, or we can throw down our gauntlet for life, for success and progress, thus bringing into full play the mysterious and miraculous forces and aptitudes for life transmitted to us at birth. This will, this attitude is not the end product of logic or thinking alone; it is a vital drive which sustains life in the complex mysteries around us in a forever incomprehensible but marvelous universe. Without it, our individual lives, a group, a civilization, a culture and humanity perish. Nothing therefore is more important than teaching children the right attitude towards life, peace and human progress. All great religions have placed the miracle of faith at the center of human progress. This is no less true today. Nothing would be more damaging to human peace and ascent than to believe that it cannot be done, that peace, justice and survival are unlikely or impossible.

In this connection, these beautiful words by Teilhard de Chardin are particularly appropriate:

> Let us not forget that faith in peace is not possible, not justifiable, except in a world dominated by faith in the future, *faith in Man* and the progress of Man. By this token, so long as we are not all of one mind, and with a sufficient degree of ardour, it will be useless for us to seek to draw together and unite. We shall only fail.
>
> That is why, when I look for reassurance as to our future, I do not turn to official utterances, or "pacifist" manifestations, or conscientious objectors. I turn instinctively towards the ever more numerous institutions and associations of men where in the search for knowledge a new spirit is silently taking shape around us—the soul of Mankind resolved at all costs to achieve, in its total integrity, the uttermost fulfillment of its powers and its destiny.[1]

It is true, humanity's piercing of the surrounding reality and its intervention as a factor of new, man-made complexities are at the source of much of today's anxiety. But the complexity and mystery of life are not worse now than they were for primitive man. For him it was an even more threatening and incomprehensible world. And we, like him, have at our disposal the great simplifying syntheses translated into human language: belief, beauty, goodness, love, peace, happiness, harmony, wisdom, knowledge, etc.—in other words, all the light, bright and positive sides of life instead of the dark, disintegrating and negative ones.

Hence, the enlightened self-interest and imperative to be optimistic, to bring into play *the miracle of faith*, to release the forces of the heart and of the soul in the largest number of people.

It is with human society as it is with the individual: we need a vision, an objective, a shore to swim towards. If not, we will drown. Life needs to be believed in, to be sustained and nourished. Hence it is our paramount duty to educate children in the art of living and happiness, in believing in humanity's success and in the establishment of a peaceful, just, brotherly and happy world.

All great prophets, visionaries and reformers understood the central importance of education. One of them said: "Give me your children, and I will give you the world." Today we should say: "Give

[1] Teilhard de Chardin, *The Future of Man* (New York: Harper Colophon Books, 1975), p. 159.

the children the right view of the world and they will give us peace."
The time has come when we must reform our curricula, reorder our
knowledge, honestly and objectively, into a vast synthesis which will
show our exact place in the universe and in time and the means of
our progress from a troubled past into a peaceful future. Yes, above
all, our first task is to put order in our knowledge, and from the
magnificent picture which will emerge will flow an immense respect
for creation and the imperative necessity for peace, justice and
fulfillment for all.

Secondly, we must re-establish the unity of science and sentiment,
knowledge and faith, the arts, humanities and spirituality, the inner
world and the outer world, in a search for the total flowering of the
human person.

Third, we must believe in peace, human ascent and justice. As for
all things on this earth, a period of preparation, of take-off is needed.
This is typically the case for economic development, and the same is
true for peace, disarmament and world-wide cooperation. The beginnings are slow, but suddenly a progress which seemed so difficult,
nay, impossible, begins to gain momentum. Proper global education
is an essential factor towards such progress and it should include
teaching the children about the instruments of peace and the first
universal organization ever on this planet: the United Nations and
its family of agencies.

Humanity has been seized by a vast, evolutionary mutation which
will permit us to progress towards both greater unity and more diversity, to understand the vast distances of the universe and the world
of the infinitely small, to grasp our position between all past and all
future, to become the responsible managers and caretakers of our
planet, and to fulfill human nature to an unprecedented extent in
all its aspects—physical, mental, moral and spiritual. We live in a
great moment in evolution. Like Darwin in the last sentence of *The
Origin of Species*, one is tempted to exclaim:

> . . . whilst this planet has gone cycling on according to the fixed
> law of gravity, from so simple a beginning endless forms most beauti-
> ful and most wonderful have been and are being evolved.

Yes, a new form of humanity most beautiful and most wonderful
is being evolved right under our eyes.

PART III

The Global Transcendence
of Religions

14

An Appeal to World Religions for Peace[1]

I would like to outline to this great gathering of religious leaders the following elements of hope in the world situation as I see them emerge in the United Nations, so that when you return to your countries you might help consolidate these trends which in my view will change the world and lead sooner or later to the type of society humans have been dreaming of for thousands of years. Among these positive elements I would like to single out the following:

First, during the last few centuries and especially since World War II, our world has finally appeared to us for what it has always been: *a global world.* For two or more million years we have lived on this planet not even knowing that it was a sphere! If our globe could speak, he would say to us:

"I pity you humans! You make me laugh! I have been rotating and circling around the sun for four and a half billion years! I have witnessed many upheavals in my flesh. I have seen continents and ice covers come and go, seas change place, mountains emerge, an atmosphere be born, vegetation arise, life develop and species evolve and disappear. You came into being only two million years ago. I have seen you crawl in utter ignorance for most of that time. Only a few hundred years ago did you at long last discover America and that I was round! And only a few years ago did you see me in my totality from outer space. I have been observing you and I want to tell you this:

"You will go nowhere if you do not remember that I will be around for several more billion years; that my body will be shaken

[1] Transcript of an address before the Third World Conference on Religion and Peace, United Nations and Princeton, August–September 1980.

by more climatic changes; that for your maximum happiness and survival you must treat and manage me with care; that you must increasingly put yourselves in my place and lift your eyes, as I do, to the sun, to the universe, to infinity and eternity of which we are only a part. After your cave age, after your tribal age, after your feudal age, after your national age, you have at long last entered *my* age: the global age. But this is still insufficient, for you have yet to enter the cosmic or divine age and see your proper place in the fathomless universe and time. You still have to become the planet of God."

And we could justifiably answer our globe: "Yes, it took us a long time, but we are there. Haven't you seen us lately make our world a global, interdependent unit through science, technology and expanding human relations? Haven't you noticed our satellites which are observing you, studying you, and linking every point of your body with others through communications? Thousands of airplanes and ships circle you. Tens of thousands of meetings and congresses are being held on your crust. We peoples of the world have never known each other so well. Our society is being more closely interwoven every day in thousands of ways into a vast interdependent, global unit. Do you think that all this will be without effects?"

And we could add another great sign of this new age and historical trend: the birth of the United Nations itself. Yes, we should never forget that the ancient dream to have a universal organization has at long last come true. I am astonished that all peoples of the earth do not rejoice at that achievement which all the great prophets, visionaries, philosophers and humanists had been dreaming of. Yes, all nations of this planet are now meeting, learning from each other and beginning to cooperate in many world agencies and programs dealing with practically every problem under the sun. How happy the Gautama Buddha, Jesus and Mahomet would be if they could see the United Nations! This is why Pope Paul VI when he visited the UN described his trip as "the end of a journey that started two thousand years ago." For the first time the dream of the Catholic (Universal) Church was fulfilled: its Pope could speak to the Assembly of all nations of earth. He asked therefore in moving terms for the support of the United Nations: "Our message is first of all a moral and solemn ratification of this lofty institution . . . convinced as we are that it represents the obligatory path of modern civilization and world peace." And Pope John Paul II after his resounding visit to the United Nations, when he left, repeated several times, with tears in his eyes, looking back at the UN buildings: "God bless the United Nations, God bless the United Nations."

Hence the need for all world religions to actively support and thoroughly explain the United Nations to their peoples, for it is here that the old dreams of humanity for peace, non-violence, disarmament, justice, world ethics and human dignity find their latest expression. This is most important, so that this organization shall never be allowed to die or to disappear but be strengthened and enlightened in the cause of human ascent. As Pope Paul VI rightly said: "This edifice that you have built must never fall again into ruins. It must be improved upon and adapted to the demands which the history of the world will make upon it." This is the new ecumenical spirit which is needed. As someone who has worked in the world organization for over thirty years, who knows it inside out from its good and its weak sides, I can only say this: it is the beginning of the fulfillment of one of the most prodigious dreams of humanity. It is the greatest hope we ever had in our divided, conflictual journey on planet Earth. We must make it work. We must help the dream come true with all our strength, all our mind, all our heart and all our soul. We need the support and the prayers of the people. We cannot win if the people do not plead with their leaders for the support and strengthening of the UN. This is the first great hopeful element which all of us can foster and nourish in order to achieve a peaceful and better world. And your help can be invaluable.

A second positive element is that we have become a new, transcended species with vastly expanded capacities, senses, knowledge and dominion over our planetary home. We were born into our particular planetary conditions with very limited senses and capacities. We have been able to achieve a tremendous miracle: that of extending practically every sense and capacity in every direction. Our eyesight did not reach more than a few kilometers, but we are now able, thanks to science and technology, to look into the far expanses of the universe, to take pictures of stars which are billions of light-years away. We can see into the infinitely small through electronic microscopes and picoscopes and observe the behavior of nuclear particles and subparticles in atomic bubble chambers. We can now hear the sounds of the universe through radio and a voice from New Delhi in New York through satellite communications. The short range of our legs has been multiplied by airplanes and other swift means of transportation. We can cross the seas, fly in the air and circle the globe in space capsules. The capacity of our brain has been multiplied thousands of times through computers and electronic devices. We have extended the capacity of our hands through incredible machines and factories. Thus, we are a new transcended species which has explored thoroughly the little corner of the universe which we occupy, and lifted our eyes vastly into the infinite.

We have made much less progress in expanding and transcending our hearts and souls, our morality and our spirituality. The great human achievements of the last few centuries have been principally in the domains of matter and mind. We have not even tried to explore what humanity could achieve if it transcended also its moral and spiritual capacities. This page has still to be written. We are only at the beginning of it. We can witness the birth of a morality in the United Nations, but immorality in this world by far still outweighs morality. Think alone of the five hundred and fifty billion dollars which are spent each year on insane, life-annihilating armaments while there are so many poor. We are still at the cave age of establishing right human relations on this planet. We have been able to look at the stars with gigantic telescopes, but has this species honestly tried to lift its heart and soul to the universe? Have we tried to become not only a global family but a spiritual family, standing in awe before the beautiful, stupendous creation? Have we really asked ourselves the fundamental question: what is this little planet in the universe and what is our purpose and destiny on it? Must we not see ourselves as a meaningful part of total creation and of the total stream of time? These are the great questions which political leaders must ask themselves. In the United Nations they have been raised very forcefully by Dag Hammarskjöld and U Thant. This again is a positive trend. Humanity, despite innumerable wars, accidents, errors and foolishness, has been able during the two million years of its story to maintain an ever ascending course. It stands today at an infinitely higher level than ever before. It is our task to bring it to even higher summits. This is where the religions have a fundamental role to play. They can coalesce, mobilize their people and demand from governments that morality and spirituality be put on a par with scientific and technological development. This is one of the greatest blessings that could happen to humanity. Otherwise science, technology and world cooperation will remain fraught with much immorality, because their ethics have been insufficiently defined. We are only at the beginning of a world ethics. In the upward march of humanity, religions can play a momentous role. They can help humanity's political progress to transcend itself into the realms of morality and love which all great prophets heralded as the ultimate key to the problem of peace on earth. Above all, religions can help humanity better understand its right place and behavior in creation. When it comes to the mystical, extraterrestrial comprehension of the universe, religions are far ahead of science and technology, of governments and of the United Nations.

A third positive element in the world situation is that, as a result of the improvement of our senses through science and technology, we have been able for the first time ever in our evolution to draw a very simple, magnificent Copernican tapestry of all our knowledge of the surrounding physical and living world. This picture has emerged from the work of the UN agencies where all human knowledge converges. Our human race has now a prodigious view which reaches from the infinitely large to the infinitesimally small. It all falls into place. We are hanging and twirling in the universe around our sun on a given planet endowed with specific resources. We have looked at this planet from every possible angle. We have examined it, investigated it globally in a whole series of resounding world conferences. Every segment, every global aspect of our little planet has been examined world-wide. Historians someday will consider these years as a crucial turning point in evolution. As a result, for the first time, we possess a great encyclopedia of knowledge which shows us that our planet is a very special one, that it is a magnificent abode in the universe compared with so many other lifeless planets. Perhaps we are one of the luckiest celestial bodies. Perhaps the religions are right when they think that God has a special design for us. As a result, we have great responsibilities towards this lovely globe of ours. Religions are not particularly inclined towards science. This is an error, for the knowledge of this marvelous picture of creation is part of our spiritual journey.

The fourth element is no less dramatic: in recent years, humanity has not only appraised its entire planet, but it has also for the first time taken full cognizance of itself. This had never happened before. For the first time, the human race has studied, analyzed and measured itself. As recently as thirty years ago we did not even know how many people lived on this planet! Today we know how many we are, how many women and men there are, how many children, handicapped and old people there are, and what our future numbers are likely to be. Every single global aspect of the human condition, be it longevity, nutrition, literacy, the state of health, standards of life, has been examined in world conferences or in one of the UN specialized agencies. UN demographers can tell us how long people can expect to live country by country. The International Labor Organization tells us how many unemployed people there are. The Food and Agriculture Organization tells us that there are still five hundred million hungry people. All this was totally unknown only a mere three decades ago. There were not even any world statistics at the time when I joined the United Nations! There had never been any world conferences or international years on this planet. This is all happening for the first time in our two million years of evolution. Religions here again have an important contribution to make because of their long experience and knowledge with social and human problems, from childhood to death.

A fifth positive element is the sudden increase in our time perception. It is only recently that humanity really began to think about its future. In 1945 we worked from year to year. Today governments and the entire United Nations system are geared to thinking and working decades ahead. The year 2000 is the normal time span for practically every UN agency. There is a world food plan 2000, a world health plan 2000, a world literacy plan 2000, a Third UN Economic Development Decade. The human species is extending its time dimension to a tremendous extent. This is another great victory of humanity, for as we expand our time vision we discover that our planet has limits and that certain things have become impossible. We encounter limits to growth, limits to resources, limits to human longevity, limits to the life-bearing capacity of our planet. It is increasingly important for us to see our place not only in the total planet but also in the total stream of time. Here again, the religions have a great contribution to make. While governments and international organizations speak in terms of a few decades, the religions have always seen humanity in the total time frame of the universe. There is no religion that does not see life from creation to the apocalypse. What the astrophysicists tell us today about the birth of a solar system, its multibillion-year-long stability and its ultimate collapse, only to be reborn in the form of another star, is known to all major religions by instinct, by vision. Hence the religions have an invaluable experience, for they see the human race in a much more complete, integral relationship with eternity than the scientists, economists and developers of today. The religions possess the right instinct about our place in total time. Their perceptions can be of utmost importance to scientists and political men.

Finally, there is another recent discovery which the religions knew from the beginning and have been relentlessly advocating, even if their competition over this fundamental truth led to many unfortunate religious wars and behavior contrary to their beliefs: the tremendous worth, dignity and sanctity of each individual human life. The more scientists study the human person, the more they discover that it is a true miracle. No human being has ever existed before in exactly the same form and will never exist again in the same form in all eternity. Even if this were the case, the circumstances of his life would be different. So we discover that each life is unique, that each human being is an incredibly complex and marvelous entity in the infinity of cosmoses, from the infinitely large to the infinitely small, linked with all matter, elements and life, yet endowed with his own, astonishing identity. We are thus given a tremendous view of the universe in which everything is linked and yet is an entity, from a galaxy and a star to an atomic particle. We know how unique, how sacred and how soulful a member of our own family is. We know it especially at the moment of death. The same is true of every member of the human family. As a result, a human should never be killed and should never kill. He should never be harmed and never harm. He should never inflict violence or have violence be inflicted on him.

Around this view of the uniqueness and preciousness of human life turns the whole story of human rights and of the establishment of peaceful and right human relations on this planet. It is the cornerstone of the coming global civilization and an absolute confirmation of what the religions have been saying for thousands of years. Isn't it obvious therefore that the religions and the United Nations should form a great alliance in the defense of human life, so that finally peace and the sanctity and dignity of the human person will become world-wide realities in our planetary home?

These are some of the main positive trends which can be seen from the vantage point of the United Nations. Despite their idiosyncrasies, errors, reluctance and misbehavior, nations are learning their lessons and the world is changing. The human race is seeking its planetization with unprecedented intensity. The old battles of humans with the elements and with each other will soon come to an end through very fundamental and powerful imperatives of evolution. The next stage will be our entry into a moral global age—the global age of love—and a global spiritual age—the cosmic age. We are now moving fast towards the fulfillment of the visions of the great prophets who through cosmic enlightenment saw the world as one unit, the human race as one family, sentiment as the cement of that family and the soul as our link with the universe, eternity and God. As Kant said:

"The star-studded sky above us and moral consciousness in us."

This is the message I would like you to take home to your people. Ask them to cherish their United Nations, to have faith and to pray for us.

15

Pope Paul VI's Doctrine of Peace

During my many years with the United Nations, I had occasion to observe the important role of Pope Paul VI in world affairs and matters of peace. He was a dear friend of former Secretary-General U Thant, whom I often heard speak of him with great fondness and admiration. Pope Paul was one of the few people, a group of very special persons, with whom U Thant was in constant spiritual communion. Later I had the privilege of accompanying Secretary-General Waldheim to Rome when he visited the Holy Father for the first time. I can remember vividly how large the issue of peace loomed in the spirit and heart of His Holiness. There is no doubt that Paul VI, together with John XXIII and John Paul II, will be remembered as the three great Popes of Peace, pioneers of a momentous transcendence of the Catholic Church into the New Age.

I have read much of what Paul VI wrote and said about human values and peace. His thoughts, writings and pronouncements constitute a unique doctrine of peace for our time. I hope that scholars and political scientists will bring out someday the richness, depth, vision and timeliness of that doctrine. Let us not forget that the Catholic Pope, like the Secretary-General of the UN, is a global, ecumenic man who has the whole world and its people at heart.[1] His thoughts and actions are therefore of utmost importance to the world community.

The following are a few comments on some of Pope Paul VI's fundamental ideas. They are based primarily on the remarkable an-

[1] Dag Hammarskjöld once observed that there were two Popes on this planet: a spiritual Pope in Rome and a civilian Pope in New York, namely, the Secretary-General of the UN.

nual messages issued by him on the occasion of the Day of Peace on January 1, which he instituted and which is always a very special event for the United Nations.

Pacts Must Be Observed

One of the cardinal principles in the Pope's doctrine is that pacts must be observed (*pacta servanda sunt*). This is the central theme of his message for 1976, "Real Weapons of Peace." How familiar it sounds to the minds of the delegates to the United Nations! Personally, I came to the conclusion long ago that the single most important way to achieve universal peace would be the strict observance of the United Nations Charter and the solemn pledge never to break it under any circumstances, which is, alas, not the case. Governments, when they break the Charter for selfish reasons, always think that they break it only a little bit. In reality they break it entirely and make the international system of security unworkable and untrustworthy. The Charter, it cannot be repeated often enough, is one of the most remarkable pacts of all times. It contains all necessary principles, methods, procedures and rules of conduct to prevent conflicts and to ensure peaceful relations among nations. A full, universal, honest, unreserved and painstaking adherence to its spirit and provisions by all members would make it the most effective instrument of peace ever. This in turn would forge the conditions under which nations would entrust their security to their collective organization rather than to arsenals of weapons or the armed protective wings of powerful tutors and military alliances.

Peace Depends on You Too

How right the Holy Father was when in his 1974 message he recalled this fundamental truth of human society. Peace is not the sole matter of governments and international agencies. Peace is the matter of every human being. In the end, total peace, justice, understanding and happiness in the world can only be the sum total of the peace, justice, understanding and happiness of all individuals, families, cities, nations, races, continents and cultures. Peace is interdependent in time and in space. The sense of peace, justice and understanding of a statesman may have been taught to him as a child by his parents, by the example of a public leader or by a good teacher. And the world may benefit immensely from that circumstance if, at a moment of crisis, that leader extends his hands to his neighbor instead of seizing arms. A single act of peace is never lost. It has mysterious, far-reaching effects in the total world fabric.

There rests an immense power for peace in the four and a half billion inhabitants of earth. People can be the masters of world peace if they work for it, if they insist on it, if they take an interest in their first universal institutions and give them their strength, their minds, their hearts and their spirits, a fact to which no government can remain insensitive. Thus, nothing in my view could do more for the strengthening and effectiveness of the United Nations than a good understanding, knowledge and wholehearted support by the public. Peace or war may depend on it. Generation after generation will have to be educated in matters of peace and global living, if peace is to become a permanent feature of this planet.

Disarmament

His Holiness repeatedly insisted on disarming as the primary condition for peace. Whatever justifications a state or group of states may have for resorting to armaments for their security, no universal person or institution can ever lend support to the idea of a planet of armed nations. From the standpoint of the earth, armaments are a folly, a disgrace and an intolerable waste. They are a folly when one thinks of the type of insane, life-annihilating weapons which are being master-minded and accumulated on our fragile globe, in the air, on the soil, in the soil, on the seas and in the seas. They are a disgrace, for they cast a severe doubt on human intelligence and on the validity of the earth's present political system. They are an intolerable waste when one thinks that five hundred and fifty billion dollars are being squandered each year on armaments—the equivalent of total world expenditures on health and education—when so many hundreds of millions of human beings cry out for food, medical care, schools and shelter on our planet. As the Pope once remarked, armaments kill, even if they are not used: they kill scores of children and people who could have been saved from hunger, malnutrition and malady.

The scandal has reached such proportions that renewed attempts at disarming are being incessantly launched by the United Nations. Even if there is little chance for early world disarmament, this must be repeated time and again, and it must remain one of the first priorities of the United Nations. There is even more reason to eradicate armaments from this planet than there was to eradicate smallpox. All conceivable files and proposals for disarmament are ready. They have been painstakingly worked out over the last three decades. All depends on the will of the peoples and nations, especially the big nations who bear the main responsibility in this matter.

If You Want Peace, Work for Justice

How pertinent are these words chosen by His Holiness for the title of his peace message in 1972! Injustice is one of the main arguments adduced by its victims to justify and advocate violence and war. The idea of a "holy" or "just" violence has not yet been eradicated from the mind of man. When utter despair sets in, it takes a saint not to think of violence and rebellion as a means of achieving justice. How can we envisage a peaceful, brotherly world, for example, if the fantastic injustices between rich and poor are allowed to prevail on our planet? The drafters of the Charter saw it most clearly when they considered economic and social progress to be one of the main foundations of peace. We see this also when attempts are being made to stem such new forms of international violence as hijacking, the taking of hostages and terrorism. The perpetrators often tell us that, despairing of finding a peaceful solution to such problems as independence, crying social and economic inequalities or the regaining of a homeland, they have no other ways but violence. We can have no illusion: the problem of world justice has been clearly and forcefully placed before states and the United Nations. Its definition and attainment represent one of the most staggering world-wide challenges of our time.

Promotion of Human Rights

In "Promotion of Human Rights, the Road to Peace" (1969 message), again His Holiness touched on one of the fundamental causes of discontent and conflict on our planet. The United Nations is often criticized for not doing enough in this field. In my opinion, historians looking back someday at the last decades of our century will recognize that the United Nations' definition of the inalienable rights of the human person has been one of the greatest collective philosophical achievements of humankind.

The question here again is one of faithful and strict compliance by governments. Much remains to be done in this respect, but at least the world community is on the right track, despite considerable difficulties stemming from divergent views regarding the position of the individual within the various social and political groups of which he is part. With time and persistence, all violations of human rights will have the same fate as slavery and racism.

Consciousness of Human Brotherhood

In his 1971 message, His Holiness reminded us forcefully of the basic truth that "Every man is my brother." Nothing, indeed, in the long run will contribute more to the forging of a peaceful and orderly society than the recent emergence of a true world-wide community. Prophets and philosophers had all perceived the fundamental unity and brotherhood of humans, but for the first time in all our long journey such a community is now being truly born. This is due primarily to the tremendous strides in science and technology which have revealed the immensely complex natural interdependence of everything on earth and have promoted over a short few decades a no less astoundingly dense and irreversible network of man-made interdependencies. Willingly or not, no nation desirous of surviving in these circumstances can afford not to pray and work for peace. This is our greatest chance of all times. One can see it well at the United Nations, where behind protracted political difficulties and idiosyncrasies the human community is fashioning an unprecedented system of world agencies and instrumentalities which play a vital role in the probing, monitoring and assessment of our total planetary home as well as in the guidance of human behavior and destiny in it. In my view, the numerous UN agencies, world conferences, meetings and endeavors are a direct, most concrete biological manifestation of the nascent efforts of the human species to establish itself as one interdependent, fulfilled and peaceful community in harmony with its planetary ecosystem.

If You Want Peace, Defend Life

In his 1976 message His Holiness dealt with the ultimate goal of all our efforts: the defense of life. In the great universal school of philosophy which the United Nations has become, it is more and more apparent that humanity is setting the highest objectives ever for human life. Priority has been given first to the attainment of a good physical life for all, in terms of food, health and shelter, and of a decent mental life through education, without which there can be neither dignity nor understanding of the miracle of life. In those countries where these two objectives have been attained, people in increasing numbers, especially youth, are demanding a new dimension of life: they insist on the establishment of a moral society, the right not to kill, not to wear arms, and the establishment of morality, honesty, trust and integrity in all walks of life, public and private. This trend has emerged in the UN where more and more codes of ethics and rules of conduct are being requested on subjects as diverse as biological engineering, the comportment of the police, the transfer of technology, and transnational corporations.

Everything is beginning to fall into place. We have acquired during the last few years a remarkable knowledge of all major global conditions of our planet. The challenge is now whether harmonious cooperation can be established between all social and political groups so that each human being, this miracle of creation and unique cosmos, will be able to achieve full consciousness of life—physical, mental, moral and spiritual. Yes, if we want peace, the first step is to defend life and to realize its uniqueness, sanctity, inalienability, sovereignty and miraculous character.

* * *

The Pope's rich doctrine of peace evokes innumerable other thoughts and comments. May I simply join in His Holiness' optimism and belief in the human race. Yes, as he exclaimed, peace is possible. Yes, disarmament is possible. Yes, justice is possible. Yes, human dignity is possible. Yes, a planet of love is possible. We may stand on the threshold of one of the greatest periods ever in evolution, if follies and accidents can be prevented. Humanity's incredible achievements in the realms of science, technology and thought can now be matched also in the social, humanitarian, ethical, moral, political and spiritual fields. It is through the development of ties of sentiment, love, understanding, give and take, truth, altruism, compassion and global order, and through a full realization of the miracle of life, that we will be able to embark upon the next segment of our prodigious journey in evolution. Pope Paul's vision and doctrine of peace, which translate into modern terms the eternal message of

Christ, are luminous guideposts on our road to becoming the planet of God.

As Teilhard de Chardin announced:

> The day will come when, after harnessing the ether, the winds, the tides, gravitation, we shall harness for God the energies of love. And, on that day, for the second time in the history of the world, man will have discovered fire.

16

The Visit of Pope John Paul II
to the United Nations

One day, after the session of the Economic and Social Council in Geneva, as I was prepared to leave for a visit to my relatives in Alsace-Lorraine, I received a phone call from Secretary-General Waldheim.

"Robert, you may know that I have invited Pope John Paul II to visit and address the United Nations. He has just accepted and will come to New York in October. I wish to appoint you as my personal representative to organize and coordinate the visit. Could you come on Sunday to my hotel for a first meeting with the Pope's representatives, who will be coming from Rome?"

That meant the end of our planned journey to my home region but also the beginning of one my most interesting assignments in the United Nations. The details, incidents and multifaceted aspects of that event could fill a separate volume, for the public has no idea how many delicate and fascinating problems such a visit involves. I will only mention a few of them, each a major headache:

— How much time would the Pope spend in the UN and what time would be left for New York City? (This raised considerable problems with the Archdiocese of New York.)
— Would it be a visit to the UN, as was Pope Paul VI's trip in 1965, or would it be a visit which would start on United States soil? (This raised major protocol problems.)
— Who would receive him at the airport, what authorities would

be allowed to greet him, to shake his hands and to make speeches?

— What security and what media coverage would there be at the airport?

— How would the cavalcade proceed from the airport to New York, what route would it follow, what traffic control and security arrangements would be made?

— Who would receive him at the entrance of the UN? Who would take the elevator with him? Who from the Vatican and from the cardinalate would accompany him?

— What exact timetable and route would he follow in the UN, minute by minute, including time to wash his hands?

— What heads of state and foreign ministers would he see, collectively or separately?

— How much time and talks would he have with the Secretary-General?

— The exchange of gifts and the taking of official photographs.

— Television arrangements with more than one hundred countries for the televising of the visit.

— The accommodation of three thousand journalists, six hundred of them accompanying the Pope from Rome; the issuance of passes to them and their stationing along the route taken by the Pontiff to and in the UN.

— The exposure of the UN staff to the Pope, including some sick members who wanted a healing benediction from him.

— The speeches he was to deliver to different audiences in five different rooms; their readiness and distribution in many languages, without any advance leakages to the press.

— Who would be admitted to the General Assembly Hall (a major headache)?

— How would the cardinals, the Pope's entourage, the distinguished guests, the press, the Catholic organizations, etc., be seated?

— Where and with whom would the Pope have luncheon?

— Who would be invited to the afternoon reception at which His Holiness would meet individually a long list of personalities, including all heads of state and ministers of foreign affairs present at the General Assembly, all ambassadors of the one hundred and fifty-four member nations and their wives, many New York guests and U.S. personalities?

— What final speeches would be delivered?
— Arrangements for the departure of the Pope.

And I could mention many, many other problems and headaches. Looking back at the event, I feel as though I exercised the function of a space flight director, who has to think of every possible detail and circumstance that might go wrong, or of a theater manager, who has to spend hundreds of hours on stage and backstage to provide the public with a smoothly running, perfect, beautiful two-hour show. Some of my friends asked me afterwards: "We didn't see you much on television among the people surrounding the Pope." Well, one doesn't see the space flight director and theater manager either!

Throughout the entire visit, until the very last moment, I was checking on details and potential mishaps. For example, while the official party of the Secretary-General went to receive the Pope at the airport, I was following a last time the Pontiff's itinerary at the UN, impersonating him and trying to find out if there could still be something that might go wrong. On that last rehearsal I found that two TV platforms, built during the night, were obstructing the route! I also discovered a lady who was placing tons of green plants on the platform where the Pope and the Secretary-General were to greet guests during the afternoon reception. I asked her:

"What on earth are you doing here?"

"I am the lady from the contracting firm which provides the flowers and green plants for UN receptions."

"Dear madam, not only is this platform going to look like a funeral scene, but do you see those platforms for TV and photographers across the room? They will take innumerable pictures and views of the guests being greeted by His Holiness, and each of the pictures is going to show palm leaves growing out of the head of the Pope, the Secretary-General and the guests! It will be a disaster. Could you remove all these tall plants and leave only a row of small flowerpots and plants?"

Thank God, all went well. A little before 6:00 P.M., Cardinal Cooke reappeared in his magnificent garments, ready to take delivery of his Pope. I handed His Holiness to him at 6:03, with only three minutes' delay and without any scratch or incident. I was physically and psychologically exhausted, happy that it was all over but also the proud possessor of a magnificent golden pectoral Crucifix given to me by His Holiness in appreciation of my efforts.

I apologize for all these details, which are only incidental to my subject, but I thought that they might be of some interest to the reader.

Regarding the substance and historical significance of the Pope's visit, I would have this to say:

First of all, any visit of the Pontiff of the Catholic Church is of utmost significance. One could trace the world's main historic events for the last two thousand years by studying the Popes' visits, non-visits, voluntary visits and forced visits away from Rome. Just remember the Pope's compelled visit to Rheims for the coronation of the Emperor Napoleon! Pope Paul VI inaugurated the Popes' modern visits around the world. Very symbolically and understandably, his first visit was to the poor: he visited Bombay for the International Eucharistic Congress. His next visit, at the invitation of U Thant, was to the community of nations in New York. He was so particular about that point that he did not even stay overnight on U.S. territory. Pope John Paul II changed that style and wanted to be exposed primarily to the people rather than to officialdom. But, for both, the UN was one of the most important, if not the most important, places on earth. As Pope Paul VI put it in his address to the General Assembly:

> "We have been journeying long and we bring with us a long history; we here celebrate the epilogue of a toilsome pilgrimage in search of a conversation with the entire world, from the day the commandment was given to us: 'Go and bring the good tidings to all peoples.' And it is you who represent all peoples."

Or in the words of John Paul II:

> As a universal community embracing the faithful belonging to almost all countries and continents, nations, peoples, races, languages and cultures, the Church is deeply interested in the existence and activity of the Organization whose very name tells us that it unites and associates nations and States. It unites and associates: it does not divide and oppose. This is the real reason, the essential reason, for my presence among you.

Secondly, on the occasion of Paul VI's visit, I was lucky to have been given by U Thant's family an unpublished text by the former Secretary-General covering a number of subjects which he had not treated in his memoirs. Among these was his invitation to Pope Paul VI to visit and address the United Nations.

Here are extracts from that text:

. . . Did I leave out anything of historical significance during my decade with the U.N. Secretariat? Yes, I must mention the historic visit of His Holiness Pope Paul VI to the United Nations on October 4, 1965. The story of my invitation and of the Pope's kind acceptance goes back to an event at Bombay on December 4, 1964.

The Pope had gone to Bombay to attend the International Eucharistic Congress. At a meeting with a group of journalists during his three-day stay in the Indian city, he addressed through them an appeal to the world. In part he said:

"We entrust to you Our special message to the world. Would that the nations could cease the armaments race, and devote their resources and energies instead to the fraternal assistance of the developing countries! Would that every nation, thinking thoughts of peace and not affliction and of war, would contribute even a part of its expenditure for arms to a great world fund for the relief of the many problems of nutrition, clothing, shelter and medical care which affect so many peoples!"

These words, coming from the head of a great religion, were in line with my own thoughts which I had expressed on several occasions. I had said repeatedly that the widening gulf between the rich and the poor countries was far more serious and ultimately far more explosive than the division of the world into East and West based on ideological differences. Moreover, I felt that the General Assembly Hall of the United Nations had been the forum for statesmen and politicians; economists and sociologists. From time to time why should not this great hall be the forum for spiritual and religious leaders? I discussed the idea of extending an invitation to His Holiness to address a special meeting of the General Assembly with the President of the 19th session of the General Assembly, Ambassador Alex Quaison-Sackey of Ghana. He was enthusiastic.

I immediately asked Pier Pasquale Spinelli, Under-Secretary and head of the European office of the United Nations at Geneva to sound out the Vatican confidentially if His Holiness would be agreeable to address the General Assembly if a formal invitation were to be sent to him. Mr. Spinelli, an Italian, and one of the wisest men who ever served the United Nations, made discreet soundings, and reported to me that if I were to extend an invitation, the reply would be affirmative.

And U Thant later in the text had this to say on the address of His Holiness to the General Assembly:

The scope of the speech covered the essential provisions of the United Nations Charter. He touched on themes which were also not in the Charter. "The edifice of modern civilization must be built on spiritual principles, which alone cannot only support it, but also illuminate and animate it," he said. As one who believes in the moral and spiritual development of man, I was deeply moved. In fact the Pope's visit to the United Nations was not only of symbolic significance, but his speech was of historic importance. It left a lasting impression on the assembled diplomats of all religious denominations.

Thirdly, as the reader can well imagine, there was a very considerable intellectual and political preparation for the Pope's visit. One can visualize all the consultations that took place at the Vatican to prepare the form and the contents of the visit, in particular the Pontiff's major address to the General Assembly and his four other speeches. Bishop Marcinkus, my counterpart at the Vatican, told me that he had a reproduction of Harry Anderson's famous painting, *The Prince of Peace*, showing Christ knocking at the UN building, placed on one of the itineraries of the Pope in the Vatican. He casually made the Pope stop in front of it and said to him: "This is what you are supposed to do in New York." I answered Marcinkus: "You are wrong. Jesus is already inside the UN building."

I myself was asked for my expectations from the Pope's visit, and this is what I said in an editorial in the *Diplomatic World Bulletin*:

I expect his visit to be a resounding expression of support and encouragement for the UN, at a time when this first universal organization meets with dangerous cynicism, misunderstanding and lack of faith, especially on the part of the media. The Pope's mere presence at the UN, even if he did not pronounce a word, will be of tremendous importance.

I expect the Pope in his address to the General Assembly to lift the hearts and minds of governments, to give them a vision of what the world can be and should be as we approach the bimillennium, and to renew our faith that humanity can fulfill its ancient dreams of peace, harmony, brotherhood and personal dignity.

I expect the Pope to add a spiritual dimension to the emerging world vision which today, of necessity, gives priority to the physical and mental well-being of humanity, but must also be extended to an understanding and appreciation of the miracle of human life and of our planet in the vast universe and stream of time.

I expect the Pope to lift the hearts of all international servants of the UN and of its specialized agencies and programs, so that this first group of human beings who come from all quarters of the world and who work together for the good of humanity can bring forth new visions in philosophy, sociology, ideology and spirituality centered on the UN's noble objective of "unity in diversity."

I expect the Pope's visit to be a great, moving event which would make the hearts of the world's four and a half billion people beat together for a moment.

I expect the Pope's visit to engender in many hearts a profound prayer for peace, for kindness, for human brotherhood and for the success of the world-serving United Nations.

Basically and foremost, the Pope came to the UN unimpressed and uninfluenced by anyone and delivered his own, deeply felt, unique message, the product of his entire life and most intimate thinking. With the exception of a few protocol and diplomatic niceties, his message was entirely written in his own hand. I know this very well: for purposes of the media, we tried to have him keep his speech to thirty minutes or to one hour sharp. He insisted on more time and obtained this compromise: the entire written text would be left intact, but he would refrain from reading certain parts of it to keep it down to one hour. Until the actual delivery, no one knew what he would delete, for I saw three of his aides follow the text frantically during the meeting, deleting from it what he had omitted.

What was the main message of the Pope? While peace had been the main theme of Pope Paul VI's address in 1965, human rights, or rather the sanctity, sacredness and centrality of the individual human person, was his main theme. His speech is a classic on the subject. It merits reading and rereading, and it continues to be quoted often in UN speeches. I really wish that someday a book containing the UN speeches of the two Popes and their yearly messages on the Day of Peace might be published for wide distribution. The result would be a kind of Bible for modern times. The two following quotations are illustrative of the speech:

"The questions that concern your functions and receive your attention—as is indicated by the vast organic complex of institutions and activities that are part of or collaborate with the United Nations, especially in the fields of culture, health, food, labour, and the peaceful uses of nuclear energy—certainly make it essential for us *to meet in the name of man in his wholeness,* in all the fullness and manifold riches of his spiritual and material existence. . . .

"Each one of you represents a particular State, system and political structure, but what you represent above all are *individual human beings;* you are all *representatives of men and women, of practically all the people of the world,* individual men and women, communities and peoples who are living the present phase of their own history and who are also part of the history of humanity as a whole, each of them a subject endowed with dignity as a human person, with his or her own culture, experiences and aspirations, tensions and sufferings, and legitimate expectations. This relationship is what provides the reason for *all political activity,* whether national or international, for in the final analysis this activity comes *from man,* is exercised *by man* and is *for man.* And if political activity is cut off from this fundamental relationship and finality, if it becomes in a way its own end, it loses much of its reason to exist. Even more, it can also give rise to a specific alienation; it can become extraneous to man; it can come to contradict humanity itself. In reality, what justifies the existence of any political activity is service to man, concerned and responsible attention to the essential problems and duties of his earthly existence in its social dimension and significance, on which also the good of each person depends."

He of course, like Paul VI, reminded the world assembly of the imperative of the spiritual:

"The progress of humanity must be measured not only by *the progress of science and technology,* which shows man's uniqueness with regard to nature, but also and chiefly by *the primacy given to spiritual values* and by *the progress of moral life."*

It is perhaps this central role of the human person in his thought and life which explains best the tremendous charisma of John Paul II. I observed him closely during his speeches and his encounters with individual persons: his "charm," or rather the love and liking people feel for him, is the product of his own love and concern for each individual human person, met alone or in a group. He "descends" to the person and to the group. He lives them. He senses the whole, total person or the soul of a group, and submits his entire being, mind, heart and soul, to the comprehension of that person or group, and what they expect from him in terms of help, healing, elevation, hope and inspiration. What lessons I learned from him during that short intensive day! Indeed, in our age, people are sufficiently educated and sophisticated to expect a leader to embody the teachings and morality he professes. They can no longer be fooled. They instinctively and unmistakenly feel the charisma, the honesty, the living embodiment of goodness, kindness and love in the master, in the good leader of people. This explains the resonance and irradiation of Pope John Paul II far beyond his Catholic flock. The people of this planet are thirsty for loving, good, ethical, moral, pure and disinterested leaders and public servants, for individuals whose hearts, minds, actions and souls unreservedly embrace the entire world, the entire human race, the last of our brethren and sisters, the last misery and poverty on earth, and God in heaven. Such appeared to me John Paul II.

And to the first group of world servers of this planet he gave the measure and limits of our lives, by comparing us to the stonecutters of a cathedral. In his view we were not likely to see the finished monument of universal peace, of fraternal collaboration and of true harmony between people, but sometimes we would catch a glimpse of it, in a particularly successful achievement, in a problem solved, in the smile of a happy and healthy child, in a conflict avoided, in a reconciliation of minds and hearts achieved. "But know that your work is great and that history will judge your achievements with favour."[1] These words apply to all men and women of good will around this planet who have thrown down the gauntlet for a peaceful, happier and godlier society. Thank you, dear John Paul II, for your blessed visit and for your benediction of the world organization.

[1] United Nations press release, GA/6014 of October 2, 1979.

17

The Reappearance of Christ[1]

You have asked me the question: What does the reappearance of Christ mean in the political, religious and educational fields? To that question I can only answer with a few perceptions, insights and foresights which have grown upon me after working for so many years at the United Nations. It is indeed a place where every day you can see the entire globe, its entire people and the entirety of their dreams, agreements, disagreements, conflicts and evolution. Since everything culminates in this organization and you observe it on a daily basis through the documents you read and the meetings you attend, seeing men and women from various nations trying to find a new path of human destiny, you end up asking yourself: "What does this all mean? Where are we? Is what I am being told the truth? What is happening on this planet? At what moment of evolution or history are we? What is life? What does this complexity mean? What do all our discoveries signify? What do all those divergent views coming from around the globe mean? Is this all vanity? Does it make any sense? Is this a ridiculous planet in the universe? Or on the contrary is what is happening making sense? Does it respond to something? Are we not the partners, the participants, and the instruments of something that goes far beyond us, that was started a long time ago and which will lead to a greater, more beautiful, higher planetary civilization?" These are questions I am asking myself every day. I will give you the answers I have arrived at, especially in the last few years, because I believe that our view is beginning to be clearer.

[1] Transcript of an address to the Arcane School Conference, New York, August 12, 1979.

Things are beginning progressively to fall into a pattern which we had not seen before, because it couldn't be seen, and which foreshadows the world predicted two thousand years ago by someone who had the most luminous insights into the mysteries of life on this planet and in the universe, namely, Christ. This is why, from all I have learned in this global organization, I am more and more drawn to some of the very simple but extremely important teachings of the Christ and of all the great prophets and visionaries. I am increasingly convinced that what they foresaw is beginning to become a reality on this planet and that humanity is transcending or metamorphosing itself into what those great dreamers, visionaries and prophets envisioned. This is what I believe I am living in the glass house on the East River of New York City.

The story, of course, is far from complete: it is only a beginning, the embryo of the world it will be in a few decades, but nevertheless something deep-seated is happening. Things seem to be falling into the following patterns:

At Long Last, a Universal Organization

For the first time ever on this planet, we have a universal organization and global, interdependent thinking. This has never happened before in the political history of this planet. But it is exactly what the great prophets predicted. They always saw the world and humanity as a totality. Today the people sitting in United Nations meetings are forced to see the planet and the human family in their entirety. This is a great new paradigm, an enormous advance in human history, the full significance of which most people do not yet grasp. Only future historians who look back at this last part of our century will be able to understand what really happened on planet Earth.

A Copernican View of Creation

The second element is that the total explosion of knowledge of the human species, which has been so tremendous in the last two hundred years and especially since the end of World War II, has fallen into a prodigiously beautiful pattern. It is a knowledge that goes from the infinitely large to the infinitely small. It is a Coper-

THE REAPPEARANCE OF CHRIST

nican view of what the mind has produced, analyzed and pierced in the surrounding reality. I am speaking now only of the mind because the last few centuries were essentially centuries of the supremacy of the mind. It is not necessary to trace the history of why this was so. It was the age of reason, of the mind and of science.

This has produced something incredible: we have been able as a species, as humans, to penetrate far and deep into creation. We have a tremendous knowledge of the universe, of the galaxies, of our solar system. We know the composition of the soils and atmospheres of other planets. We have put man into space; we have satellites turning around this planet. We know our atmosphere, our biosphere, our lithosphere, our hydrosphere, our deserts, our arable land, our mountains, our polar caps, our underground resources of water and minerals. We have penetrated, analyzed, classified and studied everything we could reach from the vastness that surrounds us to infinitely small matter. This is one picture which emerges now in all its splendor. In other words, the human mind has pierced a reality that always existed around us but which we had not penetrated.

We have transcended ourselves with our minds; we have metamorphosed our senses to better understand our planet and the universe in which we live. This is a tremendous advance. And the picture is magnificent. In the end, scientists all tell us that as they reach farther into the universe and find galaxies, spheres of galaxies and innumerable spheres within these galaxies—a world that is ever larger and more incredible—they are still unable to understand the original cause of it all. They are unable to grasp the notion of infinity, and as they go into the infinitely small, you will hear the same answer: that the discovery of further particles and subparticles is endless, that it is an incredible world which fills them with awe for creation. Therefore, scientists and all those who deal with knowledge in the end have only one answer to the mysteries of the universe, namely, that there must be a cause, there must be a reason, there must be a scheme, there must be a universal law. The mathematicians have looked for this law; the biologists have looked for it; the universalists have looked for a universal principle and the theologians have encountered God, the Creator, the alpha and omega of everything. We have now come to the end of the road. The age of reason has been exploited and the result of its discoveries is a magnificent description of the universe, as beautiful as it was seen to be by the prophets. Because they looked into the universe and up to the stars, they always had the concept of the totality of creation.

Our Place in Time

There is another element which is progressively falling into place. It is the concept of time. We see how humanity is forced all of a sudden to extend its time dimension far into the past and far into the future. I have never seen anything like it. When I joined the UN we were not looking far into time. We were just coping with the immediate issues. We have a tendency to forget how recent our knowledge is. It was only in the seventeenth century that Bishop Ussher tried to give a date to our earth. He came to the conclusion that it was born in 4004 B.C.! Then Georges Louis Leclerc, Count de Buffon, in his natural history estimated its age to be five hundred thousand years. Today we have been able to date this planet and its moon at four and a half billion years! You can imagine the prodigious jump humanity has made to date its own home from about six thousand years to four and a half billion years! Astrophysicists further tell us that this planet will be spinning around its sun for another six to eight billion years. This is a new vision which is imposing itself increasingly on the world. It is called, as far as the past is concerned, the preservation of species, of the elements, of nature, of the great monuments and achievements of humankind.

As for the future, it is called the Bimillennium, and is concerned with the economic development of the poor countries, the future of the world climate, of world population, the survival and future of humanity. Year after year one can see the time dimension of our efforts on this planet reach farther into the future. Futurology is a new discipline which was born only since World War II. More and more people are beginning to realize that any correct thinking and behavior on our earth must not only take into account the next twenty or one hundred years but the totality of the time span allotted to this planet. This will cause quite a revolution in thinking and behavior. And again you come to a very simple conclusion: the prophets, Buddha, Christ, all saw it that way. I do not believe there is a single religion on earth that has not conceived our destiny from creation to the apocalypse. Probably one of the most accurate religions in terms of astrophysics is the Hindu religion with its Year of Brahma, a very long period of hundreds of millions of years, marked by creation, preservation, destruction and again creation, preservation and destruction. This is exactly the birth of a star, its preservation through stable hydrogen explosions in the sun, and finally its disintegration again into the universe, where each atom of this present planet and solar system will be reborn in another solar system or star. Thus scientists in the last few years have simply confirmed what the great prophets and outer-space emissaries had proclaimed.

Humanity as an Entity

There is a third element which is becoming increasingly clear. It is the discovery of humanity as an entity. All our history over thousands of years has been the history of groups: tribes, religions, cities, languages, nations. It was always a history based on a group somewhere in the world, a constantly shifting civilization, the story of some major power located in one place on the planet or another. For the first time, in the last thirty years, delegates, scientists, thinkers and servers in the United Nations have discovered that the supreme concern on this planet is humanity itself. This is why, despite all the differences and the fighting for interests, in any United Nations meeting there is, at the end, an adaptation, a greater understanding, because the delegates begin to speak and to act increasingly in the name of humankind. After each successful meeting a sense of happiness radiates from the delegates. It may have been a meeting on human rights, on world population, on natural resources, on human life, be it children, adults, youth or the elderly. The delegates all know that they have participated in global history. This has never existed before on this planet! There have never been any universal meetings like those of the United Nations. Behind the loud words and claims, there is the upsurge of a great tranquil, evolutionary wave towards the protection, survival and fulfillment of the human race on planet Earth. This is now very clear.

Has it occurred to you that the only people who ever took a census of the population of this planet were the Romans? This is why Jesus was born in Bethlehem. Since then no similar censuses were taken until after the Second World War, when the United Nations organized true world censuses. Humanity is now counted and inventoried. We know how many we are. We know our age, our literacy, nutrition, health, levels of development, longevity. All this for the first time has been looked at in its totality, the final objective being to make out of this human family a peaceful, happy entity, in which someday there will be no further need for arms, suspicion, violence and injustices. It is a prodigious story that is unfolding right under our eyes. It is making a little progress each year in some direction. The United Nations is much more than a political organization, it is a paradigm, the expression of a deep, evolutionary change which in the long run will transform the world for the best.

I could also speak of the individual, the uniqueness of each human person, the story of human rights, the individual as a unique cosmos linked with everybody else and with all the elements of this planet. We are unique but we are also interdependent and part of the entirety of creation. That is another truth which was proclaimed by all great religious prophets and which is becoming clear to the international community.

A Holistic View

When you look at the totality, then you see that the picture looks more or less the way all the great religions saw it thousands of years ago, and that year after year the advance, the perception of the human species, through its world organizations is moving more and more towards moral and spiritual relationships. Of late, "economic development" has been replaced by "economic, social, cultural and spiritual development." We find these words in UN reports, in speeches by high UN officials and delegates, in the declarations of human rights. In the World Health Organization a debate on the importance of the soul for the health of the individual has begun. A "holistic approach" is noticeable everywhere. I have never seen anything like it. A completely new dimension is entering the United Nations: holistic medicine, holistic development, concern with the whole human being and with the whole of humanity.

Three hundred years ago Leibniz predicted that humanity would be so thrilled with its scientific discoveries that for centuries it would concentrate on innumerable separate sciences. But he also foresaw that a time would come when humanity would again need to see the totality, the universality, the spiritual dimension of it all. This time seems to have come.

Personally, I was very lucky to be closely associated with the thinking of Dag Hammarskjöld and U Thant. Both of them in different ways were absolutely convinced that the road to happiness and peace went through spirituality. They were emphatic about it in their speeches, writings and conversations. They both attributed to spirituality the highest function in guiding societies on earth. One can begin to see therein the political realization of old visions which were much greater than the one we have today. In the meantime we have made enormous progress on the scientific and material side. We must be grateful for it. Our life span is now much longer than it was at the time of Christ. We know much more than at his time. We therefore cannot condemn the magnificent results of the age of reason and science. But it is now also quite apparent that, after having been successful on the material scene, we must make equal progress in the moral and spiritual spheres.

Concentration on the faculties of intelligence and reason has yielded a golden age of science and progress for humanity. Suppose we concentrated as much energy on the faculties of the heart and the soul? What marvelous benefits we would reap for the further transcendence and fulfillment of the human race: peace, kindness, justice, non-violence, beauty, respect and love for our miraculous planet.

Perhaps such concentration is now indispensable in order to safeguard the benefits yielded by the age of science and intelligence.

Everyone has a different perception of the Christ. I am a Catholic. I have read his sayings many, many times and I have my perception of what the Christ means. In my view He means the following: He is always speaking of the heavenly Father. He always asks us to lift our spirits and to look at the heavens. Secondly, He was the great advocate of love as the ultimate answer to human problems. He also always spoke of peace. "Peace be with you, my peace I leave with you." He further always saw the light. Probably He distinguished himself from all other great visionaries by never accepting duality, the shadows, the dark sides, by being always entirely on the side of light and life: "Follow me and you will see the light." Finally, for me He means belief in resurrection.

Our Father

In my own life and in the world today I can see these messages reappear very potently. For example, it is our knowledge which forces us to look again at the heavens and the stars, to see ourselves as part of the infinite universe and to have endless respect for the Creator, for the Father, as well as a deep thankfulness for the tremendous gift of life and for being able, as distinct from animals, to perceive the greatness of the universe. The prayer, "Our Father," which the Christ has given us himself remains as valid today as ever.

Love

As for love, it is remarkable that both Dag Hammarskjöld and U Thant left us a message of love at the end of their lives. This is extremely important because today our world has become so complex, our knowledge has reached such phenomenal proportions and the interconnections between all the layers of knowledge are such that finally the human person cannot take it any more. As a result, the individual abandons, retreats, withdraws from society or from science, doesn't want to hear anything any more, and is beset by more anxiety than ever before. The words "love" and "faith" combine again into one of those incredible syntheses that the Christ has held before us. We can never understand this earth in its complexity, we can never understand a woman or a man in their complexity; but we can love our planet, love our life, love a person. In the end, given the complexity of the political affairs of this planet, both Dag Hammarskjöld and U Thant came to the conclusion that one could solve them only through love or serene submission to the superiority of creation, in other words, by not wanting to be a master of the planet or of other persons, but by being a servant of that planet and of the people, a servant in time and in space. The more we advance in evolution, the more we will rediscover the tremendous, simplifying, all-encompassing, metascientific virtues of love.

Peace

Peace . . . well, this is the whole United Nations. Peace between nations, peace between groups, peace between races, peace between men and women, peace between generations, peace between all humans, peace with nature. In other words, reciprocal respect and adaptation towards harmonious, happy living. One could say in one sentence that what is happening in the United Nations is a search for a consensus in diversity, a unity that constantly grows while diversity constantly grows too. We are more distinct persons, one from another, than ever before in evolution and this diversification relentlessly continues. It is one of the miracles of evolution on this planet that we move both towards greater unity and cooperation and towards greater diversification and individuality! Again, confronted with such a phenomenon, we find a great simplifying concept left to us by the Christ: peace, or the right, harmonious relations between all groups and all peoples, between humanity and the planet, between peoples and the heavens, between peoples and eternity, while each human being is a unique, unrepeatable child of God and embodiment of the universe.

Light

Light . . . here again I do not know what we would do in the United Nations if we were not constantly on the side of light, of hope, of what is good, what is progress, if we were not constantly believers that it can be done, that we must always throw down our gauntlet for life, for civilization, for the further progress of humanity. This was the Christ one hundred per cent, to the point that He let himself be killed to prove that He would never utilize the methods of darkness, brutality, and evil He condemned on this planet. This is one of the most difficult, most challenging and deepest stories in our history. The largest majority of the people of this planet still believe that it is power, gain, war and coercion that can bring them happiness. We are a minority of people and institutions who believe like Christ that one can never employ the methods one condemns in others, even at the peril of one's own life. This is what is called the miracle of faith, a mystery, a miraculous cement that holds together an individual life as it holds together collective lives. There is nothing we need more in today's world than faith, the belief that goodness and peace can win, the refusal to give up under any circumstance, the molding of every defeat into a victory, of every darkness into light. I wish scientists would study the "miracle of faith." Much of our social future would benefit from their findings. The Hindus call it *prana*, "the vital." It is indeed a vital principle, the energy, the motor of the upward path of human civilization, of our broadening into ever larger discoveries, of our elevation and metamorphosis into an ever greater understanding of the universe and of the divine.

Resurrection

Lastly, there is Christ's message of resurrection. Many people on this planet do not believe in it. But I have lived with a man like U Thant, who constantly held that we were coming from somewhere and that we were going somewhere, that not to believe this made no sense, that whatever he did at any moment of his life would have an impact on the future of humanity to all eternity. He called it the *karma*, or the law whereby no good action is ever lost. Today the biologists tell us that this makes very good sense, because our genes are registering our attitudes, our behavior and our progress, generation after generation. Consequently, our acts and thinking will be transmitted to our descendants. We will be resurrected materially in other life forms on this planet and ultimately into atoms of other stars, but most of all, we will continue to live by the contribution we have made to humanity's improvement through our deeds, thoughts, love and reverence for life during our own incarnations.

Ecumenism

So everywhere I look—and I am not a theologian or a philosopher, I am just a United Nations official trying to make a little sense out of all this—everywhere I see the Christ's luminous messages. They are all still among us, they are coming again to the fore ever more potently. In the present global world they have to express themselves in the ecumenism of religions. The world's major religions in the end all want the same thing, even though they were born in different places and circumstances on this planet. What the world needs today is a convergence of the different religions in the search for and definition of the cosmic or divine laws which ought to regulate our behavior on this planet. World-wide spiritual ecumenism, expressed in new forms of religious cooperation and institutions, would probably be closest to the heart of the resurrected Christ. I would wholeheartedly support the creation of an institutional arrangement in the UN or in UNESCO for a dialogue and cooperation between religions. There is a famous painting and poster which shows Christ knocking at the tall United Nations building, wanting to enter it. I often visualize in my mind another even more accurate painting: that of a United Nations which would be the body of Christ.

I would also like to see published someday a Bible which would show how the United Nations is a modern biblical institution, bent on implementing world-wide the wise precepts and divine commandments of the Bible. I would like to see the same thing done for all great religious or sacred books, such as the Koran, the Grant Sahib, etc.

The ecumenical teachings of the Christ—peace, justice, love, compassion, kindness, human brotherhood, light, faith, rejoicing at life, looking at the heavens and at the Father—must also find their way in world-wide global education. We must give the newcomers into the ceaselessly renewed stream of human life the right education about their planetary home, about their human family, about their past, present and future, about their place in the universe and in time, so that they can flower to their utmost beauty—physically, mentally, morally and spiritually—and become joyful and grateful members of the universe or kingdom of God.

18

Letter to a Canadian Monk

Dear Abbot Veilleux,

I want to comment immediately on the essay you sent me on the role of the monastic subculture in the formation of the monk. You are absolutely right in raising questions which are on the minds of a growing number of people nowadays, namely:

1. How can I cope with the bewildering complexity of knowledge, problems, interdependencies, possibilities, views, aspirations, beliefs, values, dreams and claims to all sorts of rights in this world? Could withdrawal, solitude, faith, meditation and prayer be the answer to my quest for happiness?

2. We know so much about this world and humanity but, like Faust, we are not wiser than before. May the answer be in mysticism, love for God, poetry, escape of the individual from the earth to the divine?

3. In the West, we have food, shelter, health, hygiene, security and education and yet we do not seem to be much happier than before. Why is that? How, when and where can we find happiness?

4. What is the purpose of life? Why am I here? Was there anything before me and will there be anything after me? Who am I? How do I relate to the rest of the world, to the people, to the heavens and to eternity?

5. How can there be peace, goodness and happiness on this planet? How can the sins of institutions, particularly of nations, be coped with? How can they continue seeking endless power instead of serving the people and humanity?

In your efforts at total rethinking, it would be good to establish this *problématique* of our time, taking into account the profound historical dichotomy which exists between the developed and the developing countries. In the latter, survival at birth, food, a decent life, education, hygiene and longer lives are the priorities. This is why materialism has a much greater justification in these countries. One might even say that materialism is the first spirituality. First one has to live.

You should ignore totally all earlier thinkers, including Plato, Hegel, Kant, Marx, Nietzsche, etc. We live in a completely different world and time. If they were alive today, they would be the first to discard their theories and offer new ones more appropriate for our era. They would probably say that care for our planetary home and for the survival and happiness of the human race are the predominant problems of our time. Ours is a period of a magnitude and of potential human development of which they did not have the faintest idea.

Facing this *problématique*, you have the eternal monastic or "self-apartheid" solution as one of the multiple possible answers. The question is: what can monks offer the individual of our time, what can they offer the world, what can they offer powerful institutions?

And the answers can be quite simple: in the monasteries of the world, all humanity is already united with itself and with the heavens. Or to say with young Pachomius: "To serve humanity all the days of my life, that is my wish."

Humans always need ideals to live by. Lost as we believe we are among the four and a half billion people of this planet, we need exceptional beings who give us a luminous vision, elevate us, make us feel better and help us understand how great a miracle human life really is in the universe. It is strange that solitude in a prison or in a monastery should often produce a mystical elevation and a deep spiritual experience. Perhaps prison, monasticism and the image of death are among the most powerful means to make us realize the true priorities and value of life. Some people also—and it is usually a mark of greatness—are able to touch the innermost fibers of life right amidst the action and turmoils of the world. Dag Hammarskjöld, for example, was a great mystic in action. All his work was performed in accord with this belief: "In our era, the road to holiness necessarily passes through the world of action." For him, world service was an overflow of love, of personal transcendence into the

realm of feeling for the world and for its people. He would have
agreed fully with Pachomius' exclamation. Mysticism, religion and
the awareness of death are close cousins of art and poetry: they are
all manifestations of a deep love and endless astonishment for the
mystery of life. The mystic, the religious person, the monk, the poet
and the artist, by expanding their hearts and souls into total reality,
are able to perceive the material and immaterial universe in a way
which will forever remain forbidden to the mind. Love might well
be in the end the highest perception within the reach of human
beings.

You are indeed great experts in many fields where basic rethinking
has begun on this planet: inner life, frugal life, simple life, manual
work, tilling the land, handicrafts, solitude, study, meditation, prayer
and communion with God. Hence the immense success of a
Thomas Merton with the youth of today. He had assimilated all you
had to offer and gave it back with an overflowing heart, as a master,
as a lived personal experience and with the accents of truth without
which no one believes anyone any more these days. In view of the
energy crisis, the food crisis, inflation, etc., monastic experiences
could be subjects of much scientific curiosity and inquiry, as the
Amish ways of life have recently been. You have something important to offer the world and you should be studied as possible answers to the problems of our time by psychologists, sociologists,
economists, etc.

This applies to all religions. They have ancient answers which
modern man has all too often forgotten. But religions are *dans le
monde* (in the world), whereas monasteries are apart from the
world. They keep intact in their purity the old, instinctive answers
to the mysteries and fears of life, developed by those who in all cultures consider it their vocation to pray and meditate for the entire
group. You can play today the same role you have played so often
before when the world passed through periods of confusion and anxiety. But there is not much time to lose. You must go to the heart of
the matter and do what all great monastic leaders did over the ages:
write down a set of monastic rules for our time and possibly conceive two world monastic orders, one composed of all the monastic
groups around the world living apart from the world; and another,
new order of world servers deeply immersed in the outside world—
politics, public service, business, education, art, etc. Those would
spend temporary periods in monasteries to refresh and purify them-

selves in solitude, contemplation, sunrises and sunsets, nature, communion with God, the universe and eternity, the practice of peace, serenity, service to others, frugality, poverty, humility and love, all those great virtues which are your specialty. Create such an order and I will join it forthwith, stimulated by the good example of U Thant, the Buddhist who in the middle of the world's turmoil never ceased to be a monk.

Speaking of U Thant, I have observed that his beloved classification of human needs and virtues is also the main foundation of all monastic orders: physical life (respect for one's body, manual work), mental life (learning, extended being through knowledge and understanding), moral life (practice of brotherhood, compassion, kindness and love), and spiritual life (communion with God, eternity and the universe, mystical comprehension of the cosmos). He showed us by his example how one's life can be beautifully geared to these four basic needs and qualities of humanity.

Like everything else, renewal consists in restating old eternal truths in a modern context, which today means a world-wide, universal, planetary context encompassing our enormous knowledge and extensive experience with living. You must write down the universal rules of monasticism, the essence of all that is true and meaningful to you, for you are among the truest and most advanced seekers of the truth. At the same time, the many diverse existing monastic traditions can continue to flourish in their rich diversity like the flowers of a garden. Unity in diversity is one of the basic laws of the universe, as it is the law for a garden.

In doing so, do not consult anyone but yourself and God. Do not hold meetings or ugly think-tanks. Someone has to sit down and give the first great outline. It is with reformers and visionaries as it is with all great masters: you have to do it all yourself. No one will help you, no one can do it for you, if only because the task seems insuperable. Hence, helpers tend to lose themselves in secondary, confusing, dilatory thinking and exercises. Once you have produced the first fruit which is ripe in you, then you can send it to a few friends for comments and advice. I would be very happy to be counted among those and to become one of the first members of a new world monastic order.

The path opened by Merton and by the Eastern sages must now be crowned in modern terms: with rules, structures, institutions, codes and the offering of a philosophy of divine fulfillment on earth.

We need a world organization in which all the world's monastic movements can cooperate, learn from each other, live with each other and define humanity's divine spiritual laws hidden in our hearts and in the cosmos.

Humanity is ready for a new culture. That culture must include the benefits derived from solitude, meditation, prayer and spirituality right in the middle of daily action and life. Dag Hammarskjöld and U Thant were two living examples of such modern monks, one a mystic in his own right, the other a humble Buddhist applying his faith honestly and painstakingly. There is no reason why our planet should not be a floating cathedral in the universe, a vast temple to God or a monastery. What better fate could we plan for? What a sight it would be for extraterrestrial visitors to see us as a planet of praying, grateful, heavenly beings, fully aware of the miraculous consciousness bestowed upon us in the vast universe. *Oui, le monachisme pourrait considérer le monde comme un immense monastère.* Yes, monasticism could consider the world as a vast monastery! In our era the road to sanctity passes indeed through the worlds of both action and solitude.

I hope these few thoughts from an international civil servant might be of some use to you.

May peace, love and happiness always be yours.

19

Global Spirituality, the Need for Faith
and What Sisters Can Do[1]

Many sisters would be interested in your ideas about global spirituality, especially since there is such an emphasis on evangelization these days. How did you discover a global spirituality?

I have been working in the United Nations for more than thirty years. During all these years, I saw that the problems brought to the world organization were primarily related to the physical well-being of peoples, such as the prevention of wars, hunger, sickness, epidemics, natural disasters, handicaps, etc. Then there were problems relating to the intellectual aspects of life, especially education and literacy, which enable people to have more dignified, fulfilled lives. In addition, the United Nations was getting increasingly involved with ethical and moral problems, like codes of human rights, codes of conduct for transnational corporations, the treatment of prisoners by the police, of patients by scientists and doctors, etc. If you read the Charter of the United Nations you will find it to be an ethical code, a sort of Ten Commandments for nations. However, one day someone asked me the question: "Isn't there also a spiritual dimension to the United Nations?"

At that time, I came across the views of two of our Secretaries-General, namely Dag Hammarskjöld and U Thant. They had both concluded that the physical, material, mental and moral problems of humanity could only be solved satisfactorily if we had a spiritual view

[1] A Message of Hope from an Optimist at the United Nations, interview with Sister Mary Madden, C.S.J. published in the magazine *Sisters Today*, October 1979.

of world affairs. Of course, the question arose immediately: how can one speak of a global spirituality in a world of so many religions and atheists, besides there being religions like Buddhism, Jainism and Sikhism which have no God? However, there is a common denominator when humans see themselves as part of a very mysterious and beautiful universe. From that awe emerges a spiritual approach to life. Everything becomes sacred, understandable and miraculous. How can one kill or harm anyone who is sacred? This will be the new common path or story of humanity as the human race matures and sees its stupendous place and luck in creation. Every religion tells this story in a different way, but all offer us explanations which no scientist has been able to give us regarding the mysterious force which rules the universe.

When we relate to this force, to God, everything falls into place. As long as humanity does not do this, no true, lasting answers will be found for our earthly problems. I often try to imagine what would happen if the delegates to the UN General Assembly in addition to opening each session with a minute of prayer or silence, put this question to God: "Look, dear God, here we are. We have all these problems. We are rather lost. Help us, enlighten us to see all this more clearly." I am sure the problems of the world would become much simpler to resolve if we related to someone who is above and beyond us. I hope that someday the United Nations will prepare a yearly report to God.

All religions see humankind's place in total time, from creation to the apocalypse. The soul is not merely here for a short number of solar years. We come from somewhere and we are going somewhere, as part of the great stream of the universe. If we do not see this in our lives, we cannot find happiness and serenity and adopt a right moral stand. Even biologists tell us that our behavior is recorded in genes. Scientists are convinced that the long-term view of life is the only correct way of visualizing the ascent of the human species.

So this is how I came to a global spirituality. I believe that the religions have many of the answers which the political world is seeking, because they have been here many more years than the United Nations. We should consult them. Dag Hammarskjöld and U Thant were absolutely right when they considered that world affairs needed to be inspired, guided, elevated and ruled by a global spirituality, and that political leaders needed similarly to be guided by a personal spirituality.

You are called the "optimist in residence" at the United Nations. Have you seen any miracles happening lately?

My optimism does not mean so much that I believe in miracles. The miracle is that the belief of people that something can be done produces the desired result. Optimism and pessimism both have their nutrients. As Norman Cousins has written: "Pessimism and optimism are significantly more than opposite moods. Just as despair sets the stage for its own omens, so reasoned hope provides the essential nutrients for a flowering of the spirit that enhances life, thereby contributing regenerative energies to the shared living environment." It is as with prayer, which visualizes what we deeply desire and helps it to materialize. I believe that if one feels that something is possible it becomes possible. If you feel it is impossible it becomes impossible, or its chances of becoming possible are substantially reduced. This is very important. The religions call it the mystery of faith, because it is very difficult to explain, and the miracle of faith, because it produces miracles. From the moment one has a particular faith, that faith materializes. This is true for all walks of life. If one has a tendency to feel sick, one is very likely to become sick. If one feels marvelously happy and in good health, automatically one's trillions of little cells feel it: they are anxiously awaiting this central message, guidance and encouragement to well-being. One must orchestrate with great care and optimism one's cosmos, or else the little cells find it difficult to work together in harmony, i.e., in health. Similarly, it is very important to be hopeful and optimistic in a place like the United Nations where one faces every conceivable problem and trouble in the world. As a matter of fact the United Nations is a kind of clinic for world accidents and therapy. At the UN more than anywhere else one must feel like a doctor and have reasonable hope; even if we do not succeed today, we will tomorrow. Someday even armaments will disappear from this planet. One has to keep after what one considers the truth all the time and relentlessly. I am sure that we will have peace on this planet, if we constantly believe in it. More and more people are working towards it all around the globe. Their efforts will not remain forever without effect.

Many hopes I have had with regard to the United Nations have materialized. I dreamed that it would become someday universal. It is universal today, the first world-wide organization ever on this planet. A few years ago I proposed a world conference on science and technology to Dag Hammarskjöld. I asked the question: "Why do we not apply our intelligence to the tropical and equatorial areas as we do to the northern countries?" I come from a steel and coal region in Lorraine; I often wondered whether, if coal and iron had not been located in the same place, we would have invented steel. Why don't we look at the rest of the world to see if miracles like this are not possible elsewhere? Well, we had two world conferences on that subject. Similarly, I had hoped that world concern would develop for our planet's four hundred fifty million handicapped. It took some doing, but in 1981 we finally had an International Year of Disabled Persons. A few years ago, with a few colleagues, we thought that we needed a world conference on water because what was happening with energy would also happen to our water supply. The first reaction of governments was: "Why should we have another world conference?" Well, we had it! And in the meantime water indeed became a problem of growing concern to many countries. We have also been preaching that we must prepare for the arrival of hundreds of millions of old people on this planet. Longevity is increasing. People in developing countries are also getting older. In the next twenty years there will be hundreds of millions of newly old people creating problems we have never encountered on this planet. Well, a world assembly on aging is being held in 1982. I have thus seen a good many dreams for humanity materialize. As a matter of fact there were so many of them that I have gained an unprecedented faith in the future of humanity, and hence have been called the "optimist in residence at the UN," a title of which I am rather proud. But miracles are not handed to one. One has to work for them. They are the fruit of one's faith, hope and optimism, which help nurture them and bring them forth to life and love.

At this stage of my life, after so many years of observation of the world scene, I have come to the conclusion that our planet, all life on it and in particular human life, is a manifestation of cosmic or divine forces of the universe. Within us therefore resides a basic cosmic force that impels us to respond to our evolutionary duties and to be in favor of life and of our further ascent. If we don't, we are abandoned by this central, all-pervading force and we die individually or collectively. Faith in life and in our future is therefore the most vital force we must rely on to continue successfully on our strange, unfathomable journey in the universe. This is what the

Christ and many other messengers from the outer heavens have told us: believe in life, in light, in resurrection, in the accomplishment of the will of God or the cosmos. This applies to me and to you as individuals as it applies to the entire world society.

As an international diplomat and Catholic layman, how do you see the role of sisters today in the new trend of world concerns?

Sisters can play a tremendously important role for two reasons. The first is that we have arrived at a stage of evolution when women will play a much more important role than ever before. It is not a question of equality of men and women. It goes much deeper. What is happening is that the first two or more million years of our evolution on this planet were of an aggressive nature. People had to fight for their food, for their survival, for their existence. For two million years aggression and fighting were the dominant features of this planet. Even today, groups fight for their "security" and preponderance. We have come to the point where this has reached its limits. We are now entering a period when the aggressiveness of men will give way to the values of women. Men have been the masters also of the last two or three hundred years because it was the so-called age of reason. Sentiment was pushed aside almost completely. Everything had to be done through "intelligence." That intelligence has enabled us to make fantastic discoveries, but now limitations have set in.

Reason suddenly is unable to give us the answers to the complexities of creation. This is why, at this juncture, we need to turn to other values which women possess instinctively and naturally, i.e., in a most advanced form. A woman who has a child is not reasoning with herself about the relations with the child. It is all expressed very simply and beautifully in the word "love." It is a relationship which one cannot define, which goes totally beyond reason. Since women nurture the family and the child, this is her specialty. What we need today on this planet is more love than reason. We must now fashion a moral world based on the great virtues of truth, love, compassion and beauty. The woman specializes in these virtues. Beauty is very important to her. It is the world of the woman to make her home beautiful, to make herself beautiful and to make the lives of others beautiful. And when it comes to love, it is increasingly apparent that the main challenge of our age is to love the entire creation, to love our planet, to love the human family, to love each other and to love the mysterious Creator in heaven. We have entered the great loving process of humanity. And we find again the woman as the experienced specialist, in the avant-garde of evolution.

As for sisters, they are not only women but altruistic women. They have decided to devote their lives to the service of others. Many sisters, therefore, are involved in education, taking care of the handicapped, of the elderly, of the poor, rejected and lonely. They are present at the moment of death. When my grandfather died there was a sister at his side helping him to die. There are not many people who will help you to die. Sister Teresa is the epitome of sisterhood when she exclaims:

"The poor are brothers and sisters in the same family, created by the same loving God. If you do not know them, you do not love them, and you do not serve them. We must love until it hurts."

Sisters are great specialists in suffering. We need them very much today. The sisters can be very helpful with their experience and concern for social, humanitarian issues such as those of the International Year of the Child, UNICEF, the International Year of Disabled Persons, the Refugees, the Hunger campaigns, the World Assembly on Aging. I have proposed to the Catholic authorities that they should not wait for some of these conferences to take place, but should prepare a long time ahead and gather the experience of the Church all around the world. In this way they would be able to advise the United Nations how to deal with these problems—for example, that of the elderly—because they know so much more than we. The Vatican should ask the sisters to share their wisdom and experience learned from their direct service to the poor and elderly.

Most of all, we should not forget their greatest contribution of all, that is, the spiritual dimension of the sisters' service in prayer and contemplation. Our world has a very great need for deeper spirituality. We need the sisters who are completely devoted to contemplation. They could play a very great role by praying for the peace and goodness of the world, especially for those who are involved in action for peace, like myself and all United Nations servers. What we need most in the United Nations is prayer for our success. It is faith-filled prayer that moves the mountains of misunderstanding and prejudice. I have suggested to the Vatican that there ought to be a campaign of prayer for the United Nations. The Church pays more attention to the problem of peace and not enough attention to the people and institutions already involved in bringing about peace on this planet. I could count on my fingers the rare number of times I have heard church prayers for the United Nations. And yet we need to know that you are praying for us. This will give us the strength we require to believe that peace can become a reality on our planet.

The United Nations also needs prayers because it is not infallible. Under pressure of political events, the United Nations sometimes takes a stand with which the churches do not agree. The churches may be right and not the United Nations. For example, there is the issue of population. The United Nations has adopted a world plan for action on population and the only voice against this plan was that of the Holy See. Against one hundred and fifty nations, the Holy See raised its voice in favor of life. It is true that we have a fantastic population explosion. It is true that it is no good for a woman to have seven or eight children and see them die around her because she is not able to feed them. However, we should not fall into the opposite error and suddenly rejoice at stopping life. If we could save the five hundred and fifty billion dollars spent each year on armaments, we could accommodate many more people at the banquet table of life.

The Church is right to keep an eye on issues because sometimes new ethical values coming out of the United Nations are not correct and are tinged with national, short-term interests. The Holy See has promised to support the United Nations when it is on the right road. If it is not, the Holy See, which is represented at the United Nations, will tell us. So far, the Holy See has never hesitated to tell the United Nations when it is wrong. We need the wisdom of the ages which belongs to the Church. We need most of all her prayers. Please tell the sisters to pray for us.

20

Spiritual Education: A World of Difference

The 1981 United States Convention of Catholic Educators and Librarians asked me for my views on the theme: "Catholic Education, A World of Difference." The statement I made could be equally valid for any denomination of the Christian faith, and it could be rewritten and adapted to every major faith of this planet. What lessons we would derive from such an exercise! What progress we would make towards a global spiritual understanding and teaching of our prodigious journey in the vast, mysterious universe!

Not being an educator, I have thought a lot of how I could make a useful contribution to your convention. I have come to the conclusion that I might tell you how I would educate the children of this world on the basis of my thirty-three years of experience at the United Nations and as a Catholic Christian. I will offer you a world core curriculum aimed at all grades, levels and forms of education, including adult education.

The starting point is that every hour 6,000 of our brothers and sisters die and 15,000 children are born on this planet. The newcomers must be educated so that they can benefit from the acquired knowledge, skills and art of living of humanity, enjoy happy and fulfilled lives, and contribute in turn to the continuance, maintenance and further ascent of humanity on a well-preserved planet.

Alas, many newly born will never reach school age. One out of ten will die before reaching the age of one and another four per cent will die before the age of five.

There is a second prior problem: we must try by every possible means to prevent children from reaching school age with handicaps.

It is estimated that ten per cent of all the world's children have a handicap of a physical, sensory or mental nature by the time they reach school age. In the developing countries, an unforgivable major cause is still malnutrition. I am glad to note that your convention has a special workshop on education of the handicapped. This is most timely, since the United Nations has proclaimed 1981 as International Year of Disabled Persons (IYDP) to draw the world's attention to its 450 million disabled people.

Thirdly, my ideal curriculum presupposes that there are schools for all the children of the world. Alas, this is not the case. There are still 814 million illiterates on this planet. Humanity has done wonders in educating its people: we have reduced the percentage of illiterates of the world adult population from 32.4 per cent to 28.9 per cent between 1970 and 1980, a period of phenomenal population growth. But between now and the year 2000, 1.6 billion more people will be added to this planet and we are likely to reach a total of 6.1 billion people in that year. Ninety per cent of the increase will be in the developing countries where the problem of education is most severe. As a result, the total number of illiterates could climb to 950 million by the Bimillennium.

Education for all remains, therefore, a first priority on this planet, as every Catholic missionary can tell you. This is why UNESCO has rightly adopted a World Literacy plan for the year 2000.

With all these miseries and limitations still with us, it remains important, nevertheless, to lift one's sight and to begin thinking of a world core curriculum since Catholicism, as the name indicates, is universal. The great merit of being a Catholic is to be more than a member of a nation, of a race, of a culture, of a language, of a profession. It is to be a member of the entire human family, a member of a heavenly, universal family ruled by divine precepts. Catholic education is therefore far ahead of purely earthbound, civilian education lacking a spiritual, universal dimension. This is true of all affairs of this world. After my many years of world service, I can say unequivocally that only a spiritual approach or divine consciousness will permit us to solve our earthly problems. This is what all great religious prophets, visionaries and heavenly emissaries have told us for thousands of years. This is the true meaning of ecumenism as proclaimed by Vatican II and I would hope that educators of all the major religions would put their heads together and show a confused and not very happy world the tremendous benefits to be derived from a global, spiritual education.

Several decades will still pass before nations admit the necessity of a curriculum which would encompass all national educational systems. But it will come. The new global circumstances and concerns of our planet make it imperative that we begin considering it. Today's planetary sciences and technology will unify the world in the same way as road and bridge building made the Roman Empire and railroads unified the United States as well as Russia. The challenge to Catholic education is therefore to integrate fully the advanced results of our scientific, technological and social knowledge into its universal, spiritual vision of human life and destiny in the universe and in time.

My curriculum aims at providing a simple synthesis of all the complex knowledge acquired in the last few centuries, especially during the last three decades. One of the main objectives of education is to put sense and order into things and to give the children a correct view of the planet and of the circumstances in which they will live. I outlined the need for a new educational approach a few years ago in an essay, "The Need for Global Education," which has played a part in inducing several governments, including that of the United States, to give consideration to a new type of world education.

As I do in the United Nations, where all human knowledge, concerns, efforts and aspirations converge, I would organize the fundamental lifelong objectives of education around four categories:

I. Our planetary home and place in the universe
II. The human family
III. Our place in time
IV. The miracle of individual human life

I. Our Planetary Home and Place in the Universe

The first major segment of the curriculum should deal with our prodigious knowledge of planet Earth. Humanity has been able, of late, to produce a magnificent picture of our planet and of its place in the universe.

From the infinitely large to the infinitely small, everything fits today into a very simple and clear pattern. The list of subjects in this first segment should be as follows, as we use it in the United Nations:

The infinitely large: the universe, the stars and outer space
Our relations with the sun
The earth's physics
The earth's climate
The atmosphere
The biosphere
The seas and oceans
The polar caps
The earth's land masses
The earth's arable lands
The deserts
The mountains
The earth's water
Plant life
Animal life
Human life
The earth's energy
The earth's crust and depths
The earth's minerals
The infinitely small: microbiology, genetics, chemistry and nuclear physics

At each of these levels humanity has made incredible progress and knows an enormous amount. Astrophysicists tell us how stars and planets are born and die. We know the physics, atmospheres and even soils of other planets. Thanks to man-made satellites, we have a total view of our globe, of our atmosphere, of our seas and oceans and land masses. We know our complicated climate through a new science called climatology. We know our polar caps. For the first time ever, we possess a soil and land map for the entire planet. We know our mountains. We know our total water resources. We know our deserts. We know our flora and fauna. We know part of the crust of our earth. Our knowledge reaches far down into the microbial, genetic and cellular worlds, into the realm of the atom and its particles and subparticles. We have an incredible, beautiful, vast picture of our place in the universe. If a teacher wishes to give children a glimpse of the tremendous expanse of our knowledge, all he or she has to do is to have them visit on the same day an astronomical observatory and an atomic bubble chamber!

All this knowledge culminates in the United Nations or in one of its specialized agencies or world conferences. For each of the above items, I could give vivid examples of intensive world cooperation: e.g., on astrophysics and outer space, the UN has convened two world conferences; on the climate, the World Meteorological Organization has a Global Atmospheric Research Program and convened in 1979 a first World Climate Conference; on air space and aviation, we have the International Civil Aviation Organization; on the seas and oceans, there is the UN's Conference on the Law of the Sea; the ozonosphere and the entire biosphere are of concern to the UN Environment Program. I could go on and on, down to world cooperation in genetics and microbiology in UNESCO and in the World Health Organization, and in nuclear physics in the International Atomic Energy Agency. As a matter of fact, it is absolutely essential and in our enlightened self-interest to teach the children about this international cooperation so that they can see that humanity is beginning to work together and that there is good hope for a better world. There is a dire need for a good textbook on the UN and on international cooperation for Catholic schools.

The above framework allows us to present our planetary and universal knowledge to all people and particularly to children in a simple, beautiful manner. Humanity has discovered and pierced piecemeal the reality that surrounds us, and now this knowledge falls into a magnificent total pattern which must be taught to humans from childhood on. They wish to be told about their correct place in the universe. The Greeks' and Pascal's genial view of the infinitely large and the infinitely small has been filled in by science and provides the framework for much of today's international cooperation and daily lives of peoples. We can now give children a breath-taking view of the beauty and teeming, endless richness of creation as has never been possible before in human evolution. It should make them glad to be alive and to be human. It should also prepare them with excitement for a vast number of professions and make them better and more responsible members of the human race, henceforth the caretaker of our planet.

What special contributions can a Catholic Christian or spiritual education add to these "civilian" results, which are mostly the products of the scientific and rational age by which the world has now been ruled for several centuries? There are many of them, but let me mention four principal ones:

First, the scientists have now come to the end of their wisdom. Humans are simply incapable of grasping the vastness of creation and all its mysteries. We cannot understand the notions of the infinitely large, of the infinitely small and of eternity. Even the notions of matter and energy, of objectivity and subjectivity are being challenged today. Beyond the elation at our discoveries, there is a certain despair at our incapacity to comprehend the totality. This is where spirituality or religion comes in. Science in my view is part of the spiritual process; it is a transcendence and elevation of the human race into an ever vaster knowledge and consciousness of the universe and of its unfathomable, divine character.

Secondly, our wonder at the magnificence of creation is today greater than ever. What a beautiful picture of the universe we can present to our children! We should describe it with at least as much love, poetry, exaltation and ecstasy as did the writers of the Bible. Teachers have a wonderful story to tell, stories of endless miracles from a galaxy to the genetic factory contained in a cell, from the courses of the planets to the life of a flower and the whirling of electrons in an atom. Spiritual and religious awe, endless respect for the magnificence of the universe and for the greatness of the Creator will ensue.

Thirdly, we can elicit pride at being humans, at being able, above all species, to go so far in the comprehension of the universe. We can show children and people that there is something divine, miraculous and tremendous in being human, that God must have a special design for us, that our evolution makes more and more sense, that it will continue at ever higher levels until this planet has finally become a showcase in the universe, a planet of God. This will give children a sense of participation in the building of the earth, of becoming artisans of the will of God and thus co-creators with Him.

Fourthly, as vividly described in the story of the Tree of Knowledge, having decided to become like God through knowledge and our attempt to understand the heavens and the earth, we have also become masters in deciding between good and bad: every invention of ours can be used for good and bad all along the above Copernican tapestry of our knowledge: outer-space technology can be used for peace or for killer satellites, aviation for transportation or for dropping bombs, the atom for energy or for nuclear destruction, etc.

This gives Catholic, Christian and all spiritual educators a marvelous opportunity to teach a new morality and ethics all along the scale and thus to prepare responsible citizens, workers, scientists, geneticists, physicists and scores of other professionals, including a new badly needed category: world managers and caretakers.

II. The Human Family

There is a second segment on which humanity has also made tremendous progress of late: not only have we taken cognizance of our planet and of our place in the universe, but we have also taken stock of ourselves! This is of momentous importance, for henceforth our story in the universe is basically that of ourselves and of our planet. For a proper unfolding of that story, we had to know its two main elements well: the planet and ourselves. This has been accomplished since World War II. The planetary and human inventories are practically complete.

When the UN was founded no one knew what the world population was. A UN Population Commission was created, sample surveys were conducted and agreements reached on the world-wide collection of population statistics and the holding of world censuses. We thus learned in 1951 that we were two and a half billion people. Today we are four and a half billion! A population explosion which could have gone unnoticed was detected. The necessary global warnings were given and humanity is now responding with slower birth rates to the lowering of death rates.

We have learned so much about humanity since the end of World War II: we now know how many we are; where we live; how long we live; how many males, females, youths and elderly there are. This knowledge is being constantly improved and refined. We have a quantitative knowledge of our human family which we never had before at any time in history. We know ourselves also qualitatively: our levels of living, of nutrition, of health, of literacy, of employment, etc. We also have records of our progress: we know how many literates are being added to this planet each year; we know that by eradicating smallpox the number of the blind in the world was reduced by half, etc. Incidentally, it was no small achievement to have accommodated 2 billion more people on this planet within a short period of thirty years!

The human family has looked at itself in a series of major conferences on population, human settlements, women, youth, races, economic development, etc. After the International Year of the Child, we had the International Year of Disabled Persons, and in 1982 we will hold a World Assembly on Aging. As a result of so many efforts, we have an unprecedented inventory and knowledge of humanity. That fundamental, up-to-date knowledge must be conveyed to all the children of the world.

There is a further major aspect of the human family on which we have made substantial progress during the last decades, namely, our society and its man-made groupings. We are indeed a species that likes to congregate and subdivide itself into any conceivable group based on physical, geographic, qualitative or ideological aspects: races, sexes, age groups, nations, provinces, cities, rich and poor, religions, languages, social systems, forms of government, corporations, professions, institutions, associations, etc. Many of these are inherited from the past: thus we enter the global age with more than 150 nations, 5,000 languages, scores of religions, etc. Other entities are new, such as world organizations, multinational corporations and transnational associations.

All these groups are being studied and heard in the United Nations and its agencies. What this all means is as yet little understood. Formation of entities or the social biology of the human species, from the world society to the individual, is still a rather primitive science.

The first task of the United Nations is to build bridges, peace and harmony between these groups, to listen to their views and perceptions, to prevent them from blowing each other up and endangering the entire planet, to seek what each group has to contribute, to understand their legitimate concerns, values, denominators and objectives, and to grasp the meaning of the vast and complex functioning of life from the largest to the most minute, from the total society to the individual, from human unity to an endless, more refined diversity.

It is a vast, unprecedented, mind-boggling challenge but it would help if our second great segment of the world core curriculum were organized as follows:

The Human Family

QUANTITATIVE CHARACTERISTICS

The total world population and its changes
Human geography and migrations

Human longevity
Races
Sexes
Children
Youth
Adults
The elderly
The handicapped

QUALITATIVE CHARACTERISTICS

Our levels of nutrition
Our levels of health
Our standards of life (rich and poor)
Our skills and employment
Our levels of education
Our moral levels
Our spiritual levels

HUMAN GROUPINGS

The family
Human settlements
Professions
Corporations
Institutions
Nations
Regions
Religions
Multinational business
Transnational networks
World organizations

What will be important in such a curriculum is the dynamic aspect of the relations between humanity and our planet: we now have good inventories; we know the elements of the great evolutionary problems confronting us, but we barely stand at the beginning of the planetary management phase of human history: demographic options, resources management, environmental protection, conflict resolution, the management of peace, justice and progress for all, the optimization of human life in space and in time. The

United Nations and its specialized agencies offer the first examples of attempts at global management in all these fields and must therefore occupy a prominent and necessary place in the world's curricula. The earlier we do this, the better it will be for our survival and fulfillment.

Again, what an immense contribution Catholic and Christian education can bring to a better understanding and teaching of the human family and its components: a proper population policy which respects the right to life; the equality of races; Christ's teachings and the Church's long experience with children, youth, the family, adults, the elderly; the equality of sexes, peace, justice, reverence for life; help to the poor, the downtrodden and the handicapped. The social experience of the Church vastly surpasses that of the young United Nations and its agencies. This is why the Holy See has become so close to the United Nations, offering its vision, help and experience in the solution of most difficult world problems. When I read documents emanating from the Holy See dealing with social issues, I sometimes have the impression that I am reading United Nations documents. What marvelous opportunities the UN, its agencies and its world conferences offer Catholics to participate in the making of a better world! The Holy See has fully understood it and maintains important missions at the seats of all the UN agencies. His Holiness is always ready to help the United Nations in its endeavors, the last example being his appeal for the world's handicapped on January 1, 1981, the opening day of the IYDP.

More importantly, all the teachings of Catholicism and Christianity derive from a spiritual, divine or cosmic understanding of the unity of the human race under God, of the sanctity of life and the consequent abhorrence and condemnation of war, violence, terrorism, armaments, injustices, poverty, discrimination, hatred and untruthfulness. Popes Paul VI and John Paul II in their historical visits to the United Nations and their yearly messages on the Day of Peace have articulated a full doctrine of peace and right human relations for our planet. These texts should be used in the teaching of this vital segment of the world curriculum. They go far beyond the rational and "interest" language of the political world and add a much-needed spiritual, altruistic dimension to human efforts. They dare to speak of love for our planet, for the heavens and for all our brothers and sisters, a word very little used in the contemporary political world. What beautiful teachings can unfold in Catholic schools around these concepts: concern for the environment as an act of love for our planet; concern for the poor as an act of love for all our human brothers and sisters; turning to God as a guide for our behavior, etc. What a deep truth and tremendous vision Christ has given us! No wonder He has survived all political regimes and ideologies, and He offers us today as correct universal answers to humanity's problems as ever. As a matter of fact, this is the great hour for a spiritual world renaissance. The supreme reality of the human family, universal and interdependent, as seen by Christ and by all great religious leaders must now become the world's major political objective. The time has come for the implementation of a spiritual vision of world affairs. The entire planet must elevate itself again into the spiritual, cosmic throbbing of the universe.

III. Our Place in Time

In the same way as humanity is taking cognizance of its correct place in the universe, it is now also forced to look at its correct place in time or eternity.

When I joined the United Nations in 1948 there was very little time perspective. The word "futurology" did not even exist. Some nations who had five-year economic plans were derided, because it was believed that no one on this planet could plan for five years ahead! How the world has changed since then! Today every nation is planning for at least twenty years ahead. At the world level, the UN has adopted a world economic development strategy for the 1980s; the Food and Agriculture Organization has a World Food Plan 2000, the World Health Organization a World Health Plan 2000, UNESCO a World Literacy Plan 2000; UN demographers provide us with population projections for the next hundred years and the World Meteorological Organization tries to forecast our climate for the next several hundred years.

Something similar is happening with regard to the past. Today we know that our planet is more than 4.5 billion years old and we have developed a vast knowledge of our paleontological and archaeological past. Astrophysicists tell us that our sun—a star of stabilized light hydrogen explosions—will remain in existence for another 6 to 8 billion years before we vanish again into the universe to become other stars and planets.

Thus humanity is forced to expand its time dimension tremendously into the past and into the future: we must preserve the natural elements inherited from the past and necessary for our life and survival (air, water, soils, energy, animals, fauna, flora, genetic materials). We also want to preserve our cultural heritage, the landmarks of our own evolution and history, in order to see the unfolding and magnitude of our cosmic journey. At the same time we must think and plan far ahead into the future in order to hand over to succeeding generations a well-preserved and better-managed planet. What does this mean for a world curriculum? It means that we must add a time dimension to the above layers, each of which has a past, a present and a future:

The universe:	past,	present,	future
Our sun	"	"	"
Our globe	"	"	"
Our climate	"	"	"
Our biosphere	"	"	"

etc. down to the cell, genes and the atom

The human family:	past,	present,	future
Our age composition	"	"	"
Our levels of health	"	"	"
Our standards of living	"	"	"
Nations	"	"	"
Religions	"	"	"
World organizations	"	"	"

etc. down to the individual

Taken together, our present knowledge and responsibilities on our miraculous little planet are of awesome complexity and magnitude. It will take great vision and honesty to achieve the harmony and fulfillment of our journey in the universe and in time. The time has come to look again at the totality and to be what we were always meant to be: universal, total, spiritual beings. The hour for this vast synthesis, for a new encyclopedia of all our knowledge and the formulation of the agenda for our cosmic future has struck. Like the human eye which receives millions of bits of information at every glance, we must see the total picture and beauty of our planet, of the universe and of our lives.

Here again, science and rationalism have arrived at an impasse while religions have always seen the time dimension of our journey. What lessons religions can give geneticists, evolutionists and futurologists: the belief that our good deeds will be recorded and will contribute to a better humanity and a better future life (the genetic recording of the biologists); the belief that we are coming from somewhere and that we are going somewhere (evolutionists); the belief in a millennium, in a better, more peaceful world inspired and ruled by divine or cosmic laws, the belief that in us humans there are divine, cosmic elements which will flower to the point that we will become conscious of the total universe and that the universe will become conscious in ourselves (futurologists). As Catholics would say: the incarnated God, or Christ, is in all of us and for all of us to manifest.

What a formidable force it will be when all 4.5 billion humans on this planet have become spiritual beings in the eternal stream of time, conscious of the long-term consequences of their lives and actions and no longer prone to sacrifice these for petty, short-term interests and profit.

Here again an immense and beautiful responsibility behooves all Christian and religious teachers: it is no less than to prepare universal beings ready to flower and to fulfill their divine lives or cosmic destinies, as proclaimed by all great prophets for eons of time.

This brings me to the last but not the least segment of my world core curriculum.

IV. The Miracle of Individual Human Life

It is becoming increasingly clear in our debates on human rights that the individual is the alpha and omega of all our efforts. Individual human life is the highest form of universal or divine consciousness on our planet. Institutions, concepts, factories, systems, states, ideologies, theories have no consciousness. They are all servants, instruments, means for better lives and for the increase of individual human consciousness. We are faced today with the full-fledged centrality, divinity, dignity and miracle of individual human life as proclaimed relentlessly by Jesus, irrespective of race, sex, status, age, nation, physical or mental capacity: the divine nature of the human person.

Education of the newcomers is basically the teaching of the art of living and of human fulfillment within the immense knowledge of space and time acquired by humanity. It is to make each child feel like a king in the universe, an expanded being aggrandized by the vastness of our knowledge, which now reaches far into the infinitely large and the infinitely small, the distant past and the future. It is to make him feel proud to be a member of a transformed species whose eyesight, hearing, hands, legs, brain and heart have been multiplied a thousand times. Like the early Christians, the task is to help to maturity beings who exude a resplendent joy of living, who are witnesses to the beauty and majesty of creation. Knowledge, peace, happiness, goodness, love and meaningful lives—these must be the objectives of education.

And here I would complete my core curriculum for the individual with the four segments so dear to former Secretary-General U Thant:

— GOOD PHYSICAL LIVES:

knowledge and care of the body
teaching to see, to hear, to speak, to write, to observe, to create, to do, to use well all senses and physical capacities

— GOOD MENTAL LIVES:

knowledge
teaching to raise questions, to think, to analyze, to synthesize, to conclude, to communicate
teaching to focus from the infinitely large to the infinitely small, from the distant past to the present and the future

— GOOD MORAL LIVES:

teaching to love
teaching truth, understanding, humility, liberty, reverence for life, compassion, altruism and service

— GOOD SPIRITUAL LIVES:

spiritual exercises of interiority, meditation, prayer and communion with God, the universe and eternity.

Here I have not much to say, for your knowledge and experience in these fields are far superior to mine. I tried in my book, *Most of All They Taught Me Happiness*, to summarize all I have learned on the subject. Its starting point is this simple sentence by Norman Cousins in the Preface, which I would like to see pondered by all humans of this planet:

> The tragedy of life is not death, but what we let die inside us while we live.

Its epilogue is as follows:

> Decide to be happy
> render others happy
> proclaim your joy
> love passionately your miraculous life
> do not listen to promises
> do not wait for a better world
> be grateful for every moment of life
> switch on and keep on the positive buttons in yourself, those marked
>   optimism, serenity, confidence, positive thinking, love
> pray and thank God every day
> meditate—smile—laugh
> whistle—sing—dance
> look with fascination at everything
> fill you lungs and heart with liberty
> be yourself fully and immensely
> act like a king or queen unto Death
> feel God in your body, mind, heart, and soul
> and be convinced of eternal life and resurrection.

Conclusion

In all four segments of my proposed world curriculum, the spiritual visions of Christianity and other religions are truer, deeper and more enriching than any purely rational, scientific, pragmatic, civilian education. Our lives and planet and human family advance in time as a huge living ball of changes, interdependencies, dreams and aspirations, the full significance and mystery of which will probably forever escape us. But Christ gave us hope, faith and light. He gave us his two great commandments: love the Father in heaven and love each other with all your strength, all your mind, all your heart and all your soul. His "holistic" and divinely simple teachings do in many ways enrich the marvelous discoveries of science, reason, analysis and experimentation. But the latter are not all. There is more in the heavens and on earth than in our discoveries. The unique challenge to universal spiritual education is to integrate our vast scientific knowledge, our social knowledge, our knowledge of time and of the art of living into a shining, divine, blissful vision of our miraculous journey in the unfathomable universe.

Modern Christian and spiritual teachers could well say:

"Give me your children, and I will give them the heavens, happiness, the earth and immortality."

PART IV

My Personal Global Transcendence

21

My Five Teilhardian Enlightenments

As far back as I can remember, the natural inclinations of my being have always been to love life, nature, people—especially old people, because they know so much—temples to God, sunshine, the stars, and the moon. My schoolmates used to laugh at me when I repeated my most basic conviction, namely, that life was *göttlich* or divine.

In my homeland of Alsace-Lorraine, then, I was taught that to be French or German was apparently more important than to be alive, for we were asked to give our lives for one or the other country. I learned that my grandfather had changed his nationality five times without leaving his village. I saw pictures of my father once in a German uniform, then in a French one. I was asked not to cross the Saar River, which I could see from my window. Then troops began to fill our region, fortifications were built, and twice our city was evacuated. The second time it meant war. Half of my family wore German uniforms, the other half French ones. I saw human horrors that were in utter contradiction to the beauty of nature, people, church, sunshine, the stars, the moon, and the cultures of Goethe and Racine.

After the war I decided to work for peace, and in 1948 I entered the United Nations. For the first years I worked there as an economist and I was privileged to be associated with some of the great ventures of the international community, such as the creation of the United Nations Development Program and the first world conferences. These pressed me constantly ahead toward a global view of our planet and its people.

In 1970, the year of the twenty-fifth anniversary of the UN, I was appointed director of the Secretary-General's Office. From then on I really had to have a total view and I often heard myself being described as a "Teilhardian." Father Emmanuel de Breuvery, a companion of Teilhard de Chardin, had already exposed me to the ideas and philosophy of Teilhard when I was working in the Natural Resources Division of the United Nations.[1] With Secretary-General U Thant, this exposure became ever more frequent, and now after a third of a century of service with the UN I can say unequivocally that much of what I have observed in the world bears out the all-encompassing, global, forward-looking philosophy of Teilhard de Chardin.

My own comprehension of the universal order of things took place progressively, at special moments of my life when I was challenged to explain what was going on in the world as seen from the UN. I like to call these moments my "Teilhardian enlightenments." They were all very pragmatic and arose from grass-roots observations of the world and of its people. As an economist, I had learned to observe, to analyze and to conclude. Nurtured by my love for life, for the world, the people, the moon, and the stars, a rather simple philosophy took form in me which has much in common with the vastly more prestigious cosmology of Teilhard de Chardin.

From the Infinitely Large to the Infinitely Small

The first enlightenment took place in 1973 when I was asked to speak to the American Association of Systems Analysts on the subject: "Can the United Nations become a functional system of world order?" It was on that occasion that I perceived and presented for the first time my Copernican view of world cooperation (see Part I, Chapter 3 above).

I was amazed by the simplicity of the pattern which was emerging from humanity's efforts as reflected in the United Nations. Everything was beginning to fall into place! A magnificent tapestry of our place in the universe was being woven by the world organization. A practical network of people and institutions all around the world was working on Pascal's genial view of the universe, from the infinitely large to the infinitely small. There remained a few gaps in the picture but soon they would be filled too.

[1] See *Most of All They Taught Me Happiness*, pp. 113–17.

This framework was typically Teilhardian. It was universal in scope and covered every aspect of our planetary home. Teilhard had viewed the UN as the nascent institutional embodiment of his vision. He did not live long enough to see today's formidable global enterprise of the United Nations, but the world organization reflects accurately the unified system of planetary concerns, aspirations, convergence and consciousness he had conceived.

A Biological View of Humanity

During the same year I was asked to speak at a meeting of the American Institute of Biological Sciences on "Biological Evolution and the United Nations." It was the time when the UN was embarking on the great conference on the seas and oceans. I remembered my discussions with Father de Breuvery on the astonishing, teeming biological resources of the seas and oceans. I decided therefore to speak on the UN's efforts, world conferences, and institutional arrangements in a number of major biological fields: the World Population Conference, the UN Conference on the Environment, the Law of the Sea Conference, the Habitat Conference, the Man and the Biosphere Program, etc., and I found myself suddenly exclaiming:

> "One could write a whole treatise about the birth of this collective brain and warning system of the human species. . . . All this forms part of a biological evolution. The human species continues to probe out, on an ever larger scale, the possibilities and limits of its terrestrial and perhaps tomorrow extraterrestrial habitat. This is one of the most thrilling and challenging periods of our planet's history. I am personally convinced that we will find the necessary adaptation of our brains, appetites, beliefs, feelings and behaviour to reach new equilibria and to select what is good for us instead of what is bad on our small spaceship Earth, circling in the universe, surrounded by its thin but so fantastically rich biosphere of only a few miles, containing all life of our solar system. . . ."[2]

After the speech, Professor Ernst Mayr, an anthropologist from Chicago University, commented that he had never heard the work of the UN presented in that way and that he felt he had witnessed a rare moment in evolution, namely, the birth of a new species, a metamorphosis similar to the transformation of the protozoa into

[2] Ibid., pp. 182–89.

metazoa. Perhaps indeed the human species was entering a new period of evolution, a period of planetary consciousness and global living, a fact that would be fully understood only by future generations.

If a Teilhardian had been in the audience, he would have stated most emphatically that my presentation was one long, practical illustration of Teilhard's philosophy of global evolution, of the noosphere, of metamorphosis, and of the birth of a collective brain to the human species! What was happening in the world and in the UN was just one vast confirmation of his vision. We did not have to wait for future generations to understand that we had entered the global age.

From the Infinite Past to the Infinite Future

For a couple of years I relied on these two "enlightenments" when presenting the work of the UN in my speeches and writings, and in taking further initiatives to fill the gaps in the two Copernican and biological schemes. It was not until 1975 that I made a new "find." I had been asked to speak at a joint conference of the Audubon Society and the Sierra Club on the subject "Interdependence: Societies' Interaction with Ecosystems."[3] I tried to do my best to show in a sweeping statement the main stages of our planet's evolution since its birth, our present position in time, and the recently emerging concerns about the future. Again, it was simply a schematic presentation of humanity's efforts and preoccupations as mirrored in the UN: the world agencies were increasingly called upon to deal with the past (preservation of the environment, of genetic resources, of the natural and cultural heritage), with the present (world conferences or international years on resources, water, desertification, science and technology, outer space, children, youth, women, the elderly, races, the handicapped, etc.) and with the future (development decades, climatic changes, Food 2000, Industry 2000, Education 2000, Health 2000, Environment 2000, etc.).

The world had never seen anything like it! But what was happening was in reality very simple: the human species, as a result of its

[3] The speech was published in "Earthcare, Global Protection of Natural Areas," edited by Edmond Schoffield, Westview Press, Boulder, Colorado, 1980 (pp. 583–98).

expanding knowledge, intelligence and discoveries, was suddenly forced to visualize the entire time span of our planet, reaching from our most distant astrophysical and paleontological past to the remaining six to eight billion years of our future. As a matter of fact, each layer of our Copernican reality has a time dimension, from our planet's total duration to the length of a human life, down to the infinitely brief span of an atomic particle. Moreover, everything we are doing today has a potentially lasting effect on the future.

Our planet was a teeming ball of incredible interdependencies, complexities, intensities, relationships, exchanges, streams, flows and long-term changes, floating and evolving in the universe, carrying on its crust a species which had suddenly been able to dissect, unlock, and analyze most of that fantastic reality, and which was beginning to change it in the most far-reaching fashion. What was needed was no less than a total earth science in space and in time, a science of all interdependencies, a view of the earth and of humans as one evolving entity, and a new art of planetary management and caretaking of which the first rudiments were being born right under our eyes in the world organizations.

That speech brought me one step closer to Teilhard's theory of evolution, to his view of the earth as a "living cell" as well as his outcry for responsible earth management. Teilhard had drawn his vision from his work as an archaeologist, paleontologist and evolutionary scientist. I had drawn mine from my practical observations in humanity's first planetary institutions.

A Spiritual Dimension

Two years later, in 1977, a new broadening of my views took place. The religion taught me during my youth had largely given way to the rationalism, scientism and intellectualism so prevalent in our time. I was not at all concerned with spirituality and religion in the United Nations. But as a close collaborator of U Thant, I could not fail to be deeply impressed by his view that, of all human values, the spiritual ones were the highest. I became accustomed to his familiar fourfold presentation of all human values and concerns. I also discovered that Dag Hammarskjöld, the rational Nordic economist, had ended up as a mystic. He too held at the end of his life that spirituality was the ultimate key to our earthly fate.

About that time the UN Meditation Group and the various

religions accredited to the UN asked me to speak about the spirituality of our Secretaries-General and of the UN. I noted that during most of its existence the UN had dealt primarily with the immediate, physical, material and mental needs of humanity (avoidance of war, hunger, health, education, etc.). But I had already seen the UN's scope vastly expand into space and into time. Was the UN taking moreover the path of all religions which dealt with the total human person in the total universe and total time? Was it not inevitable that the UN would sooner or later also acquire a spiritual dimension, once the other priorities of life (physical, mental and moral) had been met (*primum vivere, deinde philosophari*)?

I suddenly understood U Thant's belief that the world would be a good place to live in only when its billions of people understood that they were part of total creation; that the goodness of humanity depended on their individual goodness and internal purity; that our lives were not closed at the beginning and the end but were part of an endless stream. Then I understood Hammarskjöld, who ultimately referred for enlightenment all human problems to a greater, outside judge—to God. Then I understood better the visits of Pope Paul VI and John Paul II to the United Nations and their plea to nations to repeat their tremendous scientific and material achievements in the fields of the heart and the soul. The lawyer-economist I had been for so many years joined their ranks, for I had not received from law and economics the proper answers to the problems of life and death and of our meaning in the universe.

I have come to believe firmly today that our future peace, justice, fulfillment, happiness and harmony on this planet will not depend on world government but on divine or cosmic government, meaning that we must seek and apply the "natural," "evolutionary," "divine," "universal" or "cosmic" laws which must rule our journey in the cosmos. Most of these laws can be found in the great religions and prophecies, and they are being rediscovered slowly but surely in the world organizations.

Any Teilhardian will recognize in this the spiritual transcendence which he announced so emphatically as the next step in our evolution. He had arrived at this conclusion from both his archaeological and his theological studies. I had arrived at mine through three decades of observation and endeavors in our planet's first universal organization.

The Human Cosmos and Happiness

Accustomed now to deal with broad global problems in time and in space, and increasingly drawn by my work to universal and philosophical concepts, I needed to retain a firmer root on earth, a more immediate, concrete, tangible challenge. I found it in a question which increasingly returned to my mind. "What is in it for me? What does this all mean for the individual human person?" Creation, the universe, remote stars, the earth, spirituality and eternity are terribly big words compared with my tiny self. As an antidote to cosmic dimensions and vagueness, I began to concentrate on my own personal life, dreams, experiences, past, family, as well as on circumstances and persons who had played an important role or left a lasting impression on me. I asked myself the question: "Suppose I die tomorrow? What are the lessons I would like to leave behind, especially for my children and grandchildren?"

The answer was clear: I had to find out by recording the most sensitive highlights of my life, be it persons, events, personal conclusions or important turning points. Since my heavy duties at the UN prevented me from writing a comprehensive, well-structured work with a beginning and an end, I decided to write down my lessons from life in the form of anecdotes and stories. There were about fifty of them. When they were finished, I discovered that there was one constant thread, theme or search running through all of them: the quest for happiness.

I had always sought the maximum fulfillment of my "divine" life! I had been on the constant lookout for circumstances, examples and people who would help me perfect the art of living. I discovered that for me life had always been the highest value, a sacred gift. I had been given the incredible privilege of opening for a few years my eyes, ears, mind, heart and soul to the stupendous creation and the world around me. I had walked through the festival of life with the wondrous eyes of a child. I had lived and loved my life with every fiber of my heart, with true enthusiasm (by God possessed). And that realization gave me the clue to my place in the total scheme: the universe is made up of endless cosmoses, from the infinitely large to the infinitely small: I am one of these cosmoses, linked with everything in the heavens and on earth, endowed with a unique and unrepeatable life in all eternity, were it only because the external circumstances and companions would never be the same. How did the world at the precise moment of time when my human cosmos was inserted in it look? How did I relate to it? How did I find fulfillment in it?

Obviously it was a highly imperfect world, in which two thirds of humanity still lived in utter poverty while hundreds of billions of dollars were being squandered each year on frightful armaments. It was a highly immoral world, a largely non-spiritual world, seemingly abandoned by God to an unknown fate in the universe. I had seen all its evils, injustices, contradictions, and follies during a World War and during my thirty-three years of world service. Could I despair? Should I give up? Was the universe an immense nonsense?

No, because I was human, that is, endowed with the highest privileges and perceptions of any living species on this planet; it was up to me to sharpen these admirable instruments called doing, seeing, hearing, thinking, feeling, dreaming, hoping and loving; I could focus my attention and love from a flower or a person to the universe and God, from the infinite past to the infinite future; I could profit from the incredible expansion of my hands, arms, legs, eyes, ears and brain through science and technology; I could seek, know and feel in myself the entire universe and Godhead, for I was part of them and they were part of me; it could not be otherwise; and last but not least I was the master of my cosmos, it was up to me to guide it, to uplift it, to give it confidence and joy, to keep it in an endless, wondrous, inquisitive, searching, loving and hopeful mood. If I visualize myself as a little erect being on the surface of our whirling planet Earth among billions of other humans, I am not more than a tiny speck. And yet that speck can embrace the heavens, the earth, humanity, the past, present and future! It can be and it is an active actor and receptor of the entire universe. To be this "fullest being" is our cosmic task on earth, our sacred, spiritual duty. And to do that I don't have to wait until the whole world is perfect. Indeed, I can contribute right away my peace, goodness and happiness to the human family.

And when I die, it will by no means be the end: my matter and life will become other matter and life; my thoughts, actions and feelings will remain part of the total stock of thoughts, actions and feelings of humanity; there will have been only a change of worlds. Even after the explosion of our solar system into fathomless space, every atom of this planet will again become an atom or another star, as it has been and will be for all eternity. No, I would never understand it all, I would not even understand a small part of it, and yet to be alive, to feel it, to know what I know, to be admitted to the banquet of life on our miraculous planet was indeed a fantastic privilege, a mysterious, stupendous phenomenon or gift of God in the vast unfathomable universe.

And I wondered why all my human relatives in the affluent world did not have the same elation about life, why they did not share my enthusiasm and gratitude, why they did not consider life as great, sacred, untouchable and divine; why there was war, killing, hurting and constant debasing of life; why there was so much injustice, pessimism and lamenting; why they did not help their poor fellow humans in the Third World; why we did not all love up to the brim our beautiful planet, our skies, our waters, our mountains, our seas, our brethren the animals, our sisters the flowers, our vast human family with its teeming diversity and dreams, down to each individual miraculous, unique human being; why we did not like, observe, penetrate our self, shudder at its divine, mysterious greatness; feel God and the universe in ourselves and make shine to maximum intensity the star which each of us is in creation.

Well, even if humanity did not have its values straight and believed that wealth, power, arms, glory, a nation, a race, a religion, a business or an ideology were superior to life, I would carry the jewel of my own life preciously and unscathed through the noisy market place. Even if I was alone of the four and a half billion people of this planet who believed in the superiority, sanctity and divinity of life (and I am not alone), I would proclaim and practice this truth fearlessly, joyously and proudly to the very end, be it in prison or at the top of the United Nations.

And once more, as I arrived at these conclusions, the image of Teilhard de Chardin came back to me. This time it was not as a philosophical concept or vision, but the image of his person as described in a wonderful story by Jean Houston. As a young girl, Jean used to cross Central Park in New York on the way to school. She often met in the park an elderly gentleman, who was either sitting on a bench or walking around. She talked to him and they became friends. The gray-haired gentleman seemed constantly afloat in a strange, endless, joyous astonishment at life. He would hold a flower or an insect in his hand and infer from it the whole universe and story of creation and evolution. As William Blake said:

To see the world in a grain of sand,
  And a heaven in a wild flower;
  Hold infinity in the palm of your hand,
    And eternity in an hour.

The old gentleman had introduced himself and was known to Jean Houston as Mr. Teller, but years later, when she studied philosophy and saw a picture of Teilhard de Chardin, she exclaimed: "But this is Mr. Teller, my friend, the old gentleman in the park!"

And Fate wanted it to be that she arranged the publication of my little life stories and essays on human happiness!

At this juncture of my life, after a long, meandering search for truth, the picture I have obtained from the United Nations' global observation tower is now pretty clear. The table of contents of a new world encyclopedia is ready. The agenda for the next chapter of humanity is in sight. But this is when the real Teilhardian period begins: with this vast fundamental, well-ordered knowledge on hand we must now administer our planet well, learn the art of peaceful, personal and social living, practice justice, love and tolerance, and celebrate the miracle of life through individual peace, happiness, joy, altruism and harmony in the endless stream of changing worlds. Our new global living is so sudden, so complex, so manifold and mind-boggling, it is such a mixture of small and big, global and local, past and future, young and old, that our bewilderment and anxiety are not surprising, but rather normal. To humanity I would simply say: do not despair, but learn.

We must now prepare for a Bimillennium Celebration of Life, free of war, violence, hunger and despair; a world in which every child can keep and nourish his inborn love for life, nature, people, God, sunshine, the stars, the moon and so many other wonderful things.

22

How I Became a Spiritual Being[1]

In [your book] Most of All They Taught Me Happiness, *you wrote four chapters on U Thant, telling how he influenced your spiritual life. It is surprising how a man of a Buddhist tradition had more effect on your spirituality than someone like Thomas Merton. How do you explain this?*

I can explain this, and I feel my experience can be of value to others because it is not an infrequent one. I have never been a deeply religious person. I was raised in a good Catholic family, but for long in my life, I had never met anyone who inspired me to become a really spiritual person. Our schools in France have practically eradicated religion. Intelligence and performance are the highest virtues. As a young person, I obviously followed the prevailing ideas and values of my time and tried to do my best within their realm. At the university it was the same story. I then came to work for the United Nations where the highest virtue is not spirituality but again high intelligence and performance. Our whole world seems to be like that. One's life is unavoidably dominated by the values of the time. Of course, one prays, one goes to church and one raises the children in one's faith, but for me there has never been anything deeper than that. My readings were always in economics, politics and law. I had never found Thomas Merton included in the requirements of my reading lists.

At the age of forty-six I became director of Secretary-General U Thant's office. Here, for the first time in my life, I met a person who

[1] A Message of Hope from an Optimist at the United Nations, interview with Sister Mary Madden, C.S.J. published in the magazine *Sisters Today*, October 1979.

inspired me, a man who was deeply religious, who had a profound spirituality and code of human ethics which he applied to every moment and situation of his day. This I had never experienced. I had met people with very beautiful ideas about spirituality who did not practice what they preached. Here was a man who never spoke badly about anyone else—and God knows how many occasions he had for it!—who was always patient, widely open to others, never vainglorious, proud or demanding. To the humblest being he was most respectful and a friend. The UN guards remember him well for his immense human kindness. As one of them put it: "He could have the President of the United States waiting for him, but the first thing he would do would be to greet the guard who opened the door. Then, he would ask how you were, no matter who was there. He was one of the most marvelous human beings I ever met in my life."[2]

As I became more and more amazed at the authenticity of this man and of his actions in everyday life, I began to discuss religion with him. I tried to understand him better and found that he was simply, honestly and painstakingly applying his Buddhist faith to daily life. He was far from being a mystic like Hammarskjöld, who was in constant negotiation with God. I discovered that for U Thant there was no difference between spirituality, religion and life. Life was for him a constant spirituality. I studied Buddhism to understand him better. We became great friends. He was able to teach me what my Catholic priests had always told me, but at that time I hadn't listened. Here, in the middle of my life, was the master, the one who inspired me, someone I could imitate like a father. This has changed my life. Perhaps what we need most at this time are masters who give us the good example. And, like U Thant, they ought to include people in highest office and with wide responsibilities. All statesmen should be models and masters for their people, human beings with a deep philosophy, ethics and spirituality, as were Dag Hammarskjöld and U Thant at the UN.

From the moment I became interested in the spiritual dimension of life, everything started to change. I began to read Hammarskjöld's *Markings*. I discovered that he had found God as the Master and that he had to interpret His will as the Secretary-General of the United Nations. His preferred authors were Thomas à Kempis and

[2] UN Meditation Group, *A Salute to the UN Security and Safety Service* (Garden City, N.Y.: Agni Press, 1977), pp. 90–91.

St. John of the Cross, whom I had never read in my life. I began to read the mystics and understood much more about this new dimension of life consciousness. Some religious people began to be interested in my ideas. I was invited to participate in an East-West monastic encounter. There I discovered Merton and began to read his works. Before that I had never heard of him.

Later on I was made a member of the East-West Monastic Board because its members wanted to know what was going on in the world organization. I am learning a great deal from them and they are also learning from me. I found that most monastic orders are organized on the basis of U Thant's cherished four categories of human needs and qualities: physical, mental, moral and spiritual. I learned that he was a monk himself. Buddhists are required to go to a monastery for one month each year. Since he could not go back to a Burmese monastery, he acted as a kind of monk in the United Nations, the same way as Hammarskjöld acted as a solitary mystic in it. This has been a tremendous experience for me, and as a result I have been writing more and more about the need for spirituality as an answer to our personal as well as world problems. I would like the whole world to benefit from my experience and to derive the same enlightenment, happiness, serenity and hope in the future as I derived from my contact with U Thant. I would never have thought that I would discover spirituality in the United Nations! The same happened to the Western, rational, hyperintellectual Dag Hammarskjöld. It is a subject which therefore merits close attention. Perhaps spirituality is such a fundamental human need that it always reappears in one form or another in life and throughout history and that we are about to witness now its renaissance in a global, planetary context.[3]

[3] I am glad that Professor Ewert Cousins, head of the Fordham University Spirituality Program, has entrusted one of his students with the preparation of a thesis on the spirituality of Dag Hammarskjöld and U Thant.

23

A Proclamation of Faith

I am often asked why the United Nations occupies such an important part in my writings. There are two reasons for it: first, the United Nations has helped me to extend tremendously my consciousness of the world and of humanity. It has played for my comprehension of planet Earth and of its people the same role that thought, prayer and meditation later played for the understanding of my inner world. Secondly, there can be no doubt that the main condition for world happiness and spirituality is peace, for it is in peace only that we will be able to enjoy happiness, fully flower as human beings, and fulfill our cosmic destiny. A strengthened and actively supported United Nations can help enormously in attaining peace, human fulfillment and a better understanding of our fate. The horrid sufferings and destruction I saw as a young man during World War II could have been avoided if the people had worked harder for a strong and universal League of Nations. Adventures like those of Hitler and Mussolini might have been impossible.

I have seen the United Nations grow and greatly change since I joined it a third of a century ago. It has taught me more than any school or university on earth. It has taught me in particular to be confident in humankind's capacity to organize itself in peace, justice and happiness on our little planet. We are scarcely emerging from the political cave age. We are only in the kindergarten of the global school. Therefore, despite the frustrations and pitfalls I have known, after so many years of world service, I am today more enthusiastic than ever about the United Nations. I want to communicate this enthusiasm to the people, for nothing is more important for our future than public understanding and support for the world's first universal organization.

When I remember the sufferings and waste I saw in Europe during my youth, I cannot help feeling that humanity has covered an immense distance, that we are finally on the right road and that we will never again see a world war on this planet. For a third of a century now, all children in Europe could go to sleep every night without having to fear a war the next morning. The political wisdom achieved in Europe will now extend also to the rest of the world. We will see dialogue and cooperation progressively replace everywhere conflicts and confrontations. Someday the last decades of the twentieth century will be remembered as one of the greatest turning points in human history.

True enough, there remain immense problems, there could be less horrid nonsense, more peace and a better organization than the UN, but we have passed successfully through one of the most colossal and complex periods of change in all human evolution without slaughtering each other on a mass scale. This augurs well for the future and, since I have been privileged to work for one of the most exciting and most misunderstood organizations on earth, I wish to declare unambiguously my profound faith in the United Nations and bear witness to the human progress it represents, despite all its shortcomings, failures and errors. If someone had told me thirty years ago that I would see the degree of international cooperation and world convergence I see today, I would not have believed it. It is therefore only fitting that I proclaim my faith in an organization which will be considered someday as the paradigm of the new millennium.

Briefly, here are my articles of faith in the UN:

The UN has
- helped one billion people gain independence with a minimum of bloodshed, thus completing the historical movement started two hundred years ago by the Declaration of Independence;
- helped the emergence of the poorer countries into the modern age, providing a safety lid for the explosive feelings of our less fortunate brethren at the injustices which prevail in the world;
- provided a talking place and a meeting ground during the worst periods of the cold war;
- provided for the first time in history a code of ethics for rela-

tions between the most powerful entities on earth: armed nations;

— prevented, by its mere existence, even more national political and military adventures;
— provided a covering lid for hot conflicts, a standstill for fighting, a separation of belligerents and a talking ground between them;
— fared better with any conflict brought before it than unilateral, forceful attempts at settlement;
— been a moral force for progress toward political maturity, defusion of tensions, better understanding and reason around the world, proving that talking and listening are the beginning of wisdom and peace in human relations;
— been a platform for the expression and defense of all basic human aspirations, including those of liberty, equality and fraternity proclaimed by the American and French Revolutions on the eve of the modern age;
— enhanced immensely a planetary acceptance of the racial equality of all human beings;
— warned humanity of the immorality, inhumanity, dangers and inacceptability of armaments;
— warned humankind of its global limits and environmental constraints;
— progressively developed a functional system of world order, covering with its large number of specialized agencies and programs practically every field of human concern.

The UN is
— the first universal, global instrument humanity has ever had;
— the best chance of governments and nations to remain the permanent political and administrative units of planet Earth, provided they use and make the UN work to the satisfaction of the people;
— the place where new ethical values for nations and humanity are being formulated;
— the greatest universal collective effort ever attempted to reduce and eradicate all forms of violence from this planet;
— the best chance to keep within bounds new forms of excessive power and to develop codes of conduct for them;
— the central, permanent meeting ground of all human aspira-

tions in which will be molded a peaceful, just, safe and happy future for the human race;

— a treasure chest of world information;

— an incipient brain of the human species, registering global dangers and tendencies, keeping world conditions and phenomena under constant review, and fostering a better knowledge of our planet's resources and contraints;

— an incipient world nervous system which relays global findings and warnings to governments, local collectivities and the peoples;

— an incipient conscience and heart of humanity, which speaks for what is good and against what is bad for humans; which advocates and fosters understanding, cooperation and altruism instead of division, struggle and indifference among nations;

— an observatory into the future, since most problems facing humankind will derive from the expansion of the human race and its massive transformation of the physical and living conditions of our planet;

— an international mechanism born at the precise moment when humanity is becoming one global, complex, interdependent entity in so many respects; this will be its greatest historical chance of success and usefulness to the human race;

— the beginning of an important new story in evolution: the story of humanity as one family or one society living in one common home.

The UN should

— never be by-passed by any nation or group of nations as humanity's peacekeeping force;

— be used faithfully, in accordance with the Charter and the pledge of compliance by each member government, for the settlement of conflicts and the maintenance and strengthening of world peace;

— be further strengthened and perfected as a warning tower for global trends and menaces;

— be further developed as the planet's central data bank;

— be strengthened regionally, bringing each continent to bear its full contribution and role in the total world order;

— never be by-passed as the forum for the consideration of any problems which are of a world-wide nature and of concern to all humans;

— strengthen its links with the world scientific and academic community. The United Nations University and the University of Peace constitute, in this respect, major historical steps forward in world cooperation and human evolution;

— strengthen its links with the world's religions, since humanity will now enter its moral and spiritual age;

— further elaborate its cosmic vision by adding to its present physical, mental and moral comprehension a spiritual, mystical dimension of our mysterious journey in the universe.

Governments should

— respect, support, strengthen and constantly improve their first planetary instrument for world peace, justice, progress, diagnosis, cooperation, forecasting and management; fulfill faithfully their obligations toward the Charter, a fact which alone would bring about peace, order and understanding in the world;

— implement the recommendations of the UN, above all by putting an end to the obsolete, insane and wasteful armaments race;

— teach our children and youth about the global age, global living and the global intergovernmental instruments which have been created to help cope with global problems;

— enlist the impatience, idealism and energy of youth in building a better world, free of war, want, hatred and injustice;

— join their efforts in unprecedented ways to better explore, utilize and conserve the resources of our planet;

— promote a real revolution in world cooperation for the common benefit of the whole human race;

— better inform and educate the people about the work and efforts of the UN and its specialized agencies, thereby giving them confidence that something is being done about the problems which confront humankind on a global scale;

— enlist the support and better understanding of parliamentarians for a world cooperation which is of direct interest and consequence to their electorates;

— turn their eyes away from the past and direct them to the future;

— plan for the arrival of a few billion more people on this planet;

— extend their vision and concern to the whole planet, to all peoples and to all future generations instead of seeing, defending and promoting only narrow, immediate and transient national interests.

The people should
 — have faith in the future and give a chance to the most noble attempt at world peace and cooperation ever undertaken on this planet;
 — take an interest in the UN, its peacekeeping and peacemaking activities, its specialized agencies, its organs, its information, its studies, its meetings, its recommendations, its publications, its programs, its world conferences, its international years and its emerging global vision;
 — support, join or create volunteer groups or associations for the UN in order to be better informed about the efforts of *their* UN, and discuss the issues before it;
 — celebrate United Nations Day on October 24;
 — display the UN flag;
 — pray for the UN;
 — request that children be educated about the UN and the world's global problems, which affect every citizen;
 — demand from the news media more information about the UN, its specialized agencies, global problems and efforts for peace, justice and a better world;
 — request their political representatives to take a greater interest in world cooperation and development, which have become affairs of concern to all peoples;
 — inform themselves of the efforts of the more than ten thousand international non-governmental organizations which in a vast number of professional, humanitarian and scientific fields foster international cooperation, friendship and common concerns;[1]
 — act and behave in greater cognizance of the fact that, in a world of several billion people, peace, progress, justice, understanding and spirituality are essentially the sum total of the peace, progress, justice, understanding and spirituality of all individuals.

Religions should
 — take an active interest in the work and efforts of the UN and inform their members properly about them;

[1] The UN has entrusted to the Union of International Associations the publication of a Yearbook of International Organizations. See "Networking," by Jessica Lynack and Jeffrey Stamps, (Doubleday, 1982), Chapter 9, pp. 189–205.

— accelerate their ecumenism and create common world religious
   institutions which would bring the resources and inspirations of
   the religions to bear upon the solution of world problems;
— display the UN flag in all their houses of worship;
— pray and organize world prayers for the UN and for all
   peacemakers;
— pray God for our successful passage into the global age without
   a war or a nuclear holocaust.

24

My Creed in Human Happiness

As I near the end of my journey on planet Earth, may I dare to offer a few personal conclusions regarding the quest for human happiness:

I believe that happiness is

love for the heavens
love for our beautiful planet
love for all humankind
love for my family
love for my work
love for my miraculous life

I believe that happiness is

a personal decision
an internal readiness
the supreme harmony between senses, mind,
heart and soul

I believe that happiness is

the greatest form of freedom
the ultimate fulfillment of life
the highest transcendence of life
a powerful self-assertion

I believe that happiness

is reached through physical, mental, moral and
spiritual care and exercises

I believe that happiness can be achieved

>*through concentration upon oneself*
>*opening oneself to others*
>*elevating oneself to God*

I believe that happiness is

>*to look always at the good side of life*
>*to be in constant amazement and reverence for life*
>*to be passionate about life*
>*to be enthusiastic about life*

I believe that happiness is better than gloom

>*optimism better than pessimism*
>*hope better than despair*
>*confidence better than diffidence*
>*positive thinking better than negative thinking*
>*a smile better than a frown*
>*cleanliness better than impurity*
>*cooperation better than obstruction*
>*friendship better than hostility*
>*truth better than falsehood*
>*love better than hatred*
>*altruism better than egotism*
>*peace better than conflict*
>*serenity better than anxiety*

I believe that happiness is

>*the ultimate objective of life*
>*a sacred duty of the living*
>*an act of grace for the miraculous gift of life*

I believe that happiness is

>*to lead good physical lives*
>*to constantly broaden one's knowledge*
>*to live in peace and friendship with all our human*
>   *brethren and sisters*
>*to lead a pure inner life in harmony with*
>   *God, humanity, our planet, the universe and eternity*

I believe that happiness

> *brings health and serenity*
> *unlocks the mind*
> *broadens the heart*
> *brings us near to God and to cosmic understanding*

I believe that happiness

> *is the secret of life and youth*
> *the human answer to many insoluble questions*
> *the lamp that illuminates our amazing journey in*
>   *the vast, incomprehensible universe.*

25

Conclusion

O God, forgive me all this multitude of words which are so feeble to express my love for the greatness of Your creation. As if they were not enough—and they will never be enough—I wish to let upwell a few final waves of ecstasy.

Dear God,

Humanity has achieved marvelous successes since the advent of its scientific and industrial age. It has unlocked many secrets and mysteries of nature and of the universe. It has penetrated into every possible aspect of the infinite manifestations of Your creation. It has transcended its physical and sensory capacities to the point of becoming a different species. It has been able to accommodate thousands of millions more people in the flow of human life on this planet. It has provided for longer lives, better lives and vastly improved knowledge for large numbers of people. It has eradicated most epidemics and diseases afflicting human life. It has conquered many social inequalities and evils in human relations. It has elevated itself from a passive species dominated by nature and its environment to an active living entity able to transform, mold, manage and improve planet Earth for its flowering.

Despite all the wars, mistakes, injustices and follies of power and armaments, this has been a prodigious period of human ascent which will stand out as one of the greatest advances in our evolution. We must be thankful to You, O God, for having allowed us to transcend our physical and mental nature into such knowledge and mastery. Men and women of science who have pierced the surrounding reality and provided the basis for our conquests deserve our deepest gratitude.

But we are now entering a new age, the understanding and image of which still remain to be charted. After more than thirty years of observation and thinking from the balcony of world history at the United Nations, may I offer these suggestions and hopes for our passage into the first planetary civilization:

— It is high time for humanity to accept and to work out the full consequences of the total global and interdependent nature of our planetary home and of our species. Our survival and further progress will depend largely on the advent of global visions and of proper global education in all countries of the world.
— We must effectuate a giant leap forward into the future and henceforth see ourselves and our actions in the endless stream of time.
— There is a pressing need for a science and art of planetary management and therapy which will recognize the potentialities as well as the limits of our planet for the improvement of human life; higher global education must provide well-prepared, responsible world managers, caretakers and leaders for government, religions, firms, international organizations and transnational entities.
— While continuing to learn more about our planet and its proper management, we must now pass from the national to the planetary age and from the rational to the moral and spiritual age. We must reinsert ourselves into the total visions of the great religions and prophets. Science must take its appropriate place in these greater visions which alone can provide satisfactory answers to the mysteries of life, of the universe and of right human relations.
— The world's major religions must speed up dramatically their ecumenical movement and recognize the unity of their objectives in the diversity of their cults. Religions must actively cooperate to bring to unprecedented heights a better understanding of the mysteries of life and of our place in the universe. "My religion, right or wrong," and "My nation, right or wrong" must be abandoned forever in the planetary age.
— Since the world's religions, governments, enterprises and international organizations all work to achieve the greatest possible happiness of people, they must join their forces and cooperate

actively in order to bring about a happy, just, peaceful, prosperous and godly society on earth.

— Individual as well as collective life must be elevated from the purely material and intellectual planes to the higher summits of morality (right human relations) and spirituality (right relations with God, creation, infinity and eternity). Humans in all walks of life must contribute maximum physical, mental, moral and spiritual lives to humanity's total life. Scientists and intellectuals must strive for moral and spiritual excellence. Religious and spiritual people must appreciate and be cognizant of scientific achievements.

— Humanity must bring into full play the forces of the "mystery of faith," of hope, of belief in human life, in the progress of humanity, in greater civilization, in further evolution, in the accomplishment of a divine design. Religious and spiritual people must teach the world actively about the mystery of faith, of interiority, of mysticism, of prayer and meditation and of the happiness derived from spiritual beliefs and exercises.

— Infinitely more attention must be accorded to the great, simple and so effective concepts of love, peace, compassion, truth, purity, goodness, humility, faith, divinity, the heart, the soul, resurrection, infinity and eternity. They must become the luminous pillars of human civilization in a global, universal context.

— Now must dawn a world-wide era of supreme reverence for life, embodied in a universal, peaceful, non-violent, disarmed, just society as heralded by all great religious leaders. We must work out the rules of world harmony between all peoples, between humanity and the earth, and between humanity and the divine.

— The supreme unity of the human family, universal and interdependent, as seen by all great religions must now become a political reality; the hour has struck for the implementation of a spiritual vision of world affairs; the next great task of humanity will be to determine the divine or cosmic laws which must rule our behavior on this planet.

— We must establish a vast inventory of all our knowledge and rank everything at its right place in the universal scheme that has been revealed to us; we must rejoice at our progress and achievements and raise our sights to further objectives and summits to be attained.

— We must learn to work in common and to unite our wills,

dreams, intelligence and resources towards the fashioning of a world permitting the fullest flowering of human life everywhere.

— We must learn to adjust our individual and group interests to the supreme interests, survival and apotheosis of the human race.

— We must strive to become a majority, nay, a unanimity, of positive, hopeful, enthusiastic, life-impassioned, universe- and divinity-enamored beings.

— We must learn to refrain from exploiting and developing the negative sides of our discoveries.

— We must learn to foresee intelligently the world-wide and long-term consequences of our policies and actions, and outgrow the present primitive age of learning by accident and burning our fingers like ignorant little children.

— We must define a new world ethics.

— We must respect and love each other as unique, unrepeatable, sacrosanct miracles in the universe and in eternity.

— From the evolutionary stage of perfectly coordinated, well-adapted individual beings, we must now pass to the next stage of a perfectly coordinated, well-adapted, harmonious human society.

— We must learn to become responsible members of a newly born global family endowed with common institutions, a common brain, heart, nervous system and soul geared to our common survival and flowering on planet Earth; we must help this latest-formed and greatest entity achieve its maximum harmonious functioning and perfection within our planet's given endowment.

— We must learn to focus easily and lovingly our minds, hearts, senses and souls over the entire gamut of creation, from the infinitely large to the infinitely small, from the stars to the flowers of the earth, from the entire human family to the last of our sisters and brethren, embracing at any moment the plenitude of the miracle of creation and of being.

— We must help enhance the biological and divine law of unity in diversity in all realms of creation, from science to culture, from the human family to the individual, from God-the-unique to God-the-infinitely-diverse in the endless manifestations of matter and life.

— As the religions have done for thousands of years, we must teach humans to see at all times their right place in the universe, in the eternal flow of time, on our planet and in our human family. Ours will stand out as the epoch of most gigantic comprehension, synthesis, elevation and pacification there ever was.

— We must plan now for the year 2000 a Bimillennium Celebration of Life, the advent of an Era of Peace, of a Golden Age, of the First Millennium of World Harmony and Human Happiness in which our globe will become a showcase in the universe, a true miracle of divine fulfillment, a model of peace, justice, humaneness, love, kindness and joy in the fathomless expanses of creation.

26

Meditation

Whenever I am sad or in despair or in rebellion against the state of human affairs, all I need to do is to think of You, O God, the Father, the Creator, and all becomes bright again. "He who follows Me," said the Christ, "walks not in darkness, for he will have the light of life." From the summit of the divine, all falls into place. My unhappiness, despair or complaints become so tiny and irrelevant in the total order of things. I need You, O God and Your endless, manifold incarnations in the beauty of creation. I need You to elevate me above my miserable, ephemeral condition and concerns. I need You to give me light, faith and hope. I need You to show me the reason and beauty of the universe. I need You to give sense and purpose to my life which so often appears to me meaningless.

We humans are a great species, undoubtedly endowed with a divine nature or spark, but we shall never be able to pierce the ultimate mysteries of the universe and of life. The totality of creation and of time, the infinitely large and the infinitely small, the beginningless beginning and the endless end will forever escape us. The more we know, the less we understand the totality. Scientists can see no end to time and space. Perhaps it is all very simple, infinitely more simple than we all think, but we are not made to understand it. Hence the need to believe in You as a great, simple, limitless power, an all-encompassing mind, an all-embracing heart, an all-pervading soul endowed with all the perfections we seek on earth. Even if You didn't exist, we would have to invent You as did so many cultures and civilizations over the millennia. There must be a profound reason for You. You are as alive and indispensable today as at any other period of our journey. Once again You are the light in the darkness, the answer to our anxiety, the image of our future. Strangely and significantly enough, we have endowed You with the ultimate perfection of our senses, incapable as we are to perceive You otherwise than as we see ourselves ideally in the universe. Yes, be it You as one God or as a God in the multiple manifestations of creation, You are the ultimate, simple, glorious, reassuring, all-satisfying answer to our unpierceable mysteries. I cannot prove it? Well, when I am sad or in despair or in rebellion, I think of You and all becomes bright again: a smile appears on my face, a light shines in my eyes, a warm flood of happiness inundates my heart, a wonderful leaven elevates my entire being. I am happy, consoled, hopeful again, more joyful to be alive: the miracle of faith has operated once more. You have touched me with Your invisible, unprovable hand. This is good enough proof for me as well as for hundreds of millions of brothers and sisters on this planet. The miracle of faith is so effective, so powerful, so extraordinary, even and especially in the face of adversity, sickness and death, that humans who do not use it are simply to be pitied. It is difficult to understand that so many people can live with their eyes glued to the material and mental only, disregarding the immensity and beauty of the spiritual. And what is true of the individual is also true of a society and of the entire human family: we must re-establish You at the center of our lives and of all our efforts, we must try to better understand Your great scheme and design. We must turn to You to see right, to feel right, to think right and to manage rightly our planet and our future destiny.

Yes, we must join our Hindu brethren and call henceforth our planet "Brahma" or the Planet of God.

27

Final Prayer and New Genesis

O God, I do not know who You are, but I am in exultant joy before the magnificence of Your creation.

O God, I do not know why You gave me life, but I thank You with every fiber of my heart for having lit up in me the divine spark of light in the vast, incomprehensible universe.

O God, I know that I come from You, that I am part of You, that I will return to You, and that there will be no end to my rebirth in the eternal stream of Your splendid creation.

O God, I do not know why You created light and darkness, happiness and despair, good and evil, love and hatred, creation and destruction, matter and void, and allowed us to choose constantly between the two, but I know that it is my duty and joy to throw down my gauntlet for light, brightness, compassion, goodness, happiness, truthfulness, life, beauty and love.

O God, only You know the meaning of all there is in the heavens and on earth. Why don't You return again to tell us once more what our lives and destiny should truly be?

O God, I cannot define You, I cannot see You, I cannot perceive You, I cannot understand You, I cannot embrace You, but I can most definitely feel You, love You and know that You are.

Please, O God, have pity on us and allow us to become at long last a warless, weaponless, hungerless, horrorless, just, kind, truthful, thankful, loving and happy planet.

O God, help me to show through my life that this is the Planet of God. Please.

The New Genesis

And God saw that all nations of the earth, black and white, poor and rich, from North and South, from East and West, and of all creeds were sending their emissaries to a tall glass house on the shores of the River of the Rising Sun, on the island of Manhattan, to study together, to think together and to care together for the world and all its people. And God said: That is good. And it was the first day of the New Age of the earth.

And God saw that soldiers of peace were separating the combatants of quarreling nations, that differences were being resolved by negotiation and reason instead of arms, and that the leaders of nations were seeing each other, talking to each other and joining their hearts, minds, souls and strength for the benefit of all humanity. And God said: That is good. And it was the second day of the Planet of Peace.

And God saw that humans were loving the entire creation, the stars and the sun, the day and the night, the air and the oceans, the earth and the waters, the fishes and the fowl, the flowers and the herbs, and all their human brethren and sisters. And God said: That is good. And it was the third day of the Planet of Happiness.

And God saw that humans were suppressing hunger, disease, ignorance and suffering all over the globe, providing each human person with a decent, conscious and happy life, and reducing the greed, the power and the wealth of the few. And He said: That is good. And it was the fourth day of the Planet of Justice.

And God saw that humans were living in harmony with their planet and in peace with one another, wisely managing their resources, avoiding waste, curbing excesses, replacing hatred with love, greed with contentment, arrogance with humility, division with cooperation and mistrust with understanding. And He said: That is good. And it was the fifth day of the Golden Planet.

And God saw that men were destroying their arms, bombs, missiles, warships and warplanes, dismantling their bases and disbanding their armies, keeping only policemen of peace to protect the good from the bad and the normal from the mad. And God said: That is good. And it was the sixth day of the Planet of Reason.

And God saw humans restore God and the human person as the alpha and omega, reducing institutions, beliefs, politics, governments and all man-made entities to mere servants of God and the people. And he saw them adopt as their supreme law:

You shall love the Lord your God with all your heart, all your soul, all your mind and all your strength. You shall love your neighbor as yourself. There is no greater commandment than these.

And God said: That is good. And it was the seventh day of the Planet of God.

And the Lord looked down upon the earth and said:

And now, my children, you will know again that each of you is a miracle, a unique creation in the universe, that life is a sacred gift which you must cherish at all times, that you were engendered in my image, that happiness and paradise can be established on earth, that your beautiful, miraculous planet will still spin for eons of time in the fathomless universe, that you are its caretakers and keepers, and that when finally its end comes, every atom of it will be reborn in another star in heaven. And there shall be no end to birth, life, death and resurrection in the eternal stream of the universe which you will never understand, for this will remain forever the difference between you and Me. I will now make My peace with you and let you establish a perfect Earth. Farewell, My grownup children. At long last, you are on the right path, you have brought heaven down to earth and found your proper place in the universe. I will now leave you for a long journey, for I have to turn My sight to other troubled and unfinished celestial bodies. I now pronounce you Planet of God. Be happy. Enjoy fully your divine lives on your miraculous planet with all the care, passion, ecstasy, enthusiasm and love they deserve.

*   *   *

As for me, before leaving this planet, I would like to say this to my human brethren and sisters:

Decide to be a spiritual person
Render others spiritual
Irradiate your spirituality
Treat every moment of your life with divine respect
Love passionately your Godgiven, miraculous life
Be endlessly astonished at your breathtaking consciousness of the universe
Thank God every moment for the tremendous gift of life
Lift your heart to the heavens always

Be a cosmic, divine being, an integral, conscious part of the universe

Contemplate with wonder the miraculous creation all around you

Fill your body, mind, heart and soul with divine trepidation

Know that you are coming from somewhere and that you are going somewhere in the universal stream of time

Be always open to the entire universe

Know yourself and the heavens and the earth

Act spiritually

Think spiritually

Love spiritually

Treat every person and living being with humaneness and divine respect

Pray, meditate, practice the art of spiritual living

And be convinced of eternal life and resurrection

About the Author

Robert Muller has been serving the United Nations for 33 years. He grew up in Alsace-Lorraine, fought in the French Resistance during World War II and was captured by the Nazis. He has performed diplomatic missions all over the world and today is Assistant Secretary-General in charge of economic and social services and the coordination of the 32 specialized agencies and world programs of the United Nations. He is also the author of *Most of All They Taught Me Happiness*.

"You know, I should probably call security," I tease her. "Didn't I sign some contract about protecting the safety of others?"

"With regards to students, yes. Her, no. That beeyotch is on her own," Mel replies, putting her earrings back in and rolling down her sleeves.

"What's so funny?" Matty asks. He picks up his pace alongside of us.

"Oh man," I begin. "I wish you could have seen Mel go all gangsta on Summer in the bathroom. I thought she was gonna bust out a shank."

Matty chuckles, and asks for more details. We fill him in on the way back to our seats.

"You better watch out," he says. "She might stab you with one of her nails next time. Have you seen those things? They're scary." He trembles, jokingly.

I love that he recognizes her awful manicure as a hideous mess. "You think so. I was totally gonna get mine done tomorrow." I hold out my hands staring at them. "I was even thinking of going longer than hers, with maybe an airbrushed zebra print." I lean into him, nudging him to the side a little.

"Go for it. I think it'll put a damper on your manhunt though. Most guys aren't into artificial women," he says.

"That's bullshit," Mel calls out. "You can't tell us a guy would rather be with a girl from the itty-bitty-titty committee over a girl with melon-sized knockers." She makes sure to emphasize the volume of boobage with her hands way out in front of her.

"I would," he says, very seriously. "I like breasts that move."

Mel and I are both silent and Matty looks back and forth at both of us. "What?" he asks, running his hand through his thick hair.

"You like them to move?" Mel repeats.

I shimmy to the left and right, shaking my boobs like Jell-O Jigglers. "Like this," I tease.

"That's not exactly what I meant, but it'll work," he says. I stop jiggling. "Don't stop. You can keep going." The people in front in us look back, and I have to remind myself where we are.

"Cut it out," I tell him. "We'll have to finish this conversation later." I gesture to the folks below us.

He winks at me. "I look forward to it."

I gaze into his twinkling eyes, and am so happy we're here together and he's acting normal. I was so worried things were going to be awkward after what happened after school last week. But since then, he's been just fine. We've chatted at work, and he even helped me take a boatload of projects to my car one day. We haven't done lunch again, but I'm good with the way things have been.

"You guys just need to screw and get it over with already," Mel says, stuffing a handful of popcorn in her mouth.

I roll my eyes, and I'm just about to tell her to shut up because there're students around when Matty says, "Nah, once Shelly gets a piece of me, she won't be able to stay away. I'm not sure I'm ready for so much of a time commitment just yet. She's gonna want it all the time, and I'm pretty busy right now." He starts to snicker, but I whack him in the chest with the back of my hand. "See, we haven't even done anything yet, and she can't keep her hands off me."

He and Mel giggle, and I want to laugh because they're both full of crap, but I don't. Instead, I say, "You guys are dumb asses. Are you forgetting where we are?"

"No, Ms. Gelson, now watch your language," Matty teases me.

"All right, I'll shut up," Mel replies. "Let's watch the rest of the game."

I sit back against the bench and whip out my Red Vines. I chew on them one by one observing the teams running the ball up and down the field. Neither team has much of a passing game. And neither has a decent kicker.

I should coach this shiz.

Why haven't they recruited from the soccer team? If we had a good enough kicker, we'd have more points on the board. How can you have a team who can't kick a field goal at a minimum of twenty yards? When we march down all the way to the fifteen-yard line and don't kick the ball, I almost die. I have to bite my tongue from shouting obscenities. Sensing my frustration, Matty offers to go down to the snack bar and get some more licorice since I have already gnawed through a whole package.

I really shouldn't talk shit about our coaching staff. I sure as hell don't want the job. And if I did, I'd want to be like the coach on Friday Night Lights—a molder of men, is what I think Billy Riggins called him. When I first started watching the show, I viewed the whole first season—twenty-something episodes—in one sitting. It took almost 24 hours, and every time I started a new episode I'd laugh at myself because after about sixteen of them, I was pretty much delirious. I can still picture Chase's expression when I told him I wanted to move to a small town in Texas so I could live the football life. He told me to go to sleep and forget about it.

I still think about Texas all the time.

"Hey," Mel says, "Look who's on the field."

I sit forward, resting my elbows on my knees to peer at the sidelines. Sure enough, Summer is there, heels and all, getting in the way. The boys have to keep walking around her. It seems every time they're going to make substitutions, she's right in the path of the guys. One of the assistants finally tells her something, and she moves further away from the group and down field a bit. She really has no business being on the field. I know football and I wouldn't just occupy space without having a specific job to do.

"I'm almost embarrassed for her," I tell them. "She looks like an idiot."

"Entertaining though," Mel quips.

"I'm over it. Unlike some people," Matty drags on his words, "I'm tired of hearing about her."

Whatever.

At the games end, we pull through and win with a two-point conversion in the last few minutes. I paid enough attention to the game, in between bouts of jokes and crap talking, to chat up the highlights with my students on Monday. Mission accomplished.

"I have to pee," Mel says when we reach the bottom of the bleachers. "I'll meet you in the parking lot."

She disappears in the crowd and Matty and I continue walking.

A breeze picks up and I shiver.

Matty sheds his hoodie and hands it to me. "Here, put this on."

"No way," I tell him. "I'm the dummy who didn't bring a jacket. You stay warm."

"Just put it on," he pleads, shoving it into my hands.

Fine. I start pulling the thing over my head. The familiar earthy scent in the material makes me want to squish it up to my nose and breathe it in. Matty is significantly bigger than me and I'm swimming in his clothes. When I finally surface, he puts his hands on both sides of the hood, and pulls it down over my head. I gaze up at him as he runs his hands through my hair and frees it from the inside of the sweatshirt. I could kiss him right now. I really could. I consider my rule of no dating guys from work, and think I should really add no kissing them at work too. But standing here, looking into his ocean blue eyes I could swim in, I want him to press his lips to mine.

"Aw, now isn't that sweet," I hear the bastard say. "Is this like the new way to ask a girl to go steady? You let her wear your hoodie instead of your letterman's jacket."

Matty turns away from me, and we're both facing Chase and Summer. I find comfort in having his arm around me, resting on my shoulder. I glance at the couple before me and realize how I'm in such a better place than she is. Summer is freezing, as observed by her THOs—titty hard-ons—piercing through her thin V-neck shirt. We should all be wearing protective goggles around those things.

Chase is wearing a light hoodie under a jacket. Would it kill him to offer his coat to her? Or maybe she prefers the stylish icy look.

I'd just as soon walk away, but Matty squeezes my shoulder and says, "Summer. Quick question: does it bother you that your boyfriend is so vested in our relationship?" He points to us. "I'm glad I don't have to worry about that. Shelly doesn't even mention you guys, let alone talk smack to you right in front of me. I honestly think she could care less about either of you."

Chase opens his mouth to say something, but Matty kisses the top of my head and says, "Let's go, baby."

I put my hand up to reach his on my shoulder, and hold on to it as we walk away.

How can I possibly thank him for this later?
Hmm … I can think of a few ways.

Chapter Five

"You ready?" Mel asks me as I jump in her car. She looks great. Dark fitted jeans, tall, high-heeled black boots, lacey turquoise sleeveless top, and a few strands of colorful beads around her neck. Bright colors always look amazing against her olive skin tone. She styled her hair smooth and straight, and did her smoky-eye trick. With her wide-set eyes, she can totally pull off looking like a MAC model. Is she looking for a man too, or what? She looks hot.

Raising my brow, I tell her, "Maybe I need a makeover. Guys aren't gonna notice me next to you, hot mama."

"Don't be silly. You look great." She waves me off with a hand in my face to tell me I'm being dramatic. I flip the visor mirror down and notice I really do look good. Well, I don't want to sound conceited but I'd do me. I'd really do Mel, but I'm doable. I wish I could do a smoky-eye though. It just doesn't look the same on my almond-shaped green eyes. Believe me, I've tried. I snap the mirror shut, and she asks me, "Where to?"

"What do you mean, where to? I thought you had that part figured out. You're picking me up."

"This isn't a date, Shel. I thought you'd have a plan."

"Oh great, I finally work up the nerve to get a piece of ass and I don't even know where to look for it."

"Don't freak. Let's just think for a sec. Where do single people go to hook up?" Mel pouts her face in deep thought. *Hook up*—it sounds so dirty. Not that searching for a *piece of ass* is any better. But it's so impersonal ... like I'm looking for a male hooker or something. Great, my fiancé dumps me and I'm five seconds away from combing the boulevard looking for a man to jump my bones before I become a born-again virgin. Okay, maybe we should call it something other than hooking up. Plus, I didn't bring any cash, and I doubt if we did find a male prostitute, he'd take my bank card. I don't think they carry a credit card machine in their thongs. Maybe I can swipe it between his butt cheeks. I giggle inside. Mel yelps, "Hello! You're not helping. Where should we go?" She asks again, like two times is the magic number and I'm going to all of a sudden know where to find a man. Newsflash, if I knew where to find one, I wouldn't be in this predicament.

"I have no fucking clue. Neither one of us has been single in like ten years. The last time I was dating was in college. I'm not about to hit the library or a frat party."

She grins. "That could be fun. You wanna be a cougar?" She flutters her brows.

I punch my friend on the arm and tell her to go to hell. "Let's just go to the new wine bar." I roll my eyes in disbelief. I can't believe I just mentioned a wine bar. Gag.

"Wine? You don't even like wine."

"Well, maybe the guys will be a little bit classier than if we hit the Yard House for a long skinny tube of beer."

"Oh, honey, you're looking for a man tonight. Don't mention long, skinny, and tube in the same sentence." Mel says this with a straight face, but I can't help but laugh.

"What's wrong with long?" I ask through snorts.

"Nothing as long as it's not skinny. I'd rather have short and thick."

I smack her again. "You're bad, my friend."

Finally Mel starts her car and we are on our way to find the man of my dreams. Okay, maybe not the man of my dreams. Maybe just someone who doesn't bug the shit of me, and can take my mind off Chase, and Matty, for a while.

It's a half hour drive to the bar—which would take only ten minutes if Mel would stop being a pus and drive on the freeway—and my mind is filled with thoughts about two men who are as different as night and day. How can I be so attracted to both? I thought I had a type. I guess not, because not only do Chase and Matty look different, everything else about them is in contrast too. Chase isn't a talker, he'd prefer to go to dinner and eat in silence. When Matty and I eat together, there is a constant flow of chatter in between bites. When Chase gets angry, he attacks and tries to say anything to put you down. Matty is chill. When something bothers him, he talks it out without raising his voice. Why is it again that I still have feelings for Chase? Hmm. I guess the saying is true. Love *is* blind. And with ten years of history, I'd say it's probably deaf too.

After last week's incident with Matty and Chase at the game, I expected Matty to tell me what a jerk Chase is, but he didn't. I thanked him for making Chase and Summer look like idiots, not in those words exactly. He just waved me off like it was nothing. He did, sort of lie, to them. Mel and I talk about Summer all the time. And he made it seem like he and I are a couple. But oh well. I felt like I was on a major high when we walked away that night. I have so much respect for Matty for not saying anything bad about Chase. It would be so easy, but he just keeps his mouth shut.

Mel, on the other hand, is a different story. On the way home from the game, Mel had a trash talking fest. She unleashed years of frustration about things Chase had done or said to piss her off. Apparently, she's been biting her tongue—which is totally uncharacteristic of her—because she thought he made me happy. But now that Chase and I are over, she is no longer keeping quiet with her true feelings about my ex.

"You know, I never really thought you guys would last as long as you did. I didn't say anything because I figured you guys would break up sooner or later. But then you stayed together longer and longer, and it was too fucking late. You already loved him, and you sure as hell wouldn't have listened to me if I said anything. But now, you know he's a dick. So get on with your life. I don't give a shit if you move on with Matty or with the Paleta man, just get over Chase already." Her words have been replaying in my head, over and over again. The Paleta man? Really? I don't remember the last time I saw an ice cream man go down my street.

And if that wasn't enough, she also took the time to remind me when Chase went out of town for this job he had when we were in our credential program. He was supposed to be gone for four days but got home early and didn't tell me. Instead, he went to his friend's house, played video games and went golfing with the boys. I would've never known but his boss called for him and when I told him Chase was still out of town, he embarrassed the shit out of me when he said they had all arrived on the same plane two days earlier. I could have killed Chase. But of course, he made it sound like it was my fault he needed some 'me' time and a break from being 'married' already.

I forgave him, like the lovesick girl I was, and never spoke of it again. That is until my bestie reminded me of what a stupid ass I was to let it go. At the time, the whole thing didn't seem so bad, but now, looking back, I feel like I was such a fool.

The car turns off and the sound of Mel's favorite 80's boy band is silenced. It's fun to watch her dance to the music like we're still in junior high. After repeatedly watching the same music videos over and over again until the tape threatened to give out, we could've easily been backup dancers. I bet we still could.

"You ready?" she asks, as she opens her car door.

Well, we're here. So I guess it doesn't matter.

And just as quickly as we walk in the place, we walk out.

Bad idea. The guys at the wine bar fit into one of three categories. One: twenty-somethings in Hollister shirts who kept saying, "Dude". Two: old guys in blazers who sniffed, swished, and swirled before taking a tiny sip of wine and spitting it out. And three: the good-looking, funny guys my age who would have been totally perfect had they not been there … with their wives.

"What now?" Mel asks as she starts her car.

"Cheesecake Factory?" I suggest.

Mel sighs, "Really? Don't think you're gonna find a guy interested in women sitting at the bar there."

She has a point. "BJ's?"

"You want this hypothetical guy to watch you or a game?"

"Suck it, Mel. You decide then."

"Oh, whatever. Let's go to BJ's. I could use a Pazookie right about now."

Yum. The thought of a Pazookie sounds so much better than manhunting. If only a guy could be as sweet and delicious as a hot fudge chocolate chip cookie with ice cream on top. My mouth waters. Yes, definitely going to order dessert when we get there.

BJ's is just as crowded as I thought it would be for a Friday night. What'd we expect? After waiting forty-five minutes, we finally snag a seat at a booth in the bar area. I order a Jeremiah Red, and Mel gets some fruity concoction with a ridiculous name.

Our first drink arrives, and I can't take a sip fast enough. Oh, how I love beer. So soothing to the belly, to the mind, to the heart. I really love pushing my palette with a variety of brews. I usually just drink Hef at home—not too heavy, but not piss water either. But at a bar, I like to go a little darker, with fuller flavor.

While I concentrate on my beer, Mel looks around like a lion on the prowl for her next meal.

"I swear, all these guys look like children," she rattles. "And what's with the tight shirts? I don't want my man to wear tighter clothing than me. And the girly pants? The little boys at school gross me out with their skinny jeans, and here we have grown men wearing them."

I look around and I see what she's talking about. Looks like we walked into an ad for Abercrombie, American Eagle, and Hollister. I think I see a guy with puka shells around his neck. Nice. One dude's pants are so tight I can actually see his balls. Big huge balls.

Maybe they didn't start out so enormous, but since his blood circulation is being cut off by denim, his nuts have swelled to the size of apples. It looks painfully freakish, yet I can't tear my eyes away.

"Are you looking at the guy with the humongo testicles?" Mel asks, with a snort.

"How did you know?" I respond.

"You're eyes got huge all of a sudden," she says. "It looks like he stuffed two potatoes in his pants. Why don't his friends tell him something? I would totally tell you if your va-jay-jay was exploding out of your jeans. Poor guy is never gonna be able to have children."

"Hey ladies," a young man's voice sounds. "We were just waiting for a table to free up and noticed you two beautiful women were alone. Would you mind if we joined you?" The screech we hear is coming from a barely legal guy in baggy ass thug-life pants and a shirt three sizes too big. His friend, who has a cute face, looks just as silly as him. Is there no in-between here? These guys either look like they're sporting a camel toe in their spandex jeans or they look like they could be extras in Boyz in the Hood.

"Are you guys even old enough to sit in the bar?" I ask, teasing.

The young men smile.

Mel looks them up and down before saying, "Tell me this. Who was the most popular boy band when you were in high school?"

The guys look at each other. One of them scratches his head. "Probably the Jonas Brothers," he replies.

"Oh my God, are you kidding me?" I can't even comprehend how absolutely hilarious this is.

"Get the fuck out of here," Mel says, shooing them away with a flick of her wrist.

The toddlers disappear, and we practically bust a gut.

"That seriously had to be the funniest thing I've ever heard," I tell her.

Our Pazookie arrives and we try to stop laughing long enough to enjoy it.

"They could have at least said N'Sync," Mel says. "The Jonas Brothers? Those guys probably weren't even alive when we were in high school. We're old enough to be their mothers."

"Doesn't look like this is the place for me to get lucky either," I say.

She swirls the cookie and ice cream around on her plate before saying, "Guess it's time to move on. Third time's a charm is what they say, right?"

It's the same routine once we get in the car.

She sits in silence, as do I. How sad. Neither of us can think of any place to go in search of hot men. At this point, I'd settle for nice looking or even average, and preferably old enough to buy beer without a fake ID. How pathetic. Maybe Nick has a friend, a co-worker. We can head over to his office and I can throw myself at a cute little mail boy or something. Nah, anyone who works with him probably has as much time for me as Nick has for Mel.

The car is moving, but I have no idea where we're going. Joining a convent is starting to look appealing. Maybe she's taking me to the local nunnery. Even Mel thinks there's no hope for me. I *am* pathetic.

"Here?" I screech, looking up at the happiest place on earth. No, not Disneyland. The Yard House. "I thought I said no."

"Shel, get real. If you wanna find a guy who can hang with you, you've gotta look at some of your favorite spots. Can you really imagine being with a man who drinks wine? You know the lucky guy you marry has to love beer."

"Preferably not the kind you can see through." I have standards when it comes to my brew. "And preferably not an alcoholic either. I love my drinks but I'm not about to clean up after a sloppy drunk."

Mel ignores my last comment with a scoff and says, "This is actually a perfect spot too. It's not cheap, so guys who come here have to at least have a job."

"Well, I guess that would be a plus, huh." We chuckle. My guy definitely needs a J-O-B. "Well, if you think so, let's go for it. I could use a Guinness right about now."

"Uh-oh… jumping to the heavy stuff already."

Inside, it's crowded. No surprise there.

"Don't you dare just sit here and watch the game either. You need to exude sexiness," Mel scolds me. She adjusts her bra and her girls perk up. "Look there's a high top."

"A girl who likes sports is sexy," I tell her.

"Maybe. But a girl who can talk sports like a man is not. So you can watch, just don't frickin' commentate."

We rush over before anyone else seizes the empty seats. We settle in, order some drinks, and my eyes search the crowd. A lot of guys, who look to be my age, are sitting at the bar. Couples take up most of the tables. A group of barely legal drinkers sit in a booth covered with pints, shots, and cocktail glasses. I remember those days.

"Check him out." Mel gestures at a guy looking in our direction from a few tables away.

Good-looking, tall, wearing a black V-neck shirt. Clothes aren't too tight. I can't see his balls. Not bad. He smiles at me as he tips his glass to take a drink.

"Ain't happenin'," I tell my dear friend.

"What's wrong with him? He's into you," she responds. She's most likely right because he's still looking our way with a smile.

"Did you see his pint? It's probably a Coors Light," I yelp.

Mel shakes her head. "I've heard of a wine snob, but not a beer … beer … I can't think of anything."

"I prefer connoisseur. And I'm not going to go out with a guy who drinks piss beer."

"He's still looking at you."

"Well, he can keep looking at me all he wants." Taking a swig of my own dark, thick stout, I suck in my top lip to taste the foam of the rich head gathered on my mouth. Oh, who knew drinking a beer could sound so sexy. I lower my eyes to get a view of some of the others at the bar. "How about the guys at the end?" I suggest. There are two of them, so Mel would have to play along. But they are decently dressed and they are strikingly hot.

"Ooo. They are cute. What are they drinking?" Mel asks.

I peer at the counter in front of them, but the area is empty. "I don't know. They don't have anything yet. Maybe they just ordered."

We continue to drink and make small talk, all the while observing the two gentlemen at the end of the bar. "Wait. Look. The bartender is getting them drinks," Mel says, and I try not to stare but I'm anxious. Please let it be a decent beverage.

"Oh shit," Mel says. I must have the worst luck in the world.

"Cosmos? Really? Is this what my life has come to? I'm attracted to men who watch Sex and the City." I down what's left of my brew. "I'm destined to spinsterhood."

"Hey, that was two. The next one is gonna be the third ... and, third time's a charm." Mel tries to remain positive. Me, not so much. "Let's keep looking."

"All right, but the next one ... I'm not gonna even look at his face until I see what he's drinking," I explain. This has to work.

Mel shakes her head in disapproval.

It's hard to find a mate looking solely at beer glasses. And it's even more difficult to keep my eyes focused, so I don't look at faces. This is important though, and I can do it.

There's a table full of idiots with nothing but cider beer. I can tell from the bubbles, and the pink hue. Painted fingernails means there are women at the table. I look up. I'm right. Hmm, I'm better at this than I thought.

This is fun. Let's try again.

Lowering my eyes, I search for a table holding glasses filled with amber-colored, or darker, fluid. If I can see through the sauce, it's not worth a second look. At the very least, it should be cloudy like a darker wheat flavor. Seriously, there are over a hundred brewskis to choose from at this place, and so few people drink anything better than what equates to Budweiser. Why bother? Why not stay home and get an eighteen-pack of Natural Light for two bucks?

The next table is filled with samplers. A tray of eight small glasses of different beers. This could go one of two ways. Experienced drinkers looking to try something new, or inexperienced drinkers who don't know any better. No, I'll pass on this table. I look up. Damn, I shouldn't have. These guys are good looking. But a few of them haven't touched the darker varieties so they're definitely out of the question.

Moving on.

Tables full of women. No. Not for me.

Keep looking. Take your time.

Bingo! Man hands. I spy man hands. Some tan, some light. But strong hands, with long fingers resting or tapping on the table. One glass looks to be filled with a Hef—my assumption based on the lemon floating inside. Bars pair a Hef with lemons, I use an orange. So much better. Another glass looks like maybe a Newcastle.

Jackpot!

The last pint is topped off with what looks like a Black & Tan. The distinct layers of two different beers can be seen from way over here. This is the one and only time a pale ale is allowed—when mixed with a stout. The bartender did an expert pour. I'm dying to take a peek and see if there's a shamrock embossed in the head at the top of the glass. I'm in love with the owner of this tall boy. I want this man. I want to marry him and have his babies. I want to suck the foam off his upper lip, just like I did my own.

I blink hard and my mouth waters. I'm afraid to look up. Please don't be ugly. Please be at least semi-cute. My eyes begin to take in my future husband at his waist. A piece of his shirt is tucked in the front, out in the back. Comfort is a priority to him. I like it. He wears a worn Claremont McKenna tee, not fitted but tight enough for me to make out his muscular chest. Educated. My man went to college. Not just anyone would sport CM gear.

"Did you find him?" Mel asks. She knows. She can see the hunger in my eyes.

I look down for a moment.

"I'm scared to look," I tell her.

Mel snorts. "Can't be worse than the guy with elephantitis or the guys with the cosmos."

"Here goes nothing," I say, picking my head up slowly.

My mouth drops. And I don't know whether to laugh or cry.

Mel senses my concern. "What is it, Shel? Is he a dog?"

"He's..." I blink. "He's..." I try to swallow even though my mouth has gone dry.

Mel puts her hand on mine. "He's what, Shel?"

"He's. Matty."

Chapter Six

When I look up again, at the man I thought was going to be my soul mate, our eyes meet, and he smiles. Worries subside instantly, and I smile right back. What am I supposed to do? Run? No, I'm going to enjoy this. He passed my test. And honestly, the thought of going somewhere else makes me want to fall into a beer-induced coma, and the thought of manhunting for the rest of the night makes me want to poke out my eyes with a corkscrew. I'm fried for tonight. If talking to Matty will get me home and off to sleep sooner rather than later, then so be it. He can help distract Mel from our search for the next top man in my life.

I watch him say something to one of his friends and strut over to our table.

"Hey, ladies," Matty says, tipping his glass at us. "What brings you out tonight?"

"Beer," I say, jokingly. "Needed some beer. Lots of beer."

"That's it?" Matty questions. "You both have the *out for blood* look in your eyes, like you're on the prowl." He jokingly roars like a kitty.

Mel shrugs him off with a chuckle. "I'm married, Matt." She holds up her left hand.

"Okay, but there's nothing wrong with window shopping. You can look but you can't take any of the goods home." Matty winks at her, and turns to me "How about you, Shel?"

Mel interrupts, telling him, "We're looking for the man of Shel's dreams."

Matty turns his attention to me again. "Any luck?"

"It's been hard you know, to find the man of one's dreams based on beer selection." Mel explains, again stealing Matty's gaze from mine. It's okay though because having him near me makes me want to do things to him I shouldn't even be considering.

A chuckle escapes him. "Shel, that's hysterical. Dating a pale ale guy is simply out of the question for you, huh?" He shakes his head, but he's amused. The way he smiles with his whole face is adorable. When Chase smiled, there were times you couldn't even tell if he was genuinely happy, or just putting on a show. But with this sweet man, even with a soft smile, just the slightest lift in his mouth, you can see his happiness in his eyes, his cheeks, and the tilt of his head. He doesn't give off any fake vibes. Whatever you sense from him is always real.

"Hey, there are just some things I can't get past. Some girls can't stand a guy with girly hands, or guys who don't wear socks, or men who wear ascots. Shitty brew just happens to be a deal breaker for me," I explain. It dawns on me Matty knows my taste in beer. I smile at the thought. A flood of giddiness creeps over me, and I can't stop smiling at him. I'm trying to hold back, but it's not working. Why fight it, right?

Matty sits on the edge of one of the empty seats, and takes another swig of his darkly colored beer. "So a guy could be like nasty looking, I'm talking warts on his nose, big ole ears, and dandruff flaking out of his hair, and as long as he was drinking, let's say, Guinness, he'd fall in the 'man of your dreams' category?" he asks, lifting his arms to hang his air quotes.

I laugh at his list of yucky traits. Looking into his crystal blue eyes, I tell him, "Yes."

"But what if said Guinness was perfectly matched in a pint with a lighter beer ... such as Bass?" Matty lowers his eyes at me in anticipation of my response.

I lean forward in my seat, lost in his playful gaze. "Even better."

Mel stands up and tugs her bag over her shoulder. She puts her hand on Matty's arm and says, "Lucky for you, you're gorgeous and you have a glassful of both those beers." She coughs and rubs her throat. "I'm not feeling well." She coughs again. "Mr. Fuller, can you please give Ms. Gelson a ride home?"

Parked outside my condo, Matty and I are strangely silent. Usually, our conversations are non-stop like Rory and Lorali on Gilmore Girls, except we're far from a mother and daughter duo. I begin digging around in my bag for my keys to break the awkward spell that has occupied us for at least an entire song.

Matty turns his body toward me. "I'm glad you let me bring you home tonight."

"It's not like I had much choice. Mel practically ran out of there. She didn't even say goodbye. Bitch." Grinning, I think of my dear friend. She sure knows how to set things up. She knows *this* situation I'm in right now would've never happened if left up to me. I'd probably be curled up on her sofa with a bottle of beer in my hand watching Lifetime movies with her. I'm not sure if I want to hug her, or slap her silly. "So what were you up to tonight, before you got stuck babysitting?"

"I met some of my buddies from undergrad for a drink. Nothing big."

It hits me. "Oh shit, Matty, you didn't even say goodbye to them. I'm sorry."

"No worries. I'm sure they could figure it out." My eyes shoot up to meet his. What does that mean? "I mean, you know. I doubt they're offended or worried."

I punch him in the arm. "So you thought you were gonna walk over to us looking all cute, take me home and have your way with me like some sorority girl in heat, huh?"

"Well, not the 'in heat' part." He bursts out laughing. I punch him again but laugh right along with him.

"Since I ruined your night out with the boys, do you wanna come in? You know I have a well-stocked fridge. It'll be just like the bar, you can even tip me if you want."

"Yeah. Why not? Beats sitting in the car all night with you punching me."

We both head toward the kitchen. I stop in the hallway to kick off my heels, and Matty goes for the fridge. This shouldn't be weird. He's been here many times. He hands me a beer and settles in on one of my bar stools. I hop up on the counter and rest against the cabinets. Taking a small sip, I feel self-conscious. I know he's watching me.

Glancing back at him, the corners of my mouth turn upward in a slight smile. So this *is* different. Every other time Matty's been to my house was when Chase lived here too. He hasn't been here since I started thinking of him in a different light. Now, it's just the two of us. Alone. I'm not engaged. He's not … engaged or otherwise seeing someone. It's just Matty. Me. And my thoughts. Dirty. Naughty. Thoughts.

I have a sudden interest in him strutting over, standing right in front of me, wrapping my legs around his back, and pulling him into me. It's only after he rips off my panties and unbuckles his pants. The image is so vivid, it's like I can feel him thrusting against me. My thighs twitch with the rising heat between my legs and I have to cross them to hold back a feeling of thought provoking pleasure. Does that ever happen in real life or only in the slew of romance novels that have been filling the space in my bed every night since Chase left?

"Whatever you're thinking, it must be good," Matty says, grinning.

My face gets hot, and it's like he's been reading my mind. "Well, you know. A woman can do a lot with an imagination." I wiggle my brows at him, and a subtle grin spreads across his mouth.

Matty takes a swig of his beer, and sets it down on the counter. He runs his hand through his thick messy hair and smiles. I can't take my eyes off his mouth as he takes the few steps needed to stand before me. "A man can do a lot with his imagination too." Placing his palms flat on my thighs, his touch is like a flame burning through my skin and my temperature rises, he gazes into my eyes and I inhale a deep breath. I try to relax in anticipation of what's coming next, even though I'm sure he can hear my heart beating right out of my chest. He glances at my mouth and murmurs, "But it doesn't get fun until he makes it a reality."

His face is less than two inches away from mine. I can feel his breath on me and my head whirls with excitement. I gaze down at his lips and lean in, closing the gap between us. Matty puts his right hand to my cheek, then runs it through my hair, sweeping my long bangs out of my face. He pauses, his eyes studying every part of my face as if he's seeing me for the very first time. His hand moves to the nape of my neck and sends a rush of heat down my spine. Then he tugs at my nape to guide me in for our very first kiss.

Our lips barely touch, yet the sensation of pleasure spreads like rapid fire soaring through every cell in my body. I back away to get a glimpse of him. His eyes smile at me and instantly I'm relaxed and at home with him. He tugs on the back on my neck again, and this time the kiss lingers as his mouth presses against mine. A few soft pecks turn into harder ones before my lips part, and his tongue teases at caressing mine. He drags his tongue across my top lip, and I let out a slight whimper as my legs hug his ass, reeling him closer. With hands full of his sandy blond hair, I'm awestruck at how soft and sexy it is. Tugging gently at his lower lip with my teeth, he lets out a groan and squeezes my ass. My tongue trails the outline of his lips and then I take him in for another fierce, heavy-breathing, smooch fest.

Our tongues slide against each other, mingling in a new form of communication for two adults who were once just good friends. I can sense his feelings for me in the way we softly tangle tongues and his gentle tugs on my hair.

My girl parts throb against the hardness in the front of his pants, and I have an odd sense of awareness of how exciting it is to make out with a man as I sit on my kitchen counter pinned against my cabinets.

Making out is so much fun. *I can't remember the last time Chase and I kissed like this.*

Shit, trying to push Chase as far from my thoughts as possible, I wrap my legs around Matty tighter. He holds me closer, embracing me with his strong arms as we kiss till my lips are swollen and my chin is stinging from his stubble. Fighting the need to take a big breath, I close my mouth and our lips meet once more for a lip-locked kiss, and a series of short pecks.

"Wow, Matty," I say, returning my gaze to his and running my fingers through his locks.

"That's what I was thinking," he responds, holding me again in a tight embrace. I hug him, resting my head on his shoulder. We're silent in this hold for what seems like hours, soaking in the happiness yet worrying about what comes next. Awkwardness? More kissing? Sex? Regret?

"Matty," I mutter into his shirt.

He releases me and pecks me on the cheek. "Yes, Shelly."

"What do you think about this?"

He kisses me again, on the lips. "About this?"

"Yes. About that."

And another one on the other cheek. "I think it's great. I'm having fun. You?"

This time, I kiss him. "Yes. Yes, I am. But that's not what I meant."

"I know." He sighs. "I just wanted to enjoy the moment."

"Moment? Are you saying this is it?" My face heats with embarrassment. Maybe he didn't feel what I just felt. Maybe I was interpreting his signals wrong.

"Well isn't that what you're getting at? We can't do this. I'm not ready for a relationship. Yada yada yada." He holds my hands in his and looks at me intently, not turning away.

"Well, maybe. I don't know. I really wanted this to happen. I think I've always been curious about kissing you, what it'd be like to be an 'us'. But you're one of my best friends. This *is* fun, and I really like you. But what if it doesn't work? We have to see each other every day. It'll be weird and I don't wanna lose a friend."

Giving my hands a squeeze, he says, "I'm not going anywhere, Shel. I knew you were going to say all this and I actually had a big ol' speech planned if it came to this point. So let me give you the short version." He pauses to bring his lips to mine again. Our lips connect sending tingles from my mouth to my toes and back up again. "I know you just felt that. And I don't think it's just pure hormones talking either. We're old enough to tell a fucking awesome kiss from one you can't wait to be finished with. When I kiss you," he touches the pad of his thumb to my bottom lip, "I don't want to stop."

I remove his hand so I can think clearly. "Maybe it's just tonight, though. What about tomorrow? And the next day?"

"I don't know, but why not see where this takes us?"

His warm breath spreads across my neck, his lips brushing against me as I utter, "That sounds great and all, but honestly, I don't really think I'm ready for a relationship just yet."

"Then let's not call it one. Let's just enjoy each other's company. You can even see other people if you want so this doesn't feel too relationship-y for you." Feeling his lips touch my neck sends all common sense out the window. "What do you say, Ms. Gelson? Are we going to *not* have a relationship?"

"I think I'd like that, Mr. Fuller." My arms wrap around his neck and round two of passionate kissing begins.

When we finally come up for air again, we're lying on my sofa wrapped around each other. Our legs are intertwined, my hands are on his well-built chest, and his hands graze and singe the skin on my lower back. I could very well get used to having his soft hands all over me.

"Do you wanna stay, Matty?"

Instantly, his eyes dart to mine. "Really?"

"Yes, but not in the way you think?" I lower my head, sure that I'm blushing.

"Okay, I'd love to stay with you but what are *you* thinking?" He runs his fingers through the back of my hair so tenderly I'm not afraid to ask for what I want.

"This. I want to sleep with you, in your arms, in jammies, like this." I pause. "And that's it."

Holding my chin between his thumb and forefinger, he lifts it so my eyes stare into his. His eyes soften, so sincere, and he says, "I'd love to." He starts to unravel himself from me and we make our way to my bedroom, hand in hand.

"Give me a minute," I tell him as I go into the bathroom to change my clothes, wash my makeup off, and brush my teeth.

When I return, he's sitting on my bed with his shirt and shoes off. His bare chest is enough to send me into fits of hunger. His skin is tan and his muscles are on display even though he's not trying to flex. His shoulders are strong and broad, narrowing down to his slim waist. He rises to his feet and I sigh as I take in the full sight of him. This isn't the same body I remember from when we first met at work five years ago. He was so skinny and lanky then. Now, he is a grown man, a gorgeous one at that, and he's standing right in front of me. I press my palms to his chest, placing them just above his hard nipples. Leaning down, he kisses me on the forehead. He clasps his hands around mine and brings them to his lips, touching them softly to my fingertips. "My turn." He steps around me and disappears into the bathroom. Blowing hair out of my face, I allow myself to exhale and try to calm down from the obvious tension and attraction between us.

I'm already in bed when he returns, facing the door so I can see he's only clothed in black boxer briefs. Calvin Klein from what I can read on the wide band. Oh my! I have my own version of the Mark Wahlberg underwear ads about to get into my bed, and I just told him all I want to do with him is *sleep*.

Holy shit. I need to think of something other than this beautiful man before me, or I swear we'll be naked and doing the nasty in a matter of seconds. Fighting the urge to have sex with him was a lot easier before I saw him in his chonies. Okay, Shel, get your mind out of his pants and think of something unattractive. Hmm. Work. What's happening at work? Fuck work. Umm. Lord of the

Flies. Oh shit. Matty is fucking hot. A bunch of sniveling adolescent boys. Piggy. The conch. Okay, my thoughts are simmering.

"You okay?" he asks.

"Completely. Now get in my bed, Mr. Fuller, and sleep with me."

He smiles, shaking his head at me, pulls the covers back and enters my bed. "I love it when you talk dirty, Ms. Gelson."

I chuckle. "It does sound a little kinky. Like we're getting freaky in detention or something."

"However it sounds, I like being here with you, Shel. " He reaches for me and reels me in close. I love how he just reached over and slid me across the bed to him. Mmm... I could melt.

I pour myself into one last kiss before turning around and backing into his body, till we fit together perfectly, spooning like a couple in love. His lips graze my bare shoulder and I've never felt so treasured, so loved before in my whole life.

I slept in this very bed, in this very house with the same man for several years and never did I feel like I do right now. Here, in Matty's arms, I'm relaxed. I'm comfortable. I'm cozy and warm. And I'm happy. I could sleep like this every night for the rest of my life.

But then, tomorrow will come. And I will have to

...

Wake up.

Chapter Seven

Wake up, I hear a voice in my head. Wake up.

I roll around, tangled in my sheets, and suddenly, my eyes pop open.

Last night, I fell asleep in Matty's arms. I did. I really did. Peeling my covers back from my face, I look over at the empty space next to me and my heart drops like the thud of a bowling ball. He left. He didn't even stick around to say good morning. It's not like we did *it* or anything. We just slept. Oh son of a shiznit. Damn it. That's even more intimate than screwing for Christ's sake. I'm a frickin' idiot. I totally spooked him, didn't I? I scared him off. A wham-bam-thank-you-ma'am would've been better.

I'm such a terrible non-girlfriend. I've been out of the loop for so long, I don't know how it all works. Do I call him now? Do I pretend like nothing happened? Well, nothing did happen. What do I do? I slept, as in actual slumber, with Matty and now he's gone and I have no effing clue what to do next.

I wrestle myself out of bed, and make my way to the bathroom. Looking at myself in the mirror, my eyes try to look away from the hopeless romantic before me.

As much as I tried to fight it, deep down I think I wanted it to work. I never realized it until now. Waking up alone, after a night without sex, standing in the bathroom, I feel like total shit. The last thing I want to do is wash my face or brush my teeth. I run my fingers through my hair. *What did I do?* I silently ask, gazing down the drain of my sink. How metaphoric. My love life has totally gone down the drain. Thank God for my students and my awesome ability to teach, or I'd start posting FML all over Twitter and Facebook. Okay, maybe I wouldn't go that far. But really, I'm pretty crappy when it comes to dealing with guys.

"Good morning, Shel?" The sound of Matty's voice startles me.

I look up and see his reflection in the mirror. Leaning up against the doorframe, his arms are crossed over his chest and he's smiling. Smiling. That's a good sign, right? Well, he's here. He didn't leave. I guess I *didn't* scare him off?

"Hi," I utter back. I focus on him, right there in the mirror. He's real. Not just a mirage. He's standing right behind me. I'm tempted to pinch myself but I don't want to look like an even bigger idiot than I am.

"Why don't you do whatever it is you do when you wake up, and come to the kitchen, I got us breakfast." He takes a step toward me, bends over, and kisses me on the top of my head. I could just faint. My legs are mush, and I think my heart just stopped for a beat.

Before I can react or turn around to give him a proper hello, he's gone. Out the door, and I can hear his footsteps throughout my house.

What is it I do when I wake up? Hmm. I normally do nothing but grab a book, or watch TV with a bowl of cereal. I shut the door so I can pee in peace and try to think of what to do next. Finally, I decide to splash some water on my face, glide some deodorant on, brush my teeth, moisturize with some smelly lotion, and pull my hair up into a twist. Should I do make-up? Nah. He'll probably laugh at me for doing as much as I did already. He knows I'm simple.

Immediately, I start cracking up when I see what's on my kitchen table. Captain Crunch cereal. How does he know these things about me? First the beer, and now this. My favorite cereal.

"When was the last time you went grocery shopping?" He chuckles. "I had to go to the store. It was either that or we were going to have beer and yogurt for breakfast."

"Hey, don't judge. It's the breakfast of champions." I sit down across from him at my table. "Besides, I've been sleeping over at Mel's a lot lately."

He pours me a bowl of cereal and hands me the milk. "Will this work?"

"Hell yes, this is my favorite cereal. I could eat the whole box for breakfast, lunch, and dinner today." I stop talking so I can stuff my mouth with a giant spoonful of sweet crunchy bites.

"Ha ha. Somehow I believe that." After pouring his own bowl, he digs in too.

For a moment, there is this ease of comfort while the two of us chow down on cereal. It's anything but silent, with the loud munching of crunch berries, but it's peaceful. Every now and then, our eyes meet and we smile. Things are not at all awkward, like I imagined they would be. It feels just like any other day, except Matty was in my bed last night. But knowing that doesn't make me feel weird. If anything, it makes me grin at him again. And he smirks back at me. Just a little something to acknowledge we're thinking of each other.

Matty finishes his breakfast and pushes his bowl away from him. He dabs at the side of his mouth with a napkin and clears his throat to speak. "So what's on your agenda for today?"

I have to think about it for a second. "Not much," I say, through a mouthful of food. I finish chewing before I continue. "I was just going to kick back, relax, and watch movies until Mel calls to say she feels like getting out of the house."

"Mind if I join you? Until Mel calls, that is."

"I'd love for you to join me. But come to think of it, she probably won't call."

He looks at me confused. "Why not?"

I smirk. "She's probably hoping you're still here."

"Oh, so you just assumed I was gonna bring you home and you could have your way with me?" he says, jokingly.

"I didn't assume anything. But I'm sure Mel was hoping something would happen. So stay, relax with me," I tell him.

"Sounds good. I'm in." He stands. "Do you mind if I shower?"

"Go for it. Towels are in the cabinet in either bathroom. You can use mine or the one in the hall."

Before heading to the shower, Matty takes my bowl and his, and washes them. Who is this guy? Why didn't I sleep with him sooner? I could've had a live-in dishwasher by now. So I don't look like a lazy ass, I get up and put away the cereal and milk.

Matty is standing at my counter, wiping it down when I come from behind, placing my arms around him in a gentle embrace. I can feel the hardness of his abs beneath my fingers and I suddenly want to watch him take a shower so I can have a front row seat with a view of suds traveling down his chiseled frame. "Thank you, Matty."

He wiggles himself around so he's facing me, and holds me close to him. "Thanks for letting me stay. I had a really good time last night."

I squeeze him again before looking up. He stares down at me and I catch him glancing at my mouth. He has to know I want him to. Gazing at his full lips, I try sending him a signal that it's okay for him to lean down and go in for a kiss. And he does. Just a soft, gentle one. Our lips lock together for three or four lingering pecks lasting a few seconds each. Perfect. I love that he doesn't feel the need to shove his tongue down my throat every time he kisses me.

"About that shower," he says, "maybe I should make it a cold one."

I lean into him, grazing my waist against the swell in his jeans. If he was any taller, that ridge would be right in the valley between my breasts. "That's not such a bad idea," I snicker.

He plants a kiss on my head, and calls me a brat. On his way to the restroom, I notice he stops in the living room and grabs a bag. "What do you have there?" I ask him.

"When I went to the store, I stopped by my place to pick up a few things."

"Oh really? Confident, huh?"

"Well, yeah. I was gonna take a shower at home but I wanted to hurry and get back before you realized I was gone. I didn't want you to think I'd skipped out on you."

Who is this guy? Am I dreaming? I didn't know guys could be this thoughtful. What else have I been missing for the last umpteen years of my life?

When we're both finally showered, separately of course, (or unfortunately, depending on how you look at it) we sit down to figure out what we're going to watch.

"Your movie collection is quite depressing, Shel. Some of these don't even count. How many boxed sets of TV shows do you have?"

I laugh. I love my TV shows. I have every season of Grey's. I have most of Entourage. All of Gilmore Girls and Dawson's Creek (still can't believe Joey Potter was married to Tom Cruise—beeyotch got Pacey and Maverick). I also have the last season of Beverly Hills 90210, only because I love to watch the final episode when Donna and David finally frickin' get married. Her dress was amazing. She looked like Cinderella going to the ball.

"C'mon. I have more than just TV. Don't exaggerate. You know, we could totally have a Step Up marathon. But the last one kind of bites because Channing Tatum isn't in it." Even though I say this with the utmost seriousness, Matty laughs at me. Okay, so I was being funny but Channing so should have been in part three. In fact, the little cameo in part two really wasn't enough either, but the whole dancing on trampolines and flips was more than hot. He was on fire.

"That's it. I gotta leave. You're too much." He sets my DVDs down and starts to walk away.

He comes back chuckling, and picks up some other movies. We both giggle, flipping through my movie collection.

"How about Dear John?" I ask.

Matty takes the movie out of my hand and puts it back down in the "no" pile, which at the moment is increasing in size exponentially. He holds up She's The

Man, and asks, "Do you have every movie this guy has been in?"

"Probably." I grin.

"Stalker," he says, shaking his head.

"Don't hate. If I could get season tickets to all Channing Tatum movies, I'd pay top dollar. Oh, and for Bradley Cooper too. And Ryan Reynolds. And Ashton Kutcher. Oh, one more. Tim Riggins from Friday Night Lights, I can't think of his real name. Imagine a movie with those five guys in it. Oh my." I look up at the ceiling, picturing such a hot cast of men. It would definitely need to be an action movie, with lots of sweat. Beach scenes, love scenes. Lots of reasons to be shirtless. Some comedy too. On second thought, make it a romantic comedy with a bit of ass kicking just for the heck of it.

He snaps me out of my fantasy with a play tap to my thigh. "Shel, Riggins is a high school football player. Just a kid." Matty raises a brow at me in disgust.

"No, he's not," I say, defensively. "He's like twenty-something. I looked it up. Plus, high school boys don't look like him. At least, none of the ones I went to school with." When I watch the current 90210 and see guys like Liam and Teddy, I always wonder where they get these guys. The boys I went to high school with did

NOT look like Matt Lanter. My high school friends looked more like Malcolm in the Middle, or Doogie Howser.

"All right, all right. But if you're gonna drool over Riggs, I'll just let my eyes feast on Minka Kelly."

"Deal."

It occurs to me Matty must watch FNL too, if he knows about the cast. Oh my goodness, the pro side of my pro and cons list for dating him continues to grow. It's just the little issue of us working together that still bothers me. And the fact that he's one of my best friends and I don't want to risk losing him. Maybe those cons outweigh the long list of pros. A frown spreads over my face.

We finally settle on rotating action-suspense films with chick flicks. Up first: The Notebook. Just the thought makes me giggle. I won the first round. After slipping in the DVD, I turn around and notice Matty sitting on my sofa, with his feet propped up on my ottoman/coffee table. He looks adorable sitting there in some soccer shorts and a loose tee. Now, where do I sit? I take a few steps toward the other side of the sofa and remove one of my decorative pillows to take a seat. Matty raises his arm, inviting me to sit next to him. Okay, that's nice. I plop myself next to him, tuck my feet underneath my thighs, and get cozy. He lays his arm on my side, and his hand curves against my ass. How will I ever be able to concentrate on the movie with his hand on my ass and my cheek pressed against his shoulder? The air better kick in soon because the rubbing of our warm bodies together is going to start a wild fire.

So maybe The Notebook isn't the best idea for our first movie together, and not for the reasons previously mentioned. I'm a blubbering idiot more than once while watching the flick. This movie seriously kills me. Beautiful but heart-wrenching. But then, I remember Matty knows me. It's not like he's not aware I'm a blubbering idiot. No use in trying to act like someone I'm not.

Finally, the ultimate sex scene comes on the screen. Allie comes back to see Noah after seeing something about him in the newspaper. It's not long before they start kissing and ravaging each other up the staircase before he throws her against the wall, her legs tie around him, and they kiss fiercely like there's not a care in the world.

"Have you ever done that?" I ask him, surprising myself.

He lets out a slight chuckle. "What's that?" He knows what I'm talking about.

"Have you ever just screwed the hell out of someone like in the movie, throwing her against the wall, with your pants around your ankles like you're saving the world with this one last act of passion?"

He runs his fingers through his hair, and scratches his head. "Wow. This movie will never be the same for me again."

"I'm serious." I sit up and away from him to get a good look at his expression.

"Well, I wouldn't call what they're doing 'screwing'."

"What would you call it then?"

His hand disappears in his hair again. "Maybe I'm gonna sound like a chick, but I think they're making love."

I snicker. "Really? It's not what I picture when I think of making love."

He chuckles again. "What? You think making love has to take place in a bed, all sweet and innocent?"

"Well, yeah. Kind of, I guess." That's exactly how I imagine it. *That's* all I've been doing for the last ten years, before Chase dropped my ass and the dust started to settle down there.

"Hmm. I guess I think if you love the one you're with, anytime you have sex, it's making love." Good point.

"Even if you get *slammed* against the wall?" I ask, grinning.

"Even if you get slammed against a wall, yes. Making love can be very passionate. I think the more in love you are, the more passionate it is, and the better it feels. It's just better. I'm gonna sound like a chick again, but I like sex that's meaningful." He licks his lips. "Wait. Don't get me wrong. Cheap sex serves a purpose, but I'd rather have someone I can make passionate love to all the time than a different person every now and then just so I can blow off steam." He unleashes these words while mingling his fingers with mine.

I take a moment to consider this. He does sound like a girl. But what he says makes sense, and it sounds appealing. He wiggles my fingers in his, getting my attention, "And I guess a quickie with the one you love does the job too."

"You never answered my question?"

He seems to consider what I'm asking. "Nope."

"Do you think people really do that? Outside of movies and books? I mean, I've heard a lot of stories about real-life sex before, and never once have any of my friends shared anything even resembling Rachel McAdams and Ryan Gosling."

"That's because all the stories you've heard probably have something to do with keg parties or Margarita Mondays at Alcapulco's."

I actually laugh out loud thinking there's probably some truth to that. "You're funny," I tell him.

"As are you." He scoops me up and brings me to him for the beginning of a make-out session that rivals our on-screen counterparts. Although, his shorts aren't gathered at his ankles and I don't feel picture frames digging into my back. But this ... this is just as good. Matty slows our pace and presses his moistened lips to my swollen mouth, and I think, *I want a man who loves me enough to nail me against the wall.*

Eventually, Matty and I are sprawled out on my sofa, with my body on top of his and my knees on either side of his waist. My hair covers our faces like a curtain as I work kisses from his lips to his neck. His scent is clean and fresh, with the subtle hint of a citrusy cologne. He doesn't bathe in it. I like that. I want access to his shoulders, his chest, but this damn shirt is in my way. Instead, I nip at his neck some more as I make my way back to his jaw line, strong and sharp. My mouth comes down on his and his tongue slides against mine in slow waves of pleasure. He pauses for a beat, sucking on my bottom lip. With a hand wrapped in my hair, he pulls gently, pushing my face upward to grant him access to my neck. My weakness. Kiss my neck and it's all I can do to keep myself from letting go right now.

Matty continues to concentrate his efforts on my throat as my breathing races to almost panting. He has me where he wants me and I wouldn't stop him even if I could. This is too damned hot. With one hand still tangled in my hair, his other is full of my ass, and with each tightened grasp, I can feel him pulse through me. I let out a moan. "Oh God, Matty," I whisper, as he thrusts his hips upward showing me just how much he's enjoying this too.

He moves his hand from my bottom, wraps it around my waist, and with one swift motion, he swings me around and now I'm beneath him. We sink into my sofa, and the pillows start to close in around us. It's like Matty reads my mind. He lifts me once more, and takes me with him as he kneels to the floor. We nestle together, holding each other, and breathing heavily.

"You need a break?" he asks me, with a wink and a sly grin.

Chapter Eight

"Are you crazy?" Not like it's really a question. "No way." I take him by his neck and yank him down for another smooch.

"You're my kind of woman." He laughs into my ear, and then begins planting kisses on my neck and chest, tracing the outline of my V-neck shirt with his lips.

I bring my hands down to touch his ass. I fight the urge to lift my hips into him. Now that would be a bad idea. Moving along, I catch the edge of his shirt, and run fingers along his bare back. Stroking his soft, warm, dampened skin, I love the feel of his muscles in the palms of my hands. The more I explore, the more his shirt slides up his long torso. I tug on it. Matty understands me and with one hand, he yanks his shirt over his head.

I take a much-needed pause to enjoy the sight before me. Pressing my hands to Matty's chest, I tilt myself upward to graze his pecs with my lips. My lack of abdominal muscles sends me flat on my back wanting more. One side of his mouth rises in a smile, and his eyes crinkle at the edges. I smile back.

"You're gorgeous, Matt Fuller." His luscious mouth comes down on my neck again. I sense his teeth drag along my collarbone, and I arch my back, thrusting my hips into his swollen shaft. "You're killing me, Matty."

The heat in his eyes bears down on me. I know he feels the same.

"And you're beautiful, Shelly Gelson. Just beautiful." His soft lips brush against mine. He kisses my nose, and just underneath each of my eyes. "I love your little freckles. They make you even more beautiful." His lips graze the same area again. "Each and every one." He touches his lips to my mouth once more before he rolls over next to me, exhaling a deep breath.

Quickly, I prop up on my elbow and stare at him, lying there, breathing heavily, and leaving me hanging, but there's that smile that has me undone. The silly grin on his face and the swell in his pants tells me he's enjoying himself as much as I am. "What are you doing?" I ask him. I said I didn't need a break.

"Taking a breather," he mutters, through a chuckle.

"Why?"

"Because you're killing me too."

Oh. I see. Not only are we enjoying ourselves, but we're also frustrating the hell out of each other—in the best way possible. "Uh. What should we do then?" I ask him, honestly. Although, if the throbbing between my legs and tenderness of my breasts is meant to go away, I'm going to have to get as far away from Matty as possible. Across the Pacific doesn't seem far enough to chill the sensations I'm experiencing.

He props himself up on his elbow too, just like me and rests his other hand on my waist. Caressing my back, he tells me, "We probably shouldn't do much more than this. For now, anyway. Not until you're ready."

"Ready for sex? Matty, this isn't my first time. I am *ready* for sex." He rolls on his back laughing at my plea. I continue, "Why are you laughing at me, butthead? I'm serious."

He clears his throat and grins at me. I lean over him, resting my chin on the backs of my hands on his chest. He plays with my hair, running strands through his fingers and then letting them fall.

"I know you are, Shel, but it doesn't mean you're ready *here*." He taps on my temple. "When we make love for the first time, I want you to love *me* … entirely, and only me." The thought crosses my mind. Do I love Matty? Of course I do. He's Matty, my dear close friend. Someone who I might just want to be more than friends with. But, do I *not* love Chase anymore? That's a tough question. Sometimes I think I always will. "Don't over think this, Shel. I can see the wheels turning in your head. It'll happen."

"So you're confident I'll fall in love with you?" I ask, teasingly.

He pauses, staring into my eyes. "Never been so confident in anything or anyone in my life." He kisses my nose.

"You're serious, aren't you?" I utter.

"As a heart attack," he says, with sincerity written all over his face.

I bite my lip. He is *so* dead serious. "So what now? Until then?" I ask. It's a reasonable enough question to put out there at this point.

"This is fun. Reminds me of high school," he tells me. We chuckle. "Although in high school I, at least, got to second base."

"I think that can be arranged, Mr. Fuller," I reply. I sit up and pull off my shirt, exposing my black lacy bra. It's been awhile since I've dipped into my girly gear. I think I heard a cheer from my panties when I opened the drawer.

His eyes dart from mine to my breasts and back. "Uh, I think second base is just a little boob action … on top of clothes. Not under."

"But this is high school remember. And you don't have a shirt on. Peer pressure, you know. I don't want to feel left out. Plus, if I don't put out just a little bit, you might dump me tomorrow."

"But we're not a couple, remember. I can't dump you." His fingertips trail over my ribs and rest at my sides.

"Whatever, Matty." I kiss his lips, before lightly dragging my tongue down his neck to his chest. This man is delicious. "Just go with it."

And with that, we spend the next hour or so dry humping like teenagers on my living room floor. It feels good to be young again. Yeah right, if I had duct tape handy, I'd totally tie Matty up and have my way with him. Men are animals. It doesn't matter what his brain is thinking. His other head has a mind of its own and would gladly stand at attention for me if I needed him to. But I don't, have any tape that is. So I just enjoy the feeling of Matty's hands exploring my curves and wait. Wait to see if he has a reason to be so confident.

"Put something in with shit getting blown up," I mention, as he shuffles through my DVDs again. "No passionate love making against a wall, or we'll never make it to the credits."

"No kidding," he agrees with a snicker.

"Hey, it's not my fault you're so irresistible," I respond. He pauses for a beat, almost not long enough for me to notice but I do. "What?"

"Nothing," he says, quickly looking from me back to the movies.

"No, tell me, sucka. What's up?" I put my hand on his back.

"I was gonna say, if I'm so irresistible, it wouldn't have taken you so long to notice me, but I stopped myself because I didn't want to sound like a … "

"Girl." I finish the sentence for him. He shakes his head, embarrassed and runs his hand through his hair. I'm starting to catch on to his little nuances. He always reaches for his hair when he feels uncomfortable. It's his boyish way of blushing. "You're anything but a girl. In fact, I think I felt proof of that earlier." I move my hand from his back to his upper thigh.

He catches my hand on the way up. "Okay. Stop, Shel, or we might not get the damn movie started."

We both laugh. I love this. Endless laughter, giddiness, butterflies doing somersaults in my belly. Cute. I could get used to having Matty around on a more permanent basis.

"You know what?" He drops the DVDs on the table. "We need food. Forget the movie. Let's go eat." He's right. We haven't eaten anything since the cereal this morning and it's way past lunchtime and I do believe we worked up quite an appetite.

"But I'm not dressed to go out." I look down at my tee and yoga pants. Disclaimer: I don't do yoga. Not since I tried it one time with Mel and we got kicked out for talking. I can't shut up for five minutes, let alone sixty. And not when the three-hundred pound guy next to me is trying to fold himself into a pretzel while ridding his body of baby-poop-scented gas. Who can remain silent throughout that? Tell me, who?

"We can go through a drive-thru," he suggests. "Unless you wanna eat more cereal?"

I take a second to consider this. "While the Crunch Berries are calling my name, I think we could use some fresh air. It smells like non-sex in here and it's making me horny. Fresh air would be good."

Matty holds out a hand to me. "Let's go, horn dog."

"Good idea. Let's get some corn dogs." I can almost taste the flavors in my mouth. "Wait a minute. I'm not sure I want to put something so phallic looking in my mouth right now."

"You're so dirty, Shel." He shakes his head, yet again.

"Matty, do you need me to tone it down? My dirty mind shouldn't come as a shock. I thought I could be myself around you."

He slings his arm around me as we walk out of my house. "No, by all means, be yourself. I don't want you to put on a show for me. *But* … if I'm going to watch you put anything phallic-like in your mouth, I sure as hell don't want it to be a hot dog. So let's get a burger."

"I like the way you think," I tell him. He winks at me as I duck into his car.

The first thing I do is take my cell out of my bag to text Mel. She's probably going crazy trying to figure out what happened last night.

Me: matty slept over. No sex. were spndng day 2gthr.

Mel: what? NO Sex? why the f not?

Me: he wnts me 2 <3 him 1st

Mel: what a girl. wht r u doin now?

Me: getting food. wrkd up an appetite. making out like horny teenagers

Mel: love it! Is it true wht they say bout shoe size? ;) ;)

Me: idk. YET!!! lol

Chapter Nine

"Holy hell," I say, watching my best friend step into my classroom. "You look like shit. Are you sure you're okay to be back at work?" She's had the flu since Sunday morning. Her face looks swollen, and she looks like she needs to sleep for another five days before she can even begin to appear rested.

"Are you frickin' kidding? I'm dying to hear about your love fest with Matt. I couldn't wait another day. I'll be fine." She plops herself in a chair next to me and rests her head on my desk. "Now spill. You have twenty minutes. Give me the short but detailed version, if there's such a thing."

Her voice sounds like she's plugging her nose, and I look at the can of Lysol on my file cabinet and have to stop myself from spraying her with it. I have no desire to get sick right now and put a damper on any future 'love fests' with Matty.

Taking a swig of my Diet Coke, I think a beer would be so much better for this story, but it will have to do. I take a deep breath before I recount the details beginning with Friday night when Mel left. I can't give her the minute-by-minute play-by-play, but I'll try my best.

"Here it goes. Friday night. He took me home. Thanks." I nod at her, and she snickers. "Invited him in. Drank a beer. He kissed me. I questioned it. Not to worry. Just go with it. No strings attached. Invited him to stay. To sleep only. Slept in bed. Me in jammies. He in his boxers. Looked like Marky Mark ad, by the way. Woke up. He was gone. Almost died. He went to get breakfast. Got me Captain Crunch." Mel gasps. I nod in agreement. "We ate. He decided to stay, be lazy, and watch movies. Started with The Notebook. Got steamy." Mel's eyes get wide. "I know," I add. "So we kissed like crazy. Stopped. No sex till I'm in love with him." We both roll our eyes. "Then Matty got to second base. We bumped bare chests, not uglies. Got some burgers. Watched The Shooter. Kissed again. Think my lips will be swollen for a month. Ate cereal and beer for dinner and a Rice Krispies Treat for dessert. Slept together again. Only sleeping. Woke up and did a repeat of the day before. He went home early Monday morning to get ready for work."

Done. I lean back in my chair, out of breath, and then take another drink of my soda to soothe my parched throat.

"Fucking awesome." Mel dabs at the corners of her eyes with a tissue.

"Are you crying? Cut it out." She's so emotional all the time, crying at commercials or love songs on the radio.

She dabs again and asks, "What now? How's work been?"

"He said he doesn't want to crowd me. Or freak me out. So he's staying away during the week. He wants me to miss him, I think. And it's working. He might have lunch with me tomorrow."

"Oh, Shelly, I'm so happy for you." She rises out of her seat and hugs me. I hug her back, swaying back and forth. "I gotta run. I'll call you later to keep your mind off him. You don't want to start calling him right away and seem needy."

"Too late. I called him before you got here. No games here. If I wanna talk to him, I'll call him. If he can't handle the real me, impatient and needy, then it's not meant to be."

"Good idea," she says, leaving my room.

On my way out, I decide to stop in and check on Mel. She looked terrible today. Maybe she'll let me cook dinner for her and Nick. What am I thinking? Of course she will. I'll have to think about what I can throw together. I can't go over there with a 12-pack and beer nuts to heal her.

"Hi," I say to the stranger sitting at Mel's desk. "Is Mrs. Cruz around?"

The older guy looks up. "She went home early. I subbed for her the last part of the day. I'm just finishing up my comments to her."

"I see. Did her kids behave?" I can't help but ask. Whenever I'm out, I'm always thinking about my class and how things are going, or *not* going.

"They were perfect. They didn't even need me. Went straight to work without making a peep."

"Great. Thank you. Enjoy the rest of your day." Mel will be happy to hear this. There's nothing better than coming back after a day off and finding out your classroom is still standing.

I make a pit stop at Rite Aid on the way to Mel's. Walking up and down the aisle, I toss anything even remotely healing in my basket. Theraflu, Pepto, Tums (you never know), Motrin, cough drops, and some Nyquil (when all else fails, some decent rest always helps). I make another stop at a deli for some homemade chicken noodle and broccoli and cheese soup. And finally, I cruise through the drive-thru at Starbucks for a venti hot green tea with honey. I also add a few boxes of tea bags so I can refill her tea throughout the night.

Nick's car's not in the driveway. I swear. Would it kill the guy to leave work early and take care of his wife? I use my key and let myself in. I drop all the stuff in the kitchen. I begin to empty the bags when I hear something. It sounds like sniffling. Not like stuffy nose sniffling, but crying.

I follow the sounds to the living room, and I find my best friend balled up on the couch weeping, with crumpled up tissues all around her. Mer Der, her Taco Bell pooch team, rest at her feet. Meredith, a light brown breed, springs her head to stare me down. She decides I'm not the culprit and rests her head back on Derek, the ruffly black dog who has a coat that gleams like silk. My focus turns back to Mel and my heart breaks at the sight of her. I've never seen her like this in my whole life. Sure, she snivels at least once a day during a TV show, or when she hears the national anthem. But this is different. She looks so sad.

I kneel down before her and my throat tightens. "Melly Belly. I'm here." I pause staring at her red nose. "Whatever it is, it'll be okay." I reach out to her, pushing her tear-soaked hair out of her face. Her eyes are even more swollen than before. And it hits me. She doesn't have the flu at all. She never did. "What can I do? Do you wanna tell me what's wrong? How can I fix it?"

I continue to stroke Mel's hair while she sobs. Tears puddle in my eyes, and I can't stop them from running down my cheeks. My best friend, who may as well be my sister, is hurting and I don't know how to help. I don't know if I can and it's the worst feeling in the world.

She always manages to make me feel better whenever I'm down, which has been quite often in the last year, and here I am, at a loss. I don't know what to do.

When Chase dumped me, Mel was there in a flash. She hardly left my side. I was broken and she was there to put me back together, when I didn't think it could be done. She forced me to get back to normal after moping around for way too long.

Oh shit. It's Nick. Mother fucker. I'm going to kill him. What the hell did he do? The only reason Mel would be in this state is because that fucking asshole did something. I'm going to kill him. I think I said that already. But I am. When I find him, he better run. He better have on a Kevlar vest, a cup, and a helmet, because first I'm going to shoot him, then I'm going to kick him in the balls, and finish him off with a bat to the head. Take that, dickhead.

Mel's sobbing slows to a whimper as she tries to catch her breath. She holds my hand. She gazes down at me like she wants to tell me everything, but she's not ready. She stares off in silence, and her eyes start to flutter before shutting completely. She sounds like a baby who's cried herself to sleep. Trying not to wake her, I get comfortable sitting down beside her on the floor, still grasping her hand. I can't let go. I'll stay here as long as she needs me.

Hours later, Mel wakes me up, and I lift my head from the sofa cushion. Still holding her hand, I look up to her sorrow filled eyes. Mer Der are still at her feet, saddened eyes peering up at their mama. It must be true, dogs can sense when something is wrong.

"Are you ready to talk to me?" I ask her.

She looks up and dabs at her eyes with her free hand. "Nick and I are getting a divorce." I don't say anything. I just nod. "He's moved out. Or rather, I kicked him out." I nod again. I think I know what's coming next. "He's been cheating on me, Shel." She squeezes my hand tighter. "For over a year. They're getting married as soon as our divorce is final. He actually had the papers ready, and I signed them."

Wow. This is more than I could have ever imagined. Sure, I had a feeling she was going to confide in me about him cheating. But divorce? Already? I wasn't expecting that. And I sure as hell wasn't expecting her to tell me Nick is going to marry his mistress already. While he hasn't always been the most attentive husband, I wouldn't have thought him to be a complete jackass.

"Holy shit, Mel." What else can I say? I sit up and throw my arms around my friend. She holds onto me, crying quietly into my shoulder. No more sobs and whimpering, just silent tears. After a few minutes, she releases me and I sit down next to her on the sofa, careful not to disturb her watchdogs.

"I found out Friday night. Although, I guess I'd always suspected." Deep down, maybe I did too but I don't share this with her. "After I left you with Matt, I called Nick. He said he had about a couple hours left of work and would pick us up some dessert on his way home. I was almost here when I thought I'd surprise him. Take dessert to him, you know." God, I want to kill him. Or at least, chop off his sac. "So I got us some Ben & Jerry's and went to his office. When I pulled in, I saw them. Nick, and one of the other partners, who I know very well by the way. He had her pinned against her car. They had their arms around each other and they were talking. I parked across from them and a few cars down and they didn't even notice me. They just went on about their business, without a care in the world that both of them were cheating bastards. Talking, kissing. I went from shocked, to disgusted, to hurt, to angry. I got out of the car, and walked over to them."

"Oh, God!" My hands shoot up, covering my mouth. "What did you do?" The sound is muffled through my fingers but she hears me.

"I called him a fucking asshole, and I socked her in the face," she explains. I glance down at her hand, and sure enough, I see the yellowed skin of healing bruises. "Just a little FYI, no matter how much you want to, I wouldn't recommend hitting someone. That shit hurt like a son of a bitch. But I didn't let it show. No way. I told him he had an hour tops to get home, pack his shit, and get the fuck out. I walked back to the car and went home."

"I'm so sorry, Melly," I begin, but she cuts me off.

"He wasn't but ten minutes behind me. Fucking bastard had the nerve to tell me he talked her out of pressing charges. Like I could give a fuck." She rips tissues into pieces. "Before he packed, he gave me the gory details. They spend a lot of time together at work. More time than we do obviously." She rolls her eyes. "He planned on telling me during winter break. He thought it would give me time to recover before getting back to work. How fucking considerate of him. He already had divorce papers drawn up, giving me a good chunk of change in alimony every month. He paid off the house, and he's letting me keep it. My car too. He really took care of me. Like a fucking sugar daddy. Can't complain, huh?" She throws her hands up. "So I'll be alone now. Big fucking deal. It's not like I wasn't alone most of the time anyway. Now, I just don't have to pick up anyone's dry cleaning or shave my damn legs. I don't even have to work if I don't want to, he set me up that well."

I give her a forced smile, not sure what to say.

"Well I think that sums it up. Got any questions?" she asks.

"Want some Nyquil?" I joke, trying to lighten up the mood.

"Huh?" She chuckles. So good to hear her laugh.

"I seriously thought you were sick so I stopped and got you some soup and about twenty different types of drugs. I can go get us some wine and chocolate."

"What I really need is a shower. Don't go anywhere okay, Shel. I'll be right out." She stands and starts plucking up pieces of tissue off the sofa. It looks like a Kleenex grenade went off in here.

"Don't worry about it. I'll get this. Just go enjoy your shower. I'm not going anywhere."

As soon as she disappears down the hall, I get to work cleaning up her mess of wadded up tears and folding the four blankets she tried to hide herself in. I also turn on some lights. The house is warm and dark, and she could use some light right now.

In the kitchen, I put my drugstore back into the bag so she's not tempted to have a cocktail of painkillers, antihistamines, and cough syrup. I'll just take these home with me. I get some bowls out to serve the soup, and open a bottle of wine for her. I look in her fridge but she's out of beer. Shit. I guess I'll just pretend to have a little class tonight so I pour myself a glass too. I take a sip and the dry bitterness irritates my taste buds.

I notice Mer Der's dishes are almost empty so I refil their water and open a new can of dog food, dividing it between both of their bowls. They must recognize the sound of the can opener or smell the food because I hear the tapping of their paws on the floor before they reach the kitchen. Once I put the containers on the floor, they go to work lapping up water and chomping at their dinner.

I can hear my cell buzzing in my bag. I fish it out and answer, "Hi."

"Hey, Shel. Where you been? I tried to call you a few times. You're not bugging out on me already, are you?" Matty's voice is just what I needed to hear.

"Oh son of shitsicle, Matty. I'm kind of having a crisis right now. Mel's … uh." I'm not sure what to say. "Uh … Mel's having some problems with Nick. So I'm here with her, trying to … I don't know. I guess just being here for her. As much as I can be, I guess, without beer and chocolate." I'm babbling, I know. But, what the hell can I say without telling him the whole story? It's not mine to tell, even though I doubt Mel would mind if I told him.

"Oh. I'm sorry. Is she okay? Is there anything I can do?" he asks. I'm certain we could ask him for anything and he'd do what he could to make it happen. It's just there isn't anything. Unfortunately. I'm still not certain what I'm supposed to be doing.

"She's doing the best she can. I'm just happy to hear your voice. Everything is a big fucking mess," I explain, trying to get the words out as my throat tightens and tears threaten to spill down my cheeks.

"Well, you know I'm here if you need me. Call me, anytime. It doesn't matter how late."

"Okay, thanks, Matty. I'll come by to visit you during lunch tomorrow."

"Sounds good."

"See you."

"Bye."

I really want to see him. I wish he could drop by for a quick hug and I think I'd feel much better.

Mel and I are just finishing dinner when I get a text from Matty.

Left you a surprise at Mel's door. Hope this helps. C U 2mro! ☺

"Is that your hot piece of ass? You should go home and have him come over," Mel tells me.

"You're dumb. I'm staying here. He said he left us something," I respond. I first go over to the window to see if he's here. He's not. Unless, he's stalking us from far away with binoculars or something. Creepy. But I do see a bag on Mel's welcome mat. I open the door and bend down to open the bag. Holy shit. Matty is my hero. I kind of wish he stayed. I'd love to see his face right now, but I also know that this is some serious bestie time.

"What is it?" Mel asks, as I return with the bag.

"He brought you some more wine, me some beer. And for both of us … chocolate and Rice Krispies Treats," I announce, taking each item out and setting them on the table.

"He's sharing his goods with me too. Did you tell him what happened?" Mel asks.

"No, I didn't," I tell her, and explain I only said enough for him to know something was up.

"Oh, Shel, he better at least get a blow job for this," she says, as she opens up another bottle of wine. We giggle, and it's nice to know she hasn't lost her sense of humor.

"I'll keep that in mind."

"You better not screw this up. We've both had assholes in our lives. Matt is amazing. Don't think he's always going to be there waiting for you to make up your mind. Be good to him. He deserves it. And you deserve to allow yourself to be happy," she scolds me with a stern look on her face.

"Thanks." I pop the cap off my Hef. "I think."

"Just don't jack this up. I'm serious." Her eyes are intense, and I know this means a lot to her. She's right. Chase is an ass who dumped me. Nick is an ass who dumped her. I should be happy to have someone like Matty so interested in me.

"Don't worry. I get the message. Now, shut up and give me some chocolate." I grab a bag of little Dove bars out from under her.

She snags the bag out of my hands before I can stop her. "Your husband didn't cheat on you and ask you for a divorce. You didn't earn any chocolates. These are mine, beeyotch." It's good to see she's eating. She's lost weight this past week. It's painfully obvious. The girl has always been a size four and rarely gains a pound. She eats like a sumo wrestler and has the metabolism of a speed freak. And without eating this week, she looks a size smaller. Thankfully, Matty's chocolates will replenish some of the calories she's in need of.

"Can't argue with that. God, I wish I could've seen you punch her." I look up trying to imagine what it would be like to see my best friend throw a right hook at some bimbo in a cheesy pantsuit.

"You're telling me. I wish I could see it on YouTube right now. How badass would that be?" We both snicker at the thought. "I wonder how many hits it would get."

"A ton. It would probably trend on Twitter," I say, laughing. Both Mel and I stuff a chocolate in our mouths and enjoy the melting sweetness with silence. I take one of the blue-foiled treats in my hands, and stare at it, warm flutters move through my belly. I'll save this for later. Mel tosses me another little square chocolate, and I ask her, "Are you sure you're all right? Is there something you want me to do?" She seems fine now, but I don't think a shower can fix all the pain I walked in on earlier.

Mel downs the last of her wine. "I've been crying since Friday. I've been dying to talk to you about it and now that I have, I feel better. I already told my mom. I don't need to personally tell anyone else, so I'm good."

"You sure?"

"Totally. I can't mourn this forever. It's not like it was a shock. Fuck it. I'm gonna go out and find myself my own piece of ass." I almost spit out my beer and she continues, "And not just one either. I can't remember what it's like to have good sex. I'm going to have fun remembering. I think I'll find some young guys too. I'm not old enough to be a cougar, so you can call me a cheetah." We both laugh, until Mel starts snorting.

"You're crazy, Melly."

"I'm serious. I'm gonna find some guy to set up camp with his face in my twat. All the twenty-somethings out there better watch out. This bitch is on the prowl."

I raise my brows at her.

"Okay, late twenties. Nothing younger. I teach all day. I don't want to have to teach at night too," she says, unwrapping another chocolate.

"All righty then," I say, wide-eyed.

"Hey, you wanna come with me to get a Brazilian?" she asks.

For the second time tonight, I almost spit out my beer. "Excuse me?"

"And I'm not talkin' about the blowout either," she says, trying to clear up any confusion on my part. I wasn't confused though. I know exactly what she means. The idea of having all the hair ripped from down there just doesn't sound appealing to me. I can barely handle the hurt of getting the lips on my face done, I can't imagine waxing the lips down there too. I'd have to get an epidural or something to manage the pain. No thank you. And while I love my best friend and understand she's feeling like crap right now, I really have no intention of holding her legs to her ears while someone plucks her like a chicken.

Somehow, I think Mel is going to survive this little bump in the road just fine.

Chapter Ten

I'm back to eating in the staff lounge. Mel is tired of being cooped up in our classrooms. "We need to be around people. Making fun of everyone will make me feel better," she had said, pleading with me. Talking crap in private just isn't fun enough for her. She likes to do it right in front of her assailant's face. Everyone knows her, so it's not like it's a surprise to anyone. Most of the people she clowns on deserve it anyway.

Take Mr. Viagra—not his real name but really no man his age should be using it—for instance, he makes his rounds at all the tables with ladies at them. One day, he's sitting with the fresh crop of just out of college teachers. The next day, he's hitting on the secretaries. And the next, he's paying some attention to the more 'seasoned' teachers. Well, I guess he doesn't discriminate. He thinks he's some kind of Hugh Hefner though. How can you watch an old PE teacher like him, who's been wearing the same polyester shorts since I was a student here, and not poke fun? Poke fun! Ha! Poke fun at Mr. Viagra. I crack myself up.

And guess what? Mel does feel better. A lot better. She is so much better at being dumped than I am. Her strength amazes me over and over again.

"I can't wait for today to be over," I tell Mel and Matty. "Two weeks without grading. Two weeks of just pure non-interrupted love of … "

"Me." I look over. Really? Chase sits next to me and says, "Sorry, I just couldn't help it."

I steal a glance at Matty, who doesn't seem rattled in the slightest. "I was gonna say non-interrupted love of *sleep*. This morning, I wanted to throw my alarm against the wall. I'm so tired."

"Well, if you weren't having sleepovers during the week, maybe you could get some rest," Mel says, winking at me. Matty grins. Okay, so we haven't kept to our hands-off during the workweek agreement.

"How cute. You and Mel have been going old school staying up all night talking about boys and washing each other's hair," Chase replies, with his boyish little fake smile.

Mel shakes her head. "Oh no. Not me. I'm not the one sleeping over."

"Who then?" Chase looks at me confused.

"I don't think it's any of your business." I take a sip of my Diet Coke and sneak another peek at Matty.

The left side of his mouth turns upward in a smile. I smile back at him, and take a bite of my Classic Chicken burrito from El Pollo Loco. Yummy.

Chase pounds his hand down on the table. "Well, I think it is." People stop and stare at us. He glares at me. I catch a glimpse of Summer in the corner of my eye. She's yanking out my hair with her eyes, and I raise my hands, as if to say, I don't know what his problem is.

"Chase, stop acting like an ass," Mel tells him. "Summer's giving you the evil eye, so run along."

She's giving *me* the stink eye, not him.

He slides his chair out and leaves.

"Dude, he is so stupid," I say. I can't believe I was in love with such an idiot. Wait. I can't believe I *am* in love with that idiot. Am I still in love with him? No, I don't think so. Or maybe. I don't know. Or do I? Oh crap, I'm so confused.

My unsorted feelings for Chase are diminishing. I can see it, feel it. But something still hits me when I see him or hear his voice. I need it to go away. Quickly. So I can move on with my non-relationship with Matty.

"Thanks for not saying anything, Matty." How he keeps his composure around Chase is beyond me.

"I told you, he doesn't bother me. But, if he raises his voice to you again, I don't care if we're at work. I *will* say something. I won't allow him to treat you badly." Matty reaches over and puts his hand on mine. Without thinking, I yank my hand away. The look on his face kills me. Why did I do that? I'm so stupid.

Jacob, another history teacher, joins us, turning a chair backward and sits down with his hands resting on the back of the seat.

"Hey, what's up?" he says, looking to each of us. I want to thank him for the distraction. Maybe Matty will forget I just snubbed him, unintentionally.

"Hi," Mel says. "What are you up to?"

Matty and I nod at him.

"I just wanted to see what you're up to during break, Shelly," he says, and when I hear my name, my head pops up from my burrito to look at him. "I thought maybe we could get together."

"Really?" I say. Am I being Punk'd? First Chase. Now this. Matty is going to stop talking to me.

"Yeah, really," he says, smiling at me like we're the only two people at the table.

Matty sits forward at the table and interrupts Jacob's googly eyes. "I think it's a fantastic idea," he announces. What in the world. "Mel and I have been telling her for so long to get out and have a good time since … well, you know. Go for it, Shel."

If looks could kill, Matty would drop dead right now. What's he thinking? He can't be thinking. No man in his right mind would send the girl he is not-seeing on a date with another man. But he's asking for it.

"Sure, Jacob, why not? Call me," I respond through gritted teeth. I take his cell from his hands and program my number in it.

"Great," he says, rising to his feet. "I'll call you later."

The bell rings and we make our way out of the lounge. Mel seems as stunned as I do, speechless for the first time, and heading to the ladies room. Matty and I walk to our rooms. I wonder who will say something first. He's not so here I go.

"What were you thinking?" I ask.

His silence is anything but golden.

"Matty, come on," I urge him. "You just set me up on a date I don't want to go on. I don't want to see anyone else."

"Yes, you do," he says. "You're going to question what we have until you know you're not missing anything and until you get over Chase. So try it. I'm not worried. Go for it."

"Fine, I'll go, and when I'm home early from wherever Jacob takes me, you better be ready to let me prove to you how much I really don't need to date anyone else," I sneer, poking him in the chest.

"Wow, sounds good. Maybe you should go on a lot of dates with other men more often." He leans over and whispers in my ear, "How exactly are you going to prove it to me?"

I nudge him back with my shoulder and laugh.

Matty is about to leave me at my door, but I stop him.

"About earlier," I mutter. "I'm sorry I pulled my hand away from you. I didn't mean to hurt your feelings."

He smiles at me. "Hey, no worries. It's too soon. See ya later, Shelly."

And with that, he walks down the hall and I don't take my eyes off him until he disappears into his room. He doesn't turn back to look at me, even though I was hoping he would.

"Hey, about what happened at lunch today," I start off with Matty as we get dinner ready at my place. "Are you sure you're okay?" He seems a little quiet tonight.

"I already told you, don't worry about it," he says. "I know it was too much of a public display of affection for you at work. Since we're not technically a couple."

"I didn't mean to hurt your feelings. It's just ... I don't know. I'm not ready yet." Sounds like my theme song. I'm sick of hearing myself say those words, I can't even fathom how Matty feels.

"Hellooo," he lingers on the word. "I'm really not bothered by it so relax." He stops stirring the spaghetti and kisses my forehead. I guess he really is fine.

"Okay then. What should we do tonight? It's Friday. We're off for two weeks." I put the plates and salad on the counter.

"I thought we could just hang out. I'm a little tired. We have the rest of break to do things." Matty serves some pasta on each plate. I take them over to the table.

"Really? I was just thinking, we always stay home and chill. And we're really good at it. We should try going out and see if we enjoy each other just as much. What do you think?" Matty serves the salad, and brings the bowls over too. I place a piece of garlic bread on each of our plates and we sit down to eat.

"Going out is the easy part. How hard is it to go to the movies or see a band with someone? That doesn't require any talking or thinking. Sitting at home is the hard part. Having conversation without any other kind of entertainment is what a lot of couples fail at," he explains to me. Makes sense.

"Hmm." I consider this, looking at my ceiling fan spinning over us. "I think we have it down. We're like a professional frickin' couple in the communication department. We can talk all day and never run out of things to say. We talk while we make dinner." I gesture to our table of food. "And while we eat." I take a bite of my bread. "And while we kiss." I lean over and pucker up my lips to him, crumbs coming out of my mouth. He bends forward anyway and plants a smooch on my lips. "Dang, we're good."

"Told ya." He flashes his pearly whites, and we start eating dinner.

"So I guess tonight, we'll just have to go to bed early since we're both so tired and in dire need of relaxation." I flutter my brows.

"You look dangerous. I'm not sure I want to get into bed with you. A guy can say *no* only so many times before his woman thinks he's a tease." He tugs me toward him and runs his fingers along the curves of my round face, brushing my bangs away from my eyes.

I tap my pointer finger on his chest, and say, "Don't fool yourself, Matty. I thought you were a tease a long time ago."

We both laugh and wrap each other up in an embrace so tender I could melt. With my face pressed against his chest, my breasts planted to his hard belly, I circle my arms around his torso and run my hands up his back until they settle on his firm shoulders. His scent tickles my senses and I let out a sigh, relaxing into his hold. Melting is such an understatement.

Matty brushes his lips against my cheek softly. He then mutters in my ear, "You got me. Let's just clean this up and we can lie down and watch TV in bed." I take a peek up at him, meeting his gaze. "And I mean watch it. Really," he says, emphatically.

Lying in bed with Matty never gets old. You would think the newness and excitement would have worn off by now, but falling asleep with his strong arms around me is still as thrilling now as it was our first night together four months ago.

"I love this," I tell him, hugging his waist and pulling him closer to me.

"Not enough," he replies, kissing and stroking my hair.

"Not enough, what?" I say, pressing my lips to his shoulder.

"It's not enough to love this." He squeezes me. "I need you to love me."

I kiss his chest. "I want to tell you I love you, but I just want to be sure. No doubts. I just need more time. Plus, you want me date *other* people. Saying it would just seem so insincere. You deserve to have it all."

"I know. So let's just watch the movie." He gestures to the TV on the wall in my bedroom.

"All right," I turn around and find my snuggly place in his arms. "Fine then." I pout, jokingly. "But I don't think he just wants to rest." I say of Matty's friend throbbing against my ass.

"He never wants to rest when you're in the room," he snickers.

"It's because he's happy I'm here, and wants to see me." I turn around and cup his length in my palm. Matty gasps. "I can't let him down."

He tenses up. "You keep doing that, and he'll go down sooner than you think."

I run my hand up and down, over his boxers. "Well maybe that's what he wants. Just a little acknowledgment so he knows I care and then he can relax."

"You're killing me, Shel," he says, anxiously, with shoulders tense and his hand frozen in my hair.

Sitting up on my knees, I push Matty flat on his back. "I think I've heard that before," I say, smirking at him. I touch my lips to the center of his chest and begin placing gentle kisses all the way down to his waistband. I slide my tongue along the edges of the material and nip at the sides of his V. I surprise myself when I tell him, "Lift your ass up." He follows my orders, and I quickly yank down his undies before he can change his mind.

Matty puts his hands down to cover himself. Too cute, and I have to giggle. "What are you doing?" he asks.

I pull off my shirt and unclasp my bra. "I wanna be naked with you." I lie down beside him, and bring my mouth to his. I kiss him, passionately and deeply. Our tongues dance together as I slide my hand down to take hold of Matty's erection. He gasps again, but doesn't stop me. I smile at this thought. He allows me to explore him for the first time since we've been non-dating. I start with slow strokes, letting my senses take in the smooth feeling in my hand. How it can be so soft and hard at the same time is amazing.

I find myself breathing harder as our kiss becomes more intense. Matty has one hand in my hair and his other brushes up and down my back. The feel of his warm touch makes me squirm with pleasure, and I can't help but tighten my grasp on him. I quicken my pace, and he squeezes my back with a moan. Tearing away my mouth from his, I trail kisses along his neck and nip at his shoulder, all the while he finishes with a shudder or two. And a groan, or two. Or three or four.

I kiss him again on the lips and he presses my chest against his in a tight embrace, cupping my back with one strong hand and my behind with the other.

A beat later, Matty says into my hair, "Oops."

"What do you mean, oops? I'm proud I can do that to you. Or for you." I look in his eyes, smiling, and wiping my hand on my sheet, and dragging it over to him so he can clean up too. I almost stand up and take a bow, but I decide not to be so silly.

"Was it ever in question?" he asks, raising a brow at me.

"You never know," I sing.

"Well then, I guess I better see if I do it for you?" I smile at him wondering how exactly to interpret his response. He flips me over and onto my back in one quick motion before I have the chance to protest.

"Excuse me?" I inquire.

"Just go with it, Shel." His smile disappears into my neck. Oh holy goodness. He doesn't need to do anything else. My neck is so sensitive, I could go any second. He knows just the right combination of lips and tongue to make my toes curl. He's killing me with just his kisses. What's it going to be like when I fall in love with him and we finally take the next step? Oh, wow.

Matty's mouth makes a move to my breasts, bringing his hand up to grasp one while he holds my nipple between his teeth. Oh son of a lover. If my toes curl any tighter, I'll get a cramp. His hands feel like they're branding me as they travel down my body, his lips trailing not too far behind. "What's this?" he says, running his fingers along the band of my panties. "I thought you wanted to be naked with me." Well I did want to be naked with him, but I didn't want his bare man parts to bump against my bare woman parts because I might just die, for real.

But looking down into his eyes, I see a man with desire and I want his man parts all over my girl parts, and I don't care how frustrated I'll be when it doesn't happen. Matty sits up, tugs on the sides of my panties, and slides them down my legs before tossing them on the floor. *Thank God I shaved*, is my first thought. My

Julie Prestsater

second thought is, *Holy shit, Matty and I are completely naked in my bed.*

Matty brushes his lips against mine and I catch his bottom lip sucking it softly until he tugs away. He works his way from my mouth to my jaw, and then gently traces kisses down the center of my chest, pausing at my navel, dragging his tongue along each of my hip bones, and continuing down to where he parts my legs and, oh my ...

"You know that doesn't count right?" Matty tells me as we cuddle together in the aftermath of panting and howling, and hushed screams into a pillow.

"What's that?" I utter, still trying to catch my breath.

"You telling me you loved me." He laughs.

"Shut up," I squeal, pulling a sheet over my head.

"'Oh God, Matty, I love you' was great and all, but I have a feeling you were a little distracted."

"Just a little," I say, flipping back the covers to reveal my flushed cheeks.

"Oh God, Matty, I love you," he repeats again, giddy with giggles.

I punch him in the arm, jokingly. "Let me do that to you and let's see what comes out of your mouth."

"Uh … no thanks," he says, pulling me toward him. "I can't be responsible for what I might say if I saw those beautiful lips around me."

"So you can do it to me but I can't do it to you and we can't have sex?" I question him.

He kisses my shoulder. "Yep, not until you're in love with me."

"Well with a performance like that, how can I not be? Holy son of a cunnilingus genius. I can't remember … " I stop myself from bringing up the past.

"What can't you remember?" he asks me. I can't lie to him. And I know he wouldn't want me to.

"Let's just say, the last time someone went there was in college."

"Are you kidding me? You mean Chase didn't?" He props himself on an elbow, obviously curious. I fall to my back with embarrassment. Matty settles himself in his familiar position with one arm around me. I look up at him and try to focus in the darkness.

"Nope, he did it once when we were younger, but since we got back together post-grad, he never did it again. This whole thing. Being naked together wasn't … I don't know. It was just different. Very simple."

As hot as Chase is, you'd think sex with him would be sexy at the very least. But it wasn't. Sure, he made me want him, but not like the fire I feel with Matty. Not even close. Chase and I were only nude with each other long enough to seal the deal, clean up, get our clothes back on, and go to sleep. I can't ever imagine Chase smashing me against the wall. I don't think he and I ever had sex anywhere other than a bed. Don't get me wrong, I enjoyed making love with Chase, and I never yearned for anything else. Maybe because I didn't know it could be anything other than what it was. I guess you never miss what you never had. But now that I've felt this undeniable chemistry, I doubt I'll ever be satisfied with the in-and-out style I once knew.

He brushes his lips along my cheek. He has definitely shown me love and sex can be so much more than what I've been accustomed to. "I can't wait for you to fall in love with me, Shel." His lips meet mine, and warmth radiates my entire being.

"Neither can I," I tell him, and completely mean it.

Chapter Eleven

Date night, or day. Whatever.

Why did I let Matty talk me into this? After our hot night of unclothed ecstasy, I was surprised he still wanted me to go out with Jacob. He tried to convince me our relationship needed it. I hope he knows what he's talking about. I don't want this to backfire on us.

What happens if Jacob is this amazing man, who casts a love spell on me, and I can't tear my eyes away from him? What happens then?

Okay, so I've probably seen way too many movies, but a man can sweep a girl off her feet, right? Love at first date is possible. I think. Maybe Jacob will end up being the man of my dreams, assuming he drinks good beer and doesn't smell badly, or something. But even then, there's still another problem. He works with me. There is no way this will work out. I may have made an exception for Matty, but I refuse to do the same for anyone else.

Yet, here I am getting ready for a picnic for crying out loud. It's winter, and we're going to have lunch outdoors. Well it is 80 degrees out, but come on. I can't remember the last time I went to the park. I'm more of an indoor girl. Any place with air conditioning is perfect. Any place I don't have to worry about getting itchy from grass or bugs is also at the top of my list. What about me would give Jacob the impression that a day strolling along in a park—full of birthday parties and couples getting their pictures taken—would be my cup of tea?

Arriving at the park, it's just like I had imagined. Each shelter is occupied with balloons and families, some have bounce houses nearby. A barefoot couple in jeans and white tees are near the lake posing for what I'd guess are engagement pictures for their save-the-date cards. Classic. When I finally take the plunge, I'm wearing a tutu for my photo shoot. I don't think that one has been done.

Jacob is where he said he'd be, at the far end of the park beyond the hiking trail and under a giant oak tree. He's sitting on a large red gingham blanket and has a little matching basket perched next to him. Is this really happening? If I watched this on the LMN, I'd probably be giddy and smiling at the TV, but in real life, it is unbelievably corny. I fight the urge to laugh, instead, muffling a loud chuckle with the back of my hand. I'm not sure if he sees me yet, and I don't want to be rude. But I don't see how I'm going to make it through lunch with this muscle man who is obviously trying to compensate in the gym for his ultra feminine side.

"Hey, Shel," he says as he hops to his feet, and puts his hands on my shoulders.

"Hey," I squeal back, as I turn my head quick enough for him to peck only my cheek.

He removes his hands and wipes them on the sides of his jeans as if trying to wash away my cooties.

Gesturing to the blanket, Jacob says, "Shall we sit?"

I guess we shall. I plop my bag down and kneel to the ground, sitting crosslegged in front of him. He does the same and it dawns on me I haven't seen a boy sit crisscross applesauce since we played Duck, Duck, Goose in elementary school. His jeans tighten around his muscular thighs and I notice the thin fabric of his shirt is hugging his chest and fits snuggly around his biceps. This Mario Lopez get-up is far from the button-up camp shirts and khaki pants he wears to work. And he smells good too. Clean and minty, as if I could pop him in my mouth like a piece of sweetmint gum.

"Are you checking me out?" Jacob asks snapping me from my thoughts.

My cheeks flush with heat, and I'm thankful I have my sunglasses on. I wave him off, with a low chuckle. "Don't be silly. You checking me out?" I turn the tables on him. I have no idea what he's been doing for the last ninety seconds while I was feasting on his firm body.

"I've been doing that for months," he says with a grin.

My face warms again, and I don't know what to say. I can't imagine he'd make an ass out of himself gawking at me today. I'm just wearing a pair of jean capris and a tank with a purple shrug over it. Nothing too fancy, and not the slightest bit sexy. I applied minimal makeup and twisted my hair up in a clip. No frills at all.

I had no interest in coming out on this date so I wasn't about to get all gussied up for Jacob. But now that I've had a chance to take in the sights, I'm rethinking that decision.

"You ready to eat?" Jacob asks, bringing the basket closer to him. I nod, and he pulls out a cloth napkin and hands it to me. Nice. Still corny, but cute.

Jacob opens the top of the basket and starts passing items to me. A plate, a bag of celery sticks, and what appears to be a sandwich wrapped in butcher paper.

"So what do we have here?" I ask him. Conversation doesn't seem to be flowing freely. I'm thankful we can at least talk about food. I don't want to strike up chitchat about work, so I'm hoping something else will come to me soon.

"A veggie wrap. I don't eat animals, so it's a spinach wrap with a variety of veggies tossed in a balsamic vinaigrette. You'll love it. Won't even miss the meat," he says, tearing through the paper and wrapping his mouth around the burrito/sandwich for a ginormous bite.

I won't miss the meat. Like hell I won't. When I finally open the wrap, I peek inside at all the vegetables. Every color of bell peppers, spinach, cucumbers, beets, artichokes, and God only knows what else. Where's the beef? I'm almost afraid to take a bite. My body might reject the healthy bits in my belly and puke it all up. I've never craved a Double Cheeseburger from McDonalds so much in my whole life. Or a juicy T-bone, and I don't even like steak. But I want one right now.

I glance at Jacob who is devouring his wrap with a playful grin. He chows down on it like I'd eat a piece of chocolate, like it's making love to his taste buds. I crunch down on my first bite. The peppers leave a nasty flavor in my mouth and I'm grateful for the refreshing cucumbers or I'd probably gag. Oh, this is so not me. I'd much rather eat a PB&J.

We steal glances at each other in between bites, but there is a lack of interest and it's starting to get uncomfortable. I decide to try my luck with the celery sticks because this veggie wrap is truly making me want to run to the supermarket for a pound of the fattiest ground beef in stock.

"Oh, I forgot. Are you thirsty?" he says, digging into the basket once again.

I nod through my crunching of celery, which is so hydrating I feel like I'm drinking a gallon of water.

Jacob looks to be concealing whatever he's pouring into red plastic cups. Whew. Alcohol. Just what the doctor ordered. I lean forward to take a peek and I can't hold back the laughter. I crack up so much I have to take off my glasses to wipe my eyes.

"What?" Jacob asks innocently. "What's so funny?"

I almost fall back holding my stomach with big belly laughs that are on the verge of full blown snorting and wheezing. He looks at me like I've stabbed him in the heart, but I can't help it. I try to calm myself and concentrate on long steady breaths.

I wipe my eyes again with my napkin and take one last deep breath before telling him, "I'm sorry. I just haven't seen a wine cooler since I was in high school. I didn't realize people still drank them."

"Oh," he murmurs. He finishes pouring our drinks and hands me one. He takes a swig of his own and lets out a sigh. "I guess I drank them in high school too, but never busted the habit. I'm not a fan of beer but I can totally go for a four pack of these."

And here Matty is always concerned about sounding like a girl. Jacob definitely has him beat in that department. Red gingham, veggie wraps, and wine coolers.

Needless to say, I won't be going on a date with Jacob again.

"Well, it's official. Jacob is not the man of my dreams," I tell Mel when I stop at her house on the way home from the park.

"Duh …," she says, putting a beer and bottle opener before me. I crack off the top and down more than half the bottle.

"Do you have anything to eat? I'm starving," I tell her, placing my head on her counter.

"I thought you were eating lunch," she says. "Don't tell me you were one of those girls who only eats a salad?"

I lift my head to take another drink. "Oh no, I ate a veggie wrap and a handful of celery sticks." I twirl my finger in a circle as if to say *big whoop*.

Mel leans back against her counter with a wine glass in her hand. "Veggie wrap?"

"Yes," I groan. "He's a vegetarian." Mel almost spits out her wine. I wait for her to swallow what she has in her mouth before I tell her the rest. "And he drinks wine coolers."

Her mouth drops in complete horror. "Yeah, I know," I mutter.

She ambles to the fridge and whips out another beer for me. "You so deserve another one of these. And let's order pizza."

I down what's left of my first beer, and swipe the other one from her hand. "Meat Lovers," I tell her and we both laugh till Mel starts snorting.

Chapter Twelve

Matty and I spend most of the time leading up to Christmas at my house, messing around, watching movies, playing video games, and eating. Mel makes an appearance a few times, but for the most part we just exist … happily … together.

I'm clearing our dessert plates when Matty asks me, "So what are you doing for the holidays?"

"Going to my parents' house on Christmas Eve, and then to Mel's Christmas day. You?"

"I'm going to my folks' house too. I'm actually gonna leave tomorrow and won't be back until the day after Christmas," he explains.

"Holy shit. I'm not gonna see you for four days." My heart suddenly feels like a brick in my chest and I can't believe I'm so affected by the thought of being away from Matty for such a short time. Four days really isn't that long, but right now it feels like an eternity and he hasn't even left yet.

Matty takes a spoon from my hand and places it in the sink. He faces me and runs his long fingers through my wavy hair. "Two really. I'm not gonna leave here until the morning and I'll see you the day I come back." He reels me in for a hug, and smacks a kiss on my mouth. It eases my heartache just a little, but not much. I've gotten so used to having him around, it's going to be quiet and lonely without him. "You're gonna be so busy with your parents and Mel, you won't even miss me."

"Fine," I tell him, not entirely convinced. Resting my head on his chest, I soak in his familiar citrusy scent that brings the outdoors in to me. I gaze up into his sparkling blue eyes that crinkle at the edges and stretch my face toward his. He meets me the rest of the way for a kiss that's soft and gentle but has enough heat to send sparks all the way down to my girl parts. "We better make tonight count then."

And we do. Make it count.

Matty leaves my house in the morning to pack for his two-hour trip up the coast to see his parents.

"I miss him already," I tell Mel over coffee and donuts.

"Oh, shut your ass. He's been gone for like two seconds," she sneers, chomping on a maple bar. No sympathy from her.

"Look at us," I say, peering around my place. Not a single holiday decoration on display. "You wouldn't know it's Christmas time. I didn't even decorate around here. Neither did you." I didn't put out stockings, I didn't get a tree, and all the presents I have are wrapped in gift bags in the trunk of my car. The only thing representing the holidays is the dish of Dove chocolates on my coffee table. And that was just chance. I didn't go shopping for chocolates in green and red foils.

She waves me off, taking a drink of her Amaretto splashed cup of joe. "What the hell for? It's not like I'm going to dig out all the shit by myself just for me. Too much trouble for nothing."

She's right. I nibble on my glazed donut, savoring every bite, trying to make it last as long as possible. "This is our first holiday without Chase and Nick. Weird huh?"

"It's so fucking crazy. I can't believe it. We're gonna go home and everyone's going to be hovering all over us, checking to see if we're okay. People are gonna be talking shit, saying we can't keep a man. I bet you some people think we're lesbians."

We both laugh so hard we snort.

"I really don't look forward to my family asking questions," I confide. "They're all gonna say what a shock it was and they thought we'd be together forever. And they're sure I'll meet a decent man soon, yada yada yada."

"Well, at least they'll have something right," Mel says.

"I don't plan on telling them about Matty," I respond. "I don't want to jinx anything before it's something."

She shakes her head at me. "I've got news for you, Shel. It already is something. I don't care what you're calling it, or not calling it. You and Matty are a couple."

"No, we're not," I shout. "We're just seeing how things go. Until I'm ready. For sure. We're not rushing anything. I'm even dating other people." My mind flashes back to Jacob. And I smirk at the thought of wine coolers. He's lucky we're on vacation or it would have been all over school. He'd lose his man card for sure.

"Stop being a dumb ass. You guys practically live together, and you're doing everything short of actual penetration, so I'd say you're an effing couple. So stop being so scared and just go for it." She pours another cup of coffee, heavy on the liquor.

"You're not nice," I pout, sticking out my bottom lip.

"Well, you're not being nice to Matt. Put him out of his misery and just tell him you love him."

I suck my lip back in and scrunch my face. Suddenly I feel like I'm in knots. "But I don't know yet," I screech. "He's the first guy I've gone out with since Chase. How do I know he's not just my rebound guy? How do I know he's the one? I thought Chase was the one. Look how that turned out."

"Chase was not *the one*. He was an ass who was convenient," she says, picking out another donut from the pink box. This time, a chocolate bar.

She did not just say that. I did *not* spend practically my entire life with a man out of convenience. We were good together. We were. Really.

Mel and I pull up to my parents' house.

"You ready to be thrown to the wolves?" she asks me.

"Only if you are," I respond.

"I'm not worried about your house. They're gonna love me like always. I'm shitting my pants about tomorrow. My tías are gonna be all up in my masa," she says, waving her hand around her face. No doubt they're going to be in her business before she even walks in the door.

I put my hand up to high-five her. "True that, sister. Let's get this shiz over with, and then we can go back to my house and get drunk."

She slaps my hand with hers and we take our first step up the walk of shame to my parents' front door.

"Shelly, there you are. I was wondering when you were going to arrive," my mother sneers, taking her first jab at me. I guess fifteen minutes isn't considered fashionably late, it's just rude by her standards. As if I didn't know this already. But obviously, I don't care. Oh well. I learned a long time ago, there is no pleasing this lady.

"Nice to see you too, Mother," I say, and air kiss her cheek.

"Oh, Melissa, it's so wonderful to see you. You look great, doesn't she, Shel?" My mother gathers Mel in a dramatic embrace fit for TV when a mother gets reunited with her long-lost daughter who she hasn't seen since birth.

I roll my eyes. "Oh course she does."

Mel winks at me. If we make it out of here without me strangling my mother, I'll deserve a gold fucking medal.

My dad greets us next. He envelops me in a bear hug. "Hey, sweetie. It's nice to see you."

"Nice to see you too, Daddy," I say, as he puts me down.

"Would it kill you to visit your old man more often?" he asks, gazing down at me from his big brown eyes.

I glance over at my mom. "It might."

He gives me a disapproving look. He knows exactly what I mean, but always tries to play devil's advocate where she's concerned.

Dad turns his attention to Mel. "Hey, Melly, good to see you too. I haven't seen Nick on the street yet, but when I do I plan on having a few words with him." He holds up his fist to show us exactly what he means by words.

"Sounds good to me," she says, hugging my father. "You can throw in an uppercut for me if you want. I won't be mad at you."

He winks at her, and says, "Well, I'll leave you two fine ladies to mingle. For some strange reason, there are a lot more bachelors here than usual."

My dad bends down to whisper in my ear, "But word is you're doing fine in the *boy* department. I'm really happy about this. I've always liked Fuller."

I'm going to kill my brother when I see him.

My dad walks away and I whip my head around to see Mel with her mouth hanging open.

"It wasn't me," she says.

"I know exactly who it was," I tell her. "Ugh. And now my mom is trying to marry us off too."

Mel and I look at each other, and I frown in fear.

"I'll save you if you save me. I can't believe my mother is plotting already," I tell Mel, as I take her arm for protection. I really don't feel like meeting any bachelors right now.

"You got it," she says. "But, hey, I don't have a Matty waiting for me at home. So I may not need saving." She raises her brows at me and I jokingly smack her arm. She doesn't want to get involved with anyone my mother would deem appropriate. She's had plenty of that nonsense with Nick.

We make our way into the dining room to scope out the food. My mother always outdoes herself for Christmas: turkey, roast, mashed potatoes, too many casseroles to count, and about fifty different types of baked desserts. I don't know how I didn't learn to cook like her. Oh wait, yes I do. I'd have to be able to tolerate her long enough to actually learn from her. During the eighteen years I spent in this house, according to her, I never poured a bowl of cereal correctly.

During the holidays, I would always try to help my mother in the kitchen at the request of my dad, but she always scoffed at how I did things. Cracking an egg with two hands instead of one. Using a slotted spoon instead of a ladle. Cooking with vegetable oil when she would have used extra virgin olive oil. I could never do anything right. When I finally moved out, I did try to come over early to help out but eventually it got to the point where I am today. Showing up when everything is ready makes it a lot easier on me, and I bet on my mom too since she doesn't have to sneer at all the shortcomings her very own daughter has in the kitchen.

"Oh, Shel, use a small plate," my mother whispers, taking my dinner plate from my hands, and replacing it with a salad-sized one. "You look like you've gained a few pounds." I won't admit she's right to her face, but she probably is. I haven't had time for my regular exercise routine since Matty.

"Thanks for looking out for me, Mother," I sneer. I take her miniature plate and start piling things on.

"Hey, little sister," Tyler says. "Looks like you can use this." Thank God for my brother. What appears to be a plain Coke is actually spiked with rum. I can't very well go walking around with a bottle of beer in my hand. What would the Stepford Mother think? She'd probably faint at the sight.

"Oh, dear God, Ty, I love you." I take the drink from his hands and chug away, ignoring the burn in my throat and the bubbles exploding near my nose.

"But I'm pissed at you." I smack him in the arm.

"What'd I do?" he shrieks.

"You told dad about Matty," I squeal.

Ty rubs his forehead, "He was worried about you so I told him someone was making you feel better these days. He says he's met him before and likes him."

On the rare occasion I mixed family and friends for birthday parties or holidays, Matty had a chance to meet my easygoing dad and my overbearing mother.

"I'm sorry. You still love me?" he asks, batting his lashes.

"Yes," I concede. I rarely get to see him, so I can't stay mad at him for long.

"I know," he says, giving me a brotherly squeeze. "How ya been? How are the kiddos treating you?"

"They're all right. I have a really good group this year," I tell him. "You?"

My brother lives up north. For the most part, we communicate through email and text messages. "I have a lot of talent this year. I'm finally teaching mostly advanced classes so I get to see some really mature work."

Being a high school art teacher was my brother's goal since his passion developed in the tenth grade. He does a lot with his students. They have art shows at their school, and he really goes above and beyond anything I've seen before. And his own work is great. I can barely draw a stick figure. I'm so jealous of his talent. Maybe jealous is the wrong word. I'm more in awe of him.

"How wonderful. I'm so proud of you," I squeal. I'm so the typical little sister who adores her big brother. He's never given me any reason not to.

"Thanks, sis," he says, ruffling my hair like I'm still five years old.

I take the last sip of my drink, and shake the ice around. "Why don't you go fetch me another drink though? I've been here for less than thirty minutes and mom has already shit on me twice."

"Two times. That's it?" he teases. "She's getting soft in her old age."

"Make that two drinks," Mel says.

Tyler swoops her up in a giant embrace. "Melly Belly. Hi."

"Hey, Ty Ty," she says. "When are you gonna transfer down here and get your ass back to town. You know, all the local schools have art programs, don't you?" she says sarcastically.

"No way. Look at the air here. I can't imagine painting in this gloom every day. It'd be so depressing." He contorts his face in disgust. "But I hear they teach English at my school. You could always transfer up there." He winks at her.

"Oh hell, get a room." I look at them, still in each other's arms and walk away to get my own damn drink. Those two have been flirting like crazy since we were in high school. I always thought Mel would eventually become my sister-in-law, but when we went off to college, she met Nick. Now that dipshit Nick is out of the picture, Tyler lives about six hours away. Their timing couldn't be more off.

Maybe there's still hope. Okay, probably not but I've always thought they'd make such a cute couple. Mel could probably fit in his pocket, she's so tiny in comparison. She's this stylish little pixy girl, and my brother is tall, thin, and a casual artsy guy. Her designer boots with his worn Chucks would clash if it were any other couple, but they're individuality just complements each other. I can just picture their coffee table sprinkled with a mixture of the classics and technical books on various forms of brush strokes. She's really loud and brazen, and he's a major goofball. And they're both my best friends.

Dad was right. There *are* a lot of single men here. I take a glance at a few who look familiar but can't place their names, probably sons of my mother's friends. Just one look at their choice in beverages and I know they're not for me. Go figure. All the eligible guys in my mom's rolodex would be either wine or piss beer drinkers.

Maybe I should rethink my strategy. Not. It's working so far. No need to shake things up just yet.

"Shelly, dear, I've been looking all over for you." It's not like it would have been hard to find me, this isn't a mansion. My mother hooks her arm in mine. "I have some friends I'd like you to meet."

"Mother, I really don't want to meet a slew of horny bankers," I snicker.

She gives me a look of disapproval and I know she couldn't care less what I want.

"Mother, really. If and when I'm ready to meet someone, I can do it on my own," I say, slowing my stride, hoping she'll cut me loose.

"And look how well doing it on your own turned out for you," she barks. "You're almost forty. If I'm going to ever have grandchildren, I'm going to have to take matters into my own hands."

"Forty? Do you have some other daughter I don't know about. I'm barely over thirty. And who said anything about making babies?" The thought of letting my own children be poisoned by this woman makes me sick. I swear, if I ever have my own kids, I will be nothing like her. Nothing.

"Shush, now," is all she says.

Losing the battle to spring free, we make our way onto the patio and my mother begins her parade of men.

"You remember Michael, don't you?" she says, as if it's a real question.

Michael puts out his hand, and I take it to be considerate. I almost gag when he brings it to his lips for a kiss. Gross. I need to wash the back of my hand later. His Tom Seleck mustache takes me back to the 80s. Not even a goatee, just a mustache.

"And this is, Kevin." She whisks me off to the next gentleman who seems shy. He nods, pushing his glasses up on his nose. He's cute. And no 'stache in sight. Whew.

I put my hand out to him, and he shakes it with about as much force as a newborn puppy. "Nice to meet you, Kevin." I could just stay here and talk to Waldo all night. He seems harmless. I don't know how he made it past my mother's checklist. His mom probably lied to her. He seems a lot more appealing than the rest of these idiots in suits. C'mon, this isn't a business meeting, just a family party.

"Move along now, Shelly," my mother kindly whispers in my ear.

"I'll be back, Kevin," I say, winking at him.

"Oh no you won't." She pinches the inside of my arm. Son of a testicle. That effing hurt. Seriously, she wants me to meet these losers with tears welling up in my eyes. The sting penetrates my entire arm and I want to punch her.

"Mother, if you do that again, I'm leaving," I whisper through gritted teeth and I have to do battle with my senses so I don't pinch her back.

She ignores me, of course. "Oh, Gordon, I'm so glad you were able to make it. Your mom wasn't sure you would with all the traffic coming in from Santa Barbara." Gordon—oh no!—takes my mother's hands in his and gives her this all mothers love me grin, and he kisses both her cheeks. Gag me. "This is my daughter,

Shelly. She's a high school English teacher." And then my mother disappears. Really? This is who you leave me with Mother? Gordon? There are still at least four remaining bachelors and Gordon is the best she could do?

So the name isn't exactly becoming of him. He's not exactly what you'd picture—short, almost bald, and a bit on the chubby side—with a name like Gordon. He is, in fact, over six feet tall. He's really hulking over me like the Empire State Building. He's also pretty built. I bet underneath his suit he doesn't have an ounce of fat on him. He just exudes this kind of arrogance. Even without him saying a word, I'm already annoyed.

"So you're a teacher?" he asks, as if he needs clarification.

"Yes, I am," I state.

"Hmm," he grunts. "Very admirable."

I doubt he means it. "I don't do it for admiration."

"Yeah, well you know how the saying goes, 'those who can, do it, those who can't …'." Luckily for him, he doesn't finish his sentence. Asshole. "Let me get you a drink, Shelly." Gordon steps away for a second, and returns with a glass of champagne. Oh fuck me.

I miss my chance to get away. "Oh, no, thank you, champagne gives me a headache." I smile, fluttering my eyelashes up at him. I wonder if he can tell I'm being bitchy.

"Okay, what can I get for you then?" he asks.

"How about a beer?" I respond. "Something in a can. I think I have a pen in my bag. Bring one for yourself. We can shotgun 'em."

"Oh cool," Mel says, swooping in from behind me. "I think I have a funnel. We can totally beer bong it."

Tyler puts his arm around Mel, and adds his two cents, "Count me in. But only if you guys do the thing where you do a handstand at the same time."

Gordon looks confused, or scared, and walks away.

We watch him walk into the house before we crack up laughing. Mel starts to snort, and so does Ty.

"That was effing hilarious," I tell them. "Thank you."

"Mom is funny. That guy is way too uptight for you," Tyler says.

Mel adds, "And you didn't even throw in any of your f-bombs. He would've probably run away if he heard your typical flare for words."

"What the fuck are you bitches talking about?" I joke.

We all laugh some more.

"Is it time to go home and get drunk yet?" I ask them.

"Let's roll," Tyler says. "I'm crashing at your place. There's no way in hell I'm staying here."

"Don't forget your flannel jammies your mama bought you," Mel teases him.

"I won't. I'll even get your Pepto pink sweater with the pearly buttons too," he dishes back.

I roll my eyes at them. "I swear, you guys just need to screw and get it over with."

Tyler raises his brows at Mel, "Now that's what I call a Christmas present."

Mel puts her hand on his chest, "Hmm. I think that can be arranged, Mr. Gelson." She stands on her tiptoes and kisses his cheek. "But just one question: have you been a good boy this year?"

I think I just threw-up in my mouth.

Chapter Thirteen

"You guys better hurry up or we're going to be really late," I yell, pounding on the door to the bathroom. I can't believe my best friend and my brother are both in there. I take that back. Yes, I can.

Mel steps out first, wrapped in a towel, and runs to my room.

I shout to her, "What? No walk of shame. Just running around my house naked with my bro. Shit, you guys aren't even discreet."

"I'll be right out. I'm just gonna get my clothes on. I'll do my makeup in the car," Mel yells back, and shuts the door.

"I'm ready," Tyler says nonchalantly as he makes his way to my living room. He sits on the sofa next to me, kicks up his big black Chucks on my coffee table, like it's no big thing he was just showering with my best friend. "You look nice, sis."

"You clean up well too, bro. I take it you're coming with us today?"

"Mel invited me, so why not? Beats going back and visiting with Mom," he says, tapping his feet on the floor. He always does this when he's nervous.

"You better not be fucking with her Tyler or I'll whoop your ass. She's a little fragile right now," I try to explain.

"Mel? Fragile? You obviously don't know your best friend as well as I do," he begins.

"I would hope not," I interrupt, rolling my eyes.

"Yeah. Anyway, she's fine. It's not like this hasn't been coming for a long time. You can't tell me you're shocked we finally ... well you know," he says.

I completely understand what he's saying but it doesn't make it right. "Yeah, but I thought when it did, it would be a little more permanent. Not a Christmas present you play with and then return. It's gonna suck for her when you leave." It's only been a full day since I've seen Matty and it sucks, even though I know he's coming back tomorrow. When Ty leaves, who knows when he'll be back.

Mel comes out and plops herself in Ty's lap. "I'll be fine, Shel. Don't worry. It's all good." Her eyes are sincere and I don't sense any worry coming from her. My brother gives me a look like, *see I told you*.

Tyler taps her on the ass. "You look great too, Melly Belly. You ready?"

She jumps up and throws her hands in the air. "Let's go to my casa. Feliz Navidad."

As we walk up the path to Mel's parents' house, she takes a deep breath and exhales slowly. "Wish me luck."

She's gonna need it. Her aunts can be brutal.

"So you think your mom is gonna have a lot of hot men here to choose from?" I ask, jokingly. "I totally forgot to get Kevin's number last night." Okay, so I wouldn't have called him. Or maybe I would have. He seems like he'd be a cool guy to talk to, but not really anything beyond friendship.

"I thought you were seeing someone," Tyler questions me.

I shake my head. "No no. Matty and I aren't exclusive. I can still date other people if I want. If I find someone. No biggie."

"Right," Tyler says nodding slowly, not buying a word of it.

If I can't convince other people Matty and I aren't a couple, how can I convince myself? To be honest, I miss him so much. I haven't talked to him since he left, and my bed feels so empty. I wish I could snuggle up to him and just sleep for hours. I'm tired and I need him with me.

Fuck it. I take out my phone and text him.

Miss u. Can't wait till 2mro 2 c u. P.S. Mel is doing my bro. ;p

I flip my cell shut and follow Mel and Ty inside the house.

We immediately greet the family with hugs and kisses. This is how Mel's family does it, even if you don't know every single one of them. It takes about an hour to say hello when you arrive and about an hour to say goodbye. It's considered very rude not to follow this tradition. And I sure as hell don't want to be the white girl to offend them. Although, after twenty-two years of being an honorary member of Mel's family, I don't think they consider me the white girl anymore.

After hugging every aunt, uncle, cousin, and grandma, we finally meet up with Mel's mom.

"Melissa, thank God you're finally here. I need your help in the kitchen," Mel's mom says. She gives her mom a kiss on the cheek and disappears down the hall. So different from my mom. Mel is actually happy to see her. "Hi, Shelly, thanks for coming. It's so nice to see you as always. And, Tyler, look at you. You've grown into such a handsome man. I'm glad you could join us too. Now make sure you grab a plate and get plenty to eat. Okay." Plenty to eat. Did you hear that? I can eat as much as I want.

Tyler and I both share a hug with Mel's mom. "Thanks for having us," I tell her. "I can't wait to get my hands on some tamales. Did you make some sweet ones this year?"

"Especially for you," she tells me, poking her finger on my nose. Oh, I could hug her again. Why can't my mother love me like this? She just poked me on the nose. Aww. I think Mel's parents forget we're grown adults sometimes. But it's very endearing. At least she didn't tell me I'm fat and try to stiff me with a salad plate.

Tyler and I take turns opening our tamales and ridding them of the wax paper and cornhusks. We both get some rice and beans too. This is a whole different kind of deliciousness. I loved my mom's cooking yesterday, but it's Mel's family cooking I crave every year.

"There're a few seats right there." I gesture to Tyler and he follows me.

"Is Mel gonna eat with us?" he asks.

"Not if she wants to live." I shove a mouthful of rice and beans in my mouth. Oh goodness, I don't need Matty. I want to fill my bedroom with this stuff and eat it all night, making snow angels in a bed of refried beans. "She'll be in there for awhile, flipping tortillas and making eggs. I'm not quite sure when all the women eat. I guess they just eat and cook at the same time."

"Why do you get to eat?"

"Because I'm a guest." I take another bite of my tamale. I'm in love.

Tyler still hasn't touched his food. He looks in the kitchen. From where we're sitting we can see Mel hovering over the stove, and chatting with the ladies.

"Ty, just eat. She's fine. This is time for all of them to catch up. They actually enjoy it." I pause, gazing up at the ceiling in thought. Considering the latest events with Nick, this probably isn't very enjoyable for Mel. "Most of the time anyway. Eat, and I'll go check on her in a minute."

Tyler looks like he's about to consume his last meal. Give me a break. They were together one effing night and he's already pussy-whipped. What a wimp my brother is.

I suck down the rest of my food and walk into the hen's den, leaving my brother alone to pout like a lovesick puppy.

"Hola, chicas," I say, as I throw my plate in the trash. "How you all doing?"

Mel looks at me with a plea for help. "My aunties here are grilling me on the details of my wonderful divorce."

"Cool. So are we all in agreement the settlement should include Nick getting his balls chopped off?" I chuckle, but the others aren't laughing. Ha, they would be if this was dinnertime. But it's breakfast and we all haven't started drinking yet. Unless you count the Bloody Marys, but I think the men are the only ones throwing those back.

"Nice try, Shel, but in this house, apparently it is my fault Nick was screwing a woman at work. I must not have been doing enough to keep my husband satisfied," Mel sneers as she flips tortillas.

"Oh."

"Yeah, they also think I'm going to go into the poorhouse because I can't possibly take care of myself." Mel is seething mad right now.

"That's not true. Mel and I make the same amount and I live on my own just fine. Plus, Nick knows how much an asshole he is so he left her with plenty of money. She doesn't even need to work," I try to explain.

"That's what I tried to tell them," she cries out, tossing the warm tortillas in a dish on the counter.

One of her aunts throws her hands up. "Ay, what will the church say?"

"I don't give a rat's ass what the church says," Mel yells. "If the church is so concerned about my marriage, why didn't they pray my husband would keep his dick in his pants?" She throws a towel on the counter and walks away.

"Ooo, you're in trouble now," I say as I follow her out.

Mel sits down next to Tyler and takes a tamale off his plate. "It's about time you get to eat," he says.

She chomps off a piece and utters through a mouthful, "That's what I'm saying. They can handle the rest." She breaks off a corner of the masa and dips it into Tyler's beans. "How long have we been here?" she asks.

Tyler looks at his watch. "Almost two hours." He holds out his plate to her as she finishes chowing down.

"Long enough. Let's go," she announces wiping her hands and face with her apron.

I put my hand on her shoulder. "Melly, calm down. It's Christmas. You haven't even opened presents with your family. And your dad hasn't stopped by yet." Mel's dad is a police officer, and he's on duty. At anytime he could stop in to wish the family a happy holidays and I know she wouldn't want to miss it.

She leans back in her chair with a sigh. "We'll stay till my dad gets here, and then we're gonna go."

We both nod in agreement.

Tyler asks, "Mel, you want me to fix you something else? You didn't eat much."

"Are you kidding? Do you want them to talk more shit? If anything, I should have fixed your plate," she complains. "Did you guys get something to drink? I need some wine."

"I'll get the drinks," I offer.

When I get back from pouring Mel a glass of wine and digging up two beers for Tyler and me, she's explaining to him the archaic ideals her family has about how women are supposed to serve their men. Mel rarely served Nick. They always just got their own stuff. But it's not like Nick would have wanted her to anyway. He's not very traditional in that sense. And Ty won't be either. He will surely take care of all her needs before he ever tends to his own.

Limiting myself to one beer sucks, but Mel needs the booze more than I do. I guess being the designated driver has its perks though. I don't have to worry about peeing every fifteen minutes. Once the seal is broken, it's like a never-ending flood, and Mel has made many trips to the little girl's room to prove it.

"Daddy's here," Mel's mom tells us as she passes by.

We walk outside and as usual, Mel's dad is flashing lights and blaring different sirens. He does this for all the little kids. I can remember getting so excited when we were young and he'd put on a show. Actually, it still is a bit thrilling.

Growing up with Mel as a best friend kept us out of a lot of trouble. There were many times when we were about to do something stupid and the thought of getting arrested by one of her dad's friends, or worse, her dad, was enough to make us do the right thing. We were by no means angels, but we did opt out of some good times in fear of Mel's dad. But we opted in on some good times to piss off my mother.

"Hi, honey, Merry Christmas," Mel's dad says as he heads our way. He stops in front of her and hugs her with a tear in his eye. Daddy's little girl. Always.

"Hi, Daddy," she says, wrapping her arms around him. "Merry Christmas to you. Wish you could stay and enjoy it."

"Sorry honey, you know the drill," he says. "Hey, Shel, hey, Tyler. Good to see you." He hugs me and shakes Ty's hand. "I'm gonna go see your mother. Come for dinner next week, okay?" Mel nods, and he finds Mel's mom waiting for him on the porch.

We all look at Mel's parents in awe. After all these years, they still look like they fell in love just yesterday.

"I want a man to look at me like that," I say, not even realizing my words are said aloud.

"You already have one, beeyotch. You're just being a frickin' pansy about it," she scolds me. I don't have time to respond because she whips off her apron and tosses it at one of her little cousins. "Okay, let's go before anyone notices."

"We can't. We have to say goodbye to everybody," I remind her.

"Forget it. I'll call my mom in a few and tell her Tyler had diarrhea and we had to leave quickly."

Tyler gives her a questioning look. "Why do I have to be the one to get the shits? Did you see how much Shel ate? That would be more believable."

"Gee thanks big, bro."

"Who cares. Shel, go get our bags and meet us at the car. Don't let anyone stop you to talk. You need to do this shit Mission Impossible style or we'll never get out of here."

We're finally home and it's only then when I get a text back from Matty. It's about time.

Miss u 2. I'll b bk 2nite.

Chapter Fourteen

"Matty's coming home," I sing. "Matty's coming home." I chant this as I run around the living room. I jump up on my ottoman and do the Cabbage Patch dance as Mel and Tyler stare at me from the sofa. "Matty's coming home." Out of breath, I have to stop doing the Running Man. I collapse to the floor and try to calm myself.

"Maybe we should go to your place," Tyler says to Mel.

"No way. I want you to meet him," I say.

"Um. I don't think so. I really don't want to be a room away from my baby sister doing the nasty."

Mel chimes in, "They're not doing it." He looks at her confused. "I know. It's this agreement they have. And you gotta remember. They're not a couple." She holds up her air quotes for emphasis.

An hour later, Matty arrives bearing gifts. Four pints of Ben & Jerry's ice cream, all in different flavors. Mel and I fight over the Chocolate Fudge Brownie. I win since my *friend* brought the goods. She takes the Cherry Garcia. Matty let's Tyler choose from the last two, and he goes for some cookie dough brownie concoction. Matty is left with a mint Oreo duo.

"Damn, sis, tell the guy you love him already." Tyler says, devouring his ice cream. "I do."

"Ha ha," Matty chuckles. "She told you, huh?"

"Mel did," Tyler responds.

"So what's going on with you two anyway?" Matty asks them.

But I answer. "About twenty years of pent-up sexual tension, finally released. It was bound to happen eventually, I guess."

Matty slides the spoon from his mouth, and I want to taste his lips right now. "It's funny how you talk about it, Shel. It doesn't bother you that your bestie and your brother are hooking up?" I shake my head. Of course not. "But I doubt Tyler would let his best friend anywhere near his little sister."

"No fucking way. I'd kill him," Ty says, with a loud chuckle.

"You guys are funny. You look alike and you have the same choice of words," Matty tells us. We do look alike. We have the same green eyes, small nose, and brownish hair, although, his is a little more on the blond side. I have more freckles than he does though, on my nose and under my eyes, if you look really close. Ty has none. He got the height though, taking after my dad. My petite frame came from my mom.

Mel loves his perfectly gelled hair, and the tiny mole he has under his right eye.

I've never really thought about the way we talk though. Pretty soon, Matty's going to be cursing every other word too.

"So, you're my sister's friend? Not her boyfriend, but you stay over every night?" Tyler begins the inquisition.

"I guess you could put it like that," Matty says.

I toss a pillow at Ty. "What are you? Dad, or something?"

"It's okay Shel," Matty says, patting my leg.

"Well, it just seems a little weird you're here with her every day. You're not having sex, supposedly. And you're okay with her going out with other guys. It's just odd," Tyler continues.

"It's not like she's gone out with anyone I need to be worried about."

I butt in, "But I could if I wanted to."

"Sure," he pats my leg again.

"Why do you say it like that? You don't think I can find a decent guy to go out with me? Someone who would be worthy enough to make you worry?" I ask him.

Matty responds, "It's not like that, Shel. I think plenty of guys would want to go out with you, but it's not like you're looking. And look at Jacob, you didn't even give him a chance. Not that I wanted you to. I just don't think you're really into finding someone else."

"Yeah, you should have seen her last night. My mom tried to hook her up with some guy in a suit and Shel scared him away with talk about beer bongs," Ty explains through a light laugh.

"I didn't mention beer bongs, that was Mel," I remind him.

Mel giggles. "No, you said something about shotgunning a beer. That's much worse."

Matty laughs with the rest of them, shaking his head. "See what I mean," he says.

"Fine, when you least expect it, I'm gonna go out with some hot guy who will have you shitting your pants with nerves that I'll choose him over you."

"Go for it," he tells me, and kisses the top of my head. My heart melts, and I realize Matty's not going to have to worry about crapping in his pants anytime soon. I'm just as wimpy as my bro and I haven't even gotten laid yet.

"This is some really good ice cream, Matt," Mel says. "Thanks so much. It totally hit the spot." My best friend is trying to squash the conversation, like Matty did with the peck to my head. I'm grateful to her. I wouldn't call it an argument but it's as close as we've come to one.

Tyler looks over at her. "Did you finish the whole thing already?"

"No," she replies. "But I'm going to."

I think about my mother. "I probably shouldn't. My mother's giving me an effing complex," I say as I swirl the ice cream around in the container.

"Why?" Matty asks.

Tyler answers, "My mom told her she's getting fat."

"No, you're not," Matty says, taking offense to my mother's words. If he's going to stick around, he's going to have to get used to it. After a pause, he continues, "And it wouldn't matter if you did."

"Good answer," Mel tells him.

"I haven't been working out lately. I need to start running again," I say.

"I'm in," Mels says through a mouthful of Cherry Garcia.

"Me too," Matty adds.

Tyler adds, "I'll run with you for a few days, but then I'm heading back home."

"What happens with you two then? When you go back home?" I ask.

Mel and Tyler look at each other. They both shrug. "Nothing, I guess," Mel responds.

"Things go back to the way they were," Tyler agrees.

"Well that's jacked up," I tell them.

Mel puts her hand up, "Don't go making a big deal out of this, Shel. We got it handled."

Matty and I leave the two fuckbirds alone when we finally finish our pints of ice cream. And yes, I finished mine. So what if I've gained a few pounds. I'm not borderline obese or anything. At a very comfortable size six, I'm anything but.

Once the door is shut, I hook my fingers in the waistline of Matty's shorts and pull him toward me. I put my arms around him and run my hands up and down his back, feeling his muscles beneath his shirt. He runs his fingers through my hair and I look up at him.

"I really missed you," I tell him.

"Me too." He cups my face in his hands and leans down to cover my mouth with his. Our lips lock together again and again. He doesn't go for the tongue right away. Instead, he puckers his cool minty lips to mine, and I taste the sweetness.

"So are you ready for your Christmas present?" he asks, with a soft kiss to the tip of my nose.

I pout. "Hey, I thought we weren't going to do gifts?"

He nods. "I know, I know. Don't get too excited though. It's more like a gag gift."

I practically do the Cabbage Patch again, "Cool, I got you one, too."

I run to my closet and come back with a giant box of Rice Krispies Treats with a big red bow on top. Matty's eyes light up like I just gave him his very first tricycle. "Look, there're ninety of these little suckers in there, enough for the rest of the school year."

He hooks his arm around my neck and presses his lips hard to mine, pulling away with a "muah" sound. "Thank you, Shelly, I love it."

Then, he goes to his bag and unzips the side pocket. He comes back with a wrapped box the size of a sandwich.

He places it in my hands and gestures for me to open it. I tear the paper, and my mouth drops in surprise. I've always wanted one of these. My eyes well up. Something so simple can also be so thoughtful.

I stand on my tiptoes to pucker up for him. He bends down to meet my lips. "Thank you, Matty. Every time I use this I'll think of you."

"Well, that'll be everyday," he says teasingly of the orange slicer he bought me. He sets his box down and takes the kitchen gadget from my hands and places it on my dresser, then reels me in for another hug, lifting me off the floor and leaving my feet dangling in the air.

"Let's get ready for bed," I tell him.

We go through the routine of me using the bathroom first. I brush my hair and my teeth, and wash my face. I put on a soft cotton tank nightgown and walk outside. He's already in his boxers lying on top of the comforter, looking beautiful, and already dozing off. Poor guy is probably beat after such a long day.

I put my hand on his leg. "Matty, it's your turn."

He opens his eyes, and smiles at me. "Be right back."

When he returns to bed, he throws his big arm over me and slides me across the bed to him. I love it when he does this. It's likely I purposely lie down on the other side of the bed just so he can reel me in every night. I snuggle in with my back to him. He squeezes me tight and kisses my neck.

"I missed this so much. I'm getting very used to having you in my bed," I tell him.

"Is that a bad thing?" he asks.

I put my hand on his, as he holds me. "I don't think so."

"I think we're doing things the right way, Shel," he says into my ear.

"What do you mean?"

"We know we can sleep together and be content. As much as I want to make love to you, it's nice to know our relationship is based on more."

"I get it. Like when I was missing you, I missed your presence, your smile, your hugs, and just talking to you. It's not like I needed you because I was horny." We both let out a low chuckle. "I'm worried about Mel. I don't think she and my brother thought this through very well. I think she's going to be hurt when he leaves."

"Maybe. But she's a big girl. She knew what she was getting into. Maybe she wanted a little attention without having to have another husband right away. Maybe this will be good for her." He kisses my shoulder and starts to bring his hands up to my breasts. And then he pauses. "Do you hear that?"

We're still as possums trying to play dead. I try to focus on listening. "Oh son of a … fuck." I need to get a new bed frame for the guest bedroom. The creaking sounds are killing me. "I should have sent them to her house. How the hell am I supposed to … exist … listening to that?" We're silent as we listen again. "I need earplugs."

Matty reaches over for the remote on the end table. He turns on the TV and increases the volume. "There. Better?"

"I think I should take some Benadryl to knock myself out."

"Turn around and let me help clear your mind."

I whirl around and face Matty. "Umm ... sounds perfect."

He runs his hand along my side and just the touch of his fingertips makes me feel lightheaded. He cups my ass and warmth spreads from between my thighs down to my toes. Working his way back up to give some attention to my breasts, he pauses and I hold my breath in anticipation. We gaze at each other, lustful, wanting more but knowing we're not ready for the next step. Not just yet.

And definitely not right now. As much as I want him, I'm fighting to keep my eyes open.

"Matty, there's nothing I want more than to get naked with you and make out like we only have five minutes to live … "

"But … ," he says.

"I'm so tired," I cry out.

"Oh, Shel, I'm fucking exhausted from the drive," he sighs. "We should have come to bed a long time ago." He falls to his back, I rest my head on his shoulder and wrap my arm around his waist.

"Hold on," I say. I reach my face to his, and plant a kiss on his lips. "Good night, Matty."

"Good night, Shel." My lips brush his once more before I scoot down to my spot.

I get comfortable again, with my cheek pressed to his broad chest, and my hand resting in the band of his boxer briefs. He strokes my hair gently until I fall asleep watching very loud reruns of Friends on the TV.

Chapter Fifteen

A knock on the door wakes me from my night of peaceful rest. I hate to think I need a man to be happy, but I sure do sleep a hell of a lot better when Matty is next to me.

"Yeah," I yell. Matty moves around and throws his arm and leg across me. The feel of his warm skin on me causes me to sting with wanting. I could spend all day kissing these arms and legs and never get bored. His strong arms and big hands make me feel so protected. His muscular thighs and bulging calves, I could explore them inch by inch taking in the flicker of sunlight on the coarse golden hair of his sunkissed legs. He's beautiful.

"Wanna go to breakfast?" Tyler yells, bringing me back to reality.

Matty opens one eye to look at me. He licks his lips and I'm thinking we should pass on breakfast. He tilts his head questioning. I shrug. He says, "Why not? Let's spend time with your brother before he goes back." Damn it. He's right.

"Give us a half hour," I shout to my brother.

I hear his footsteps walking down the hall.

"How did you sleep?" Matty asks, pulling me closer to him and pressing his warm hard body against mine.

"Like a baby." I cuddle into him, spooning him like we've just made love.

"Me too." He kisses my neck. I tilt my head to give him full access. He brushes my hair aside and I feel his tongue trace along the side of my throat before a row of kisses line my shoulder. "I don't want to get up."

"Too late," I tell him rubbing my behind against his friend who is bidding me hello.

"Hey, that's just nature talking. Morning wood," he releases a slight chuckle.

As much as I want to stay right where I'm at, we're running out of time. So I roll over and off the bed. "Yeah, that's what they all say."

When we get to our favorite eatin' place, Matty runs in to a few of his buddies from college. We ask them to join us, and they do. So now's there're six of us crowded into a horseshoe-shaped booth.

The waitress comes around to take our orders and I order a classic ham and cheese omelet with a side of home fries and biscuits and gravy. Okay, so my mother's comment did not have her desired effect. I'm still eating like usual. Maybe I will try to squeeze in a run later.

"So you guys are a bunch of geniuses, huh? If you went to CM," Mel tries to make small talk.

The guys grin at each other, shrugging off the compliment.

Matty answers for them. "I wouldn't say geniuses. We all just studied a lot in high school and had high test scores. No different from you."

"Haha, you must have heard some lies about these two," Tyler weighs in. "They did anything but study. Unless you call keg parties and making out in the back row of movie theaters, studying."

"That's so not true," I say. "We didn't have kegs at the parties, just lots of bottles, and it wasn't always the last row."

"And don't forget drunken football games," Tyler adds.

"Hey, we were pretty tame though. Mel's dad's a cop so we couldn't have too much fun," I say, laughing.

Everyone begins to share their crazy high school and college moments. Matty woke up in his own vomit after his first frat party. Mel lost her underwear at a park her senior year. Jason almost made out with a dude who he thought was a girl in Hollywood. He says there's not a day that goes by he doesn't thank Matty for getting him out of that mess. He didn't exactly share how he got into the situation in the first place but I'd love to hear the full story sometime. Jackson reminds them of a time they went to a nudie bar and one of the girls had toilet paper stuck to her crotch. Wow! That has to turn a fella on. Tyler says his worst memory is walking in on Chase and me having sex in my bedroom. Why he chooses to tell that story is beyond me. I have to remind myself to kick his ass later.

"Want me to sock him, Shel?" Mel asks me from across the table.

"Yes, preferably in the balls," I reply.

Our food comes and we make small talk through bites of a mouth-watering breakfast. Matty's friends mesh well with us and they're not too hard on the eyes either. Jason is short and stocky, but lean at the same time. With very blond curly hair, green eyes, and dark tanned skin, he looks like he belongs on a surfboard. I suppose his board shorts and Hurley shirt lend itself to that theory. He has very soft features and dimples when he smiles. I seriously can't picture this guy in an office all day.

When we finish our food, we all have disgusted looks on our faces. My stomach is so stuffed, there's no way I can run today, or maybe even tomorrow. What I need is a nap.

"Son of a shithole, I don't think I need to eat for another week," I tell the group.

"I second that," Matty says, patting his belly.

"Thankfully, I haven't found a place as good as this at home or I'd be a hundred pounds heavier," Tyler says.

We all sit and chat, letting our food settle, telling more horror stories from the past.

Then Jackson asks, "So how long have you been dating Fuller?"

"Oh, we're not dating," Matty says. I wasn't even going to go there, but whatever.

"Really?" Jackson says.

Matty and I both say, "Really."

"So you wouldn't mind if I asked Shel out then?" he questions Matty.

Matty gestures to me, "Be my guest."

"Well, thanks for your permission, Dad," I say, sarcastically.

"So what do you say, Shel? How about we go out for dinner?" Jackson asks me.

The entire table silently awaits my answer. I glance at Mel, who has a raised brow. My brother puts his head down. Matty looks straight ahead.

"Yeah, why not?" I answer. Jackson is just the type of hot guy who might finally have Matty worried. I just wish the hot guy wasn't one of his friends.

"Cool," Jackson says, "I'll get your number from Fuller."

"Well, I'll look forward to hearing from you," I manage to say. What the heck did I just do? I take a long sip of my water.

"Shall we go then?" Tyler asks, thankfully breaking the awkward silence.

Mel and I both say, "Sounds good."

We make our way out of the booth, Tyler and Matty take care of the bill, we say our farewells, and we're out.

Mel texts me on our way home to tell me they're going back to her place. Great, just what I need right now. Some alone time with the friend slash unofficial boyfriend. Well, that *was* what I wanted but now I'm not so sure. I'm such an idiot.

"Are you going to say anything?" he asks me, after we buckle up in the car. "Stop worrying, Shel. I'm not angry." He puts his hand on mine and squeezes.

"How can you not be? I'm even angry with me." He was right. I really had no intention of looking for someone else to date. And Jacob just happened to be a little blip. But now, I'm going out with one of Matty's friends. That's an all time low for me.

He looks straight ahead as he drives, every so often glancing over at me, and still holding my hand. "Don't be. I'm cool with this, really."

"Why?" I don't get how this doesn't bother him. I'd be having a fit if he was going out with another girl.

"You need to do this. Jacob wasn't really a date. And you're still afraid what we have is just a rebound. I know it's not, but you don't. Go out with other guys, and see what happens. If you feel something for someone else, then I was wrong. You were right. I just don't want you to play the 'what if' game. Figure it out. We can't move forward till you do."

I mull this over in my head. Matty is right again. I'm fairly certain I already know what I'm going to find out, but I'm happy he's given me the chance to work it through on my own. Jackson is just the kind of guy to help too. He's really good-looking and he doesn't work with me.

"I do have one stipulation though," he says. "I don't mind if you go out with Jackson or whoever else a few times, but if it gets to the point where you get physical, you have to tell me. You can't expect me to sleep with you every night when you're having sex with someone else."

I turn to him, putting my hand on top of his. "I can't imagine even kissing someone other than you, and you think I'm going to go off screwing someone." Tears start to fill my eyes. I know I'm being silly, but it almost feels like we're breaking up, even though I know we're not *together*. This whole situation is just odd, and I feel miles away from Matty when he's sitting right next to me.

We pull up to the front of my house, he gets out, and comes to my door. I get out and he scoops me up in a tight hold. He whispers in my ear, "I don't think you want to screw anyone. I just want to be clear of my feelings. I love you, Shelly, and I'm willing to let you go so you can love me back."

"But what if I already do?" I mutter into his neck.

"Again, I don't want ifs, Shel. I need you to be as confident as I am. And when you are, all this bullshit will be worth it."

As we walk up the pathway to my condo, I tell him, "You're going to feel like a dumb ass when your friend sweeps me off my feet and we end up in Vegas."

He chuckles a bit before saying, "I'll risk it."

Chapter Sixteen

Jackson called. Two days after we all went out to breakfast. I think this is a bad idea, but I'm going anyway.

When Matty and I started our little fling, I knew I had strong feelings for him. He was my close friend and we got along so well. I was unsure though. Unsure if the strength of those feelings was based on my attraction to him as a friend or as a boyfriend. Or maybe I was attracted to him because he was attracted to me and Chase had just dumped me after ten years. It's always a boost to the ego for someone to show interest in you after such a nightmare.

All right, my feelings for Matt Fuller are about more than him just boosting my ego. He's a great guy and I've never had such a good time with anyone in my life, including Chase. Matty knows more about me than I know about myself half the time, and understands all the little things that make me tick. I feel so alive when I'm with him. I don't know. This whole thing is just too effing crazy to even believe. What kind of guy sends his girl on a date with someone else?

I consider what he told me. He loves me enough to let me go—very sweet—do I deserve a guy who loves me in such a way? He deserves a girl who will tell him she loves him so much she doesn't need to be let go.

"So where are you going?" Mel yells to me.

From the closet, I shout back, "Yard House. I'm meeting him there."

"Meeting him. You're already dooming this date before it starts."

I come out in fitted jeans and a black dolmon top with a silver tank underneath. "Is this too much? Does it make me look like I want him?"

"Why don't you just cancel?" she asks. "Don't you think it's rude you're totally using this guy? You know it's not gonna work and you're gonna run back to Matt."

"I'm not using him," I squeal. "I'm totally gonna give this a shot and if it doesn't work, then I get to prove to Matty I really like him and want to be with him."

Mel picks out a string of beads and hands them to me. "Are you trying to prove it to Matty or yourself?"

"STFU, Mel." I flip her the bird. She knows me too effing well.

"Well, you look great. So you better hurry up and get going. The man *not* of your dreams awaits."

"Oh he's the man of my dreams all right. I've been thinking about Jackson for the last two nights."

Mel pushes my bag into my hands and starts walking me down the hall. "Those were your nightmares, Shel, not your dreams."

We both laugh at her joke. "Bitch!"

"Have fun. But not too much fun, because I don't care if you decide to marry this guy. He's not going with us to the New Year's Eve party tomorrow."

"If I have too much fun, I may not want to go to the fucking party. So take that," I snap at her.

"Bye, Shel."

I flip her off again as I walk to my car.

I walk into heaven, take a deep breath and head to the bar. I always eat in the bar area at the Yard House. I figure the closer you are to the bar, the quicker you get your drinks. It's not necessary tonight though. I'm driving so I will stick to my one-beer limit.

My eyes take in the crowd and I spot a hand going up. Jackson. He has a booth. Perfect. We can sit across a large table from each other.

My stomach tightens as I get closer to him, and my smile is so fake I hope I don't look like I put Vaseline on my teeth.

Jackson stands to greet me and I get a good look at his outfit. This man has some style. He has on perfectly fitted jeans slung low across his waist, but not so low he needs to wear a pair of basketball shorts to cover his ass. A dress shirt is barely visible under a soft, maybe cashmere, V-neck sweater. His sleeves are pushed up revealing a dragon tat on his very muscular forearm. He's even better looking than I remembered.

"Hi, Shelly, great to see you again." He comes toward me for a hug, and kisses me on the cheek. Oh, okay. He's just a hair taller than me and I notice his blue eyes. They're not as striking as Matty's. A little dull, but pretty all the same.

"Nice to see you too," I say, sliding into the booth.

I smile like a circus clown because I don't know what else to do or say. Instead, I steal glances at his short dark hair. He's working one of those messy but styled looks.

Jackson finally breaks the silence. "I ordered us a few beers and the spinach dip to start off with. I hope you don't mind."

"Oh, sounds great. I've had the dip before. Good stuff." I nod in agreement.

The server stops by with our drinks. "Two Honey Blondes," she says, putting the pints on the table.

Are you effing kidding me? HONEY BLONDES! Son of a bitch on a stick.

"Excuse me one second," I say, slipping out of the booth.

I charge to the bathroom and fling open the door. Setting my bag on the sink, I dig around for my cell and yank it open.

HONEY BLONDE! He ordrd me a HONEY BLONDE! Cld thr b a weaker beer! R U FUCKING w/ me? Risk, my ass! u knw this wldnt work. Now get me out of it!

I snap the cell shut, and stare at my reflection in the mirror. What have I gotten myself into? Poor Jackson. I need to find him a woman. Someone who prefers weak ass beer.

I don't wait for Matty to text back. I'm going to kick his ass when I see him.

I weave through the crowds and back to Jackson.

"Sorry about that," I tell him. "Now, where were we?"

"I already got started on the dip. It's delicious. You should try it."

Anything that will get me out of small talk. I take a chip and scoop up some cheesy spinach. The server comes by to check on us again. "How we doing here?

Can I get you anything? Refill for you?" She gestures to Jackson.

I notice his beer is drained. I push my completely full pint toward him. "How about you take mine." I turn to the server, "Can I get a the darkest beer you have?" I smile. "Thanks."

"So," Jackson begins, "You're a teacher. How do you like it?"

"I love it actually. It never gets old, that's for sure. Every year is a new beginning with a new set of kids. Come to think of it, each period is a new beginning. Each class is just so different. It's like Forest Gump."

He gulps some of his brew. "How so?"

"You know, box of chocolates … yada yada." I stuff my mouth with spinach dip.

"Got it," he says, with a light chuckle. He'd be so cute if he didn't have that nasty beer in his hands. May as well be a wine cooler. I should give him Jacob's number.

The server brings over my beer and I almost hug her. Instead, I just say, "Thank you," and take the glass from her hand before it even makes it to the table. I take a swig and my belly gets warm with happiness.

"So what do you do, Jackson?" I ask.

"I'm an attorney," he says. "Corporate law. I wanted to get into engineering, but after awhile, it seemed a bit monotonous. I liked being on the debate team in high school, so law became the next obvious choice."

"Cool," I tell him. "Mel's ex-husband is a lawyer. He cheated on her with another lawyer at his firm and now they're getting married."

"Wow." He takes another drink of his beer, draining the second one. This guy drinks more than I do.

"You're not sleeping with any married partners are you?" I ask, trying to make a joke. "Holy shit."

"What? What's wrong?" Jackson asks, concerned.

"Speak of the asshole. That's Nick. Mel's ex."

He looks around as if Nick is going to have a tattoo on his forehead that says *I'm the asshole prick who cheated on my wife*.

"I haven't seen him in a long time. He didn't even notice me," I explain.

Jackson starts to scoot out of the booth. "My turn. I'll be right back."

I stare at Nick until he meets my glare. If only he could read minds. *Motherfucker!*

Oh shit. He's coming over.

"Hi, Shelly," he says. "I know you probably don't want to talk to me, but I just wanted to say hello."

"You're right, I don't want to talk to you," I sneer. I lean to get a look at the female sitting with him. "So is that the bimbo you're gonna marry?"

"Well, enjoy your date," he says, ignoring my dig, and turns to walk away.

It's like a light bulb flips on. "Wait." He turns back around. "I need you to do something for me." His face contorts giving me a look like I have crap smeared all over my face. "You owe it to me for all the shit I've had to deal with. I need to get out of here. So when the guy comes back, I need you to come over and say something to get me to leave." He rolls his eyes at me, and I slam my hand on the table. "Just do it!"

He struts away. Fucker.

The server and Jackson return at the same time. "Are you ready to order?" she asks.

"Can you give us just a few more minutes? I haven't looked at the menu." I won't feel so bad when I suddenly get sick and need to leave, if we haven't ordered yet. But once we do, I'm in this. Stuck.

Jackson takes his menu too and we both sit in silence.

"Excuse me, Shelly." I look up and Nick is standing there. God Bless him. He's still an asshole, but he's here. "I'm sorry to interrupt your dinner. I need to ask you a favor."

I introduce Jackson and Nick continues. "I just talked to Melissa and she's not doing too well. I thought you were with her and she'd be okay, but you're here. So I thought maybe you could go check on her."

"*Now*," I say, trying to sound offended.

"Yes, now. I'm pretty sure she needs you." He doesn't say anything else. He goes back to his table and pretends he's not a total dick. Good deed or not, he's still the biggest loser I know.

"I'm sorry, Jackson. I gotta go," I tell him, rushing to stand. "I'm all Mel has now, so I have to see what's going on."

"I understand. I hope everything is all right," he says.

"I'll see you," I mumble, as I practically run out.

I think I hear him say, "Call me."

When I get on the road, I make two calls.

First, I call Mel.

"Guess who just got me out of my date?" I ask, when she picks up.

"Who?"

I explain my horror story with Jackson and Honey Blondes, and then go on to tell her about how I told Nick he owed me.

"It's about time that shithead is good for something," she says, and we both laugh.

"By the way, I can't believe that woman. She looks like he pulled her out of a JC Penney catalog. Could she be more plain?" I tell her, hoping to make her happy.

"I know right," she replies with a giggle.

"You were too much sizzle for him. He can only handle the mild sauce," I tease.

"Uh huh," she agrees. "If you can't stand the heat, get the fuck out the kitchen."

"Amen," I say. "One more thing, Mel."

"What happened?" she asks anxiously.

"He got fat," I squeal.

"Yes!" she yells.

We both start busting up until I'm gasping for breath and Mel is snorting.

And then, I call Matty. I could kick his ass right now.

He answers in a playful tone, "Are you on your way to Vegas yet?"

Chapter Seventeen

It's New Year's Eve and I'm not so sure I want to go out with Matty tonight after the crap he pulled yesterday. He had a great time, along with Mel and Tyler, talking crap about how I may have missed out on a real hunk of a man just because of his piss-poor choice in beer. I could have choked him.

But who am I kidding? Of course, I want to go out with him tonight.

We convinced Ty to stay till the end of break, so he'll be joining us for the festivities this evening too, which happens to be a work party. Matty and I haven't gone anywhere together publically, where people know who we are. This should be interesting and is sure to create a lot of gossip among our colleagues. Or maybe not. It's not like we're going to walk in holding hands and make out in a corner or something. Maybe people will assume we're just friends like we've always been.

And it's not like we RSVP'd together, as a couple. Mel actually responded for all of us.

Oh well, who cares? We're just going to go—the four of us—and have a good time. Shit, I totally overthink this stuff *all* the time.

Chase is going to be there. He hasn't invaded my thoughts all vacation, and now …

Forget it. I'm not going to say anymore.

"Oh my, you guys look frickin' adorable!" I say to Tyler and Mel, when we arrive at her place to pick them up.

"That's not really the look we were going for," Tyler shrugs. "But we'll take it." He throws his arm around Mel's neck and hooks her in for a kiss.

"Oh, even more adorable," I squeal. Matty makes gagging sounds at my comments. We all let out a quick chuckle.

When you go to a pajama party, there're really only two ways to go: slutty or cozy. I always opt for cozy. There's no way I'm going to go to a party with a bunch of co-workers looking like a prostitute. Plus, we always end up drinking way beyond tipsy and acting ridiculous. I'd rather risk acting like a fool in comfortable clothing where my tits aren't hanging out. So I'm wearing my typical PJs—cropped jammy pants and a tank. Matty's wearing one of his college tees and some Family Guy boxers, with some boxer briefs underneath—I checked. I don't want his junk hanging out there for the world to see.

Against The Wall

Tyler and Mel really do look cute. He's wearing plaid flannel pajama pants—the ones my mom gave him for Christmas—with a wife beater. She's wearing the coordinating plaid pajama top, which is too long for her but she has some little booty shorts on underneath. They're matching for crying out loud. What a great idea. I wish I had thought of it. But then again, I doubt I would have asked Matty to wear similar outfits to a work party.

Like always, we're late. Parking ten houses down and across the street is evidence of that. I think we got lucky with a spot not too far away. Someone must have left and we snagged it before they could get back, because familiar cars line the road even further from us. This party is going to be huge.

The party is mostly filled with my English department colleagues. Teaching English can really facilitate the need to party. Reading paper after paper written by kids in high school who still can't decipher when to use to, too, and two or who still don't know A LOT is two words is a joke. Couple that with this insane era of technology and the need for students to write like they're sending a text message or updating their Twitter status can really drive a person to drink. Heavily. Hence my well-stocked refrigerator full of beer.

Julie Prestsater

Maybe one day, I'll just have a keg and a beer tap installed in my kitchen. I can totally picture it, a tap right next to the sink. Or a button on the fridge dispenser: ice, cold water, or Heffeweizen. Imagine it. I should patent that shit before someone steals my idea.

As we walk around and say hello, I notice there're a few people from each of the other departments sprinkled in. Mostly people my age, but some of the oldie but goodies came, the ones that can hang. Actually, some of the oldies can party harder and longer than the rest of us.

Matty and Tyler veer off from us to get drinks. Mel and I take a seat outside with some friends.

"Hey ladies," we all seem to say in unison. They stand up, and hugs all around.

Before our asses hit our chairs, Margo asks, "So Mel, who's the hot guy who was all over you when you walked in?" Here we go.

"He *is* pretty fucking hot, huh," Mel begins. My smile fades, and I roll my eyes. This is my big brother she's talking about. "His name is Tyler and I got him for Christmas." I grin. She's funny, even if she is talking about my own flesh and blood. I'd probably do the same.

"Damn, I need to have a talk with Santa," Jessica says. "All I got was a new cardigan. I hope you're enjoying your present."

"Oh, I am," Mel responds, fluttering her brows. "I've enjoyed him quite a few times actually."

The girls fling their heads back with howls.

"Okay, enough," I shout, throwing my hands up.

"What's wrong Shelly? Santa didn't bring you a man for Christmas?" Jessica says, pouting her face.

"I thought Fuller might've been your present," Margo says, with a questioning stare. She raises a brow at me. I'd love to give in and stake my claim on Matty, but I can't.

I look at Mel, not knowing what to say. "Ah, she's just pissed cause I'm talking nasty about her brother," she changes the subject for me.

"That hottie is your brother?" Jessica says.

I nod.

"Mel, you're scandalous," Margo tells her. "You can't be talking about her brother like that, in front of her anyway." She turns to me. "Shel, go get something to eat so she can give us the dirty details about your bro."

"You guys suck," I yelp.

I'm a few yards away when I hear the hooting and hollering. My brother must be good to get the cheers he's getting. Gross!

I'm almost to the coolers when I hear my name. "Hey, Shel," Chase says. He puts his arms out to hug me. I'm not sure why. With my arms at my sides, I don't reciprocate the gesture. "Happy New Year." He releases me but keeps his hands on my shoulders. "I can't remember the last time I didn't kiss you at midnight." He's drunk. His eyes and nose are red, and he's smiling like an idiot. Someone, take this guy home already.

"Well, it won't be happening tonight. So you can remember this one," I say, standoffish, wiggling free from his grip.

"Nah, we don't want to ruin tradition," he says, "not after ten years." He runs the back of his hand down my cheek. Ah, his old move that made me weak at the knees. Yet, somehow it's not working tonight.

I try to ignore him, but can't help but ask. "Where's Summer?"

He grins. "I don't know. We're done. I moved out before Christmas. She says I'm not over you, and she doesn't feel like waiting around." He cups my cheek in his hand, and I feel myself getting irritated by the look in his poop-colored brown eyes—tthe look that used to make me swoon.

He's not over me. What? He's talking crazy. The idea does peak my interest though. Thinking about Ms. McGallian breaking up with him because he still wants me is quite satisfying. Serves the skank right. And if he even thinks he still has a chance, he's effing crazy. That ship has already sailed, even if it does make me feel good to know he still thinks of me.

"What are you thinking, Shel?" he asks, taking a step closer to me.

I step back, pushing his hand away from my face. "I'm wondering why I still don't have a beer."

"No need to wonder anymore." Matty puts a cold one over my shoulder. I look back and there he is, looking concerned. I want to tell him he has absolutely nothing to be worried about, but I can't. Not here. Not now.

"Thanks, Matty," I say, and then take a drink of my opened bottle of beer. I love that he always removes the cap for me.

"What happened to Mel?" he asks me, looking around.

"She started dishing the dirt on my brother to the girls so I had to leave," I explain. I joke placing my finger in my mouth to mimic a fake gag.

"Nice," he says. "You mean you didn't want to get the low down on the squeaky springs in the guest bedroom?" A low chuckle escapes from both of us, and I lean into him just like I would at home.

Chase interrupts, bringing his voice down to a whisper, "Shelly, you're not really with this guy, are you?" He must sense the answer to his question by the look on my face. With a look of hurt in his eyes, he says, "You don't belong with him."

I put my hand on his arm and look into his eyes. "Chase, just go away. Okay," I say softly. I turn around to Matty, hook my arm in his and guide him far away from Chase. "Let's get drunk, my friend," I tell him. We stop at the bar, and he pours me a Jägerbomb—nothing like a little friendly bonding.

Hours later, there are about ten of us sitting at the dining room table playing Quarters. And we're getting hammered. I find it ironic that we're a bunch of high school teachers playing drinking games we played when we were in high school, which was a very long time ago. I guess it's a good sign we're not filling our glasses with a bottle of Boone's Farm Strawberry Hill. I saw it on the shelf at the store and was tempted to pick it up for tonight as a joke. But I didn't. I couldn't bring myself to pay $2.49 for a bottle we used to pool leftover lunch money to buy for only $1.29. That's just wrong. Inflation sucks.

"And another shot to Mel," Tyler says. After making three consecutive quarters in the miniature glass, he gets to pick someone to toss back a shot of tequila. About thirty minutes ago, I don't remember who, but someone made up this outrageous rule and it went from a fun, easygoing game to everyone getting shitty real quick.

"Damn, Ty, I'm getting slizzard," Mel says, sending everyone into bouts of laughter.

"Dumb ass, you don't have a G6. You can't get slizzard in a frickin' Prius," I joke with her. We all laugh again, and Mel starts snorting. I take a deep breath before I start wheezing like a total dork.

"That was good," Mel compliments me. She holds out her fist for a bump, and I'm so happy to oblige.

"Ty, you better stop picking on her, or you're gonna be holding her hair back later when she's puking," I warn him. It wouldn't be the first time. He always took care of Mel when we were younger.

"Thanks for reminding me," he says, after making another three bounces in. "A shot to Shel."

"You ass!" I yell at him.

"Don't worry, Shelly, I'll hold your hair back for you, babe," Chase yells from across the table.

"No thanks," I wave him off. "I'll use a clip." I down my drink. Hot and nasty—the tequila, and Chase.

"If he keeps it up," Matty whispers, referring to the endless amount of Chase's comments tonight, "I'm gonna kick his ass."

"Just ignore him. He's drunk and stupid." *And so am I*, I think. I hope Matty's not too drunk. I don't want to see him go to blows. That would totally be a buzz kill.

"I'll try," he says. I feel his hand on the small of my back and under the influence of alcohol—a lot of alcohol—tingles spread from my eyeballs to my pinky toes. I don't say anything or make a move. Matty touching me in front of people from work doesn't bother me like I thought it would. His touch always feels good, more than just good at the moment. I have to cross my legs to suppress how good it feels.

It's my turn and I haven't made one all night. I'm the worst Quarters player in the history of the game. Not much has changed since back in the day. Once, I almost broke my friends glasses, when I bounced it too hard and it flew full speed right at her eye. My friends can't help but talk shit while they wait for me to throw the coin.

"Poor, Shel. She's never gonna get lucky again," one person says.

"Yeah, she can't even use her hand to guide it in."

"It just bounces all around, but never makes it in the hole."

Nice, real nice. Somehow a drinking game involving banking a quarter in a shot glass gets turned into something sexual.

"Shut up. This is it. I can feel it," I begin.

Someone cuts me off, "That's what she said." Funny. Haha.

I adjust my grip again. "This quarter is gonna be my bitch." I bounce it on the table at an angle, and for the first time tonight, it makes it in. "Woohoo," I yell. "Go, Shel, it's my birthday, I did it. I made a shot," I sing and dance around with my hands in the air.

"Matty, you're up," I tell him, meaning he needs to take a drink, but I can't say the word because if I do, I'll have to drink too.

"Body shot," Tyler calls out. Really? My brother is the whore of rules. How many has he made up tonight? Jeez. I lost count. But shit, according to Ty—the professional Quarters player—Matty has to do a body shot off me.

I look at Tyler with a sneer, and both he and Mel are giddy as hell. They're practically jumping out of their seats. The rest of the table, including Chase, is quiet. I know my brother is enjoying this, knowing Chase is going to watch Matty lick one of my body parts. Just effing great.

Matty looks at me, and I smile. This is a bit funny. And I've been dying to touch this man all night. Finally, he has an excuse to put his mouth on me, wherever I want him to.

All the fixings are passed to us. I pull my hair over to one side, and rub a lime on the spot on my neck where it meets my shoulder. Then I shake a little salt. Did any stick or did it just go down my shirt? My train of thought is interrupted with whistles. Matty eyes are locked to mine. "Whenever you're ready," I tell him, dizzy with anticipation.

I feel his familiar arm wrap around my waist and draw me toward him. The touch of his strong hand on the small of my back squeezes my girl parts. I tilt my head to grant him access to my neck and he dives right in. His tongue is warm on my body as he licks and sucks off the salt, lingering a lot longer than necessary and sending shivers down to my core. When he's done with his taste of me, he fixes his eyes to mine again before downing the shot. I hold the lime up to my mouth, egging him on to come and get it. When his lips are close, I move the fruit out of the way to take Matty in for the kiss I've been hungry for all night. He doesn't hesitate. His lips cover mine, and then our tongues mingle, taking me to a place I've never been with just a kiss. He has one hand on my waist and the other wrapped up in my hair as our mouths continue to make love. I squeeze his hips, pressing our bodies together. He backs away planting a few kisses on the bridge of my nose and just under my eyes. I know he's smooching my freckles. I reach up to cup his face in my hands. His lips touch mine again, and my fingers rush through his hair as he trails kisses down my chin, neck, and collarbone. When he's had enough, he puts some space between us, rests his head on my shoulder and we're both still as can be, in each other's arms.

I hear a bunch of chatter all at the same time.

"Now that's one hell of a body shot."

"Just buddies, my ass!"

"They are so not just friends anymore."

"Doesn't look like she's gonna take you back, Chase."

"Wow, I think I just came!"

"Alrighty, Shel, you get to go again unless you need a minute to cool down," Tyler says. "And Fuller, watch your back. I'm gonna wipe that smile off your face when you least expect it."

Everyone laughs.

Mel chimes in, "You're the douche who just called *body shot* on your own sister. Don't get mad, Matt just full-on manhandled your baby sis." She winks at me. "She didn't look like she minded though."

More laughter.

I look up at Matty, who runs his left hand through his hair. It doesn't matter that he's had a few, he's still embarrassed. Trying to comfort him, I rest my head against his shoulder and he kisses the top of my head.

"Are we going to play or what?" Chase shouts.

Chapter Eighteen

As the countdown nears, what Chase said earlier hits me. For the last ten years, I have kissed him at midnight. Whether we were at a party, or bringing in the New Year at home, it was always Chase. It's feels a little weird we're both here, but we won't be sharing this moment together. Time to move on, I guess, but just when I think I have, things like this creep up on me.

Margot and Mel run around passing out plastic champagne flutes to everyone, while I ponder what will happen at the stroke of midnight. Someone else dishes out noisemakers. Speaking of noise, I've already heard several gunshots, which always makes me nervous. Jessica turns on the TV and changes the channel to the countdown in Times Square. Less than five minutes.

This year is going to be so different from last. Teachers usually think of a year in terms of an academic calendar, but this time, I'm going to take the plunge and make a New Year's resolution. I'm not sure what it's going to be yet, but I know it doesn't involve needing a man to be happy and fretting over jackasses who have done me wrong.

This year is going to be my bitch, just like that quarter was.

"5—4—3—2—1—Happy New Year!" is heard all around.

This first person I celebrate with is Mel. We hold out our arms and give each other the biggest girly hug ever. "I love you," I tell her. And she tells me the same.

Next, I hug my brother. It's comforting to have him here, and in this moment, I really feel how much I miss him and wish he'd come home.

And then … Matty. I fling my hands around his neck and yank him down for my first New Year's kiss. He lifts me off the ground and hugs me so tightly I feel it in my ribs. I lift my legs to encircle his waist and I don't want to let go.

"Sorry," I say into his ear. "I couldn't resist."

"Shh… This is perfect." He kisses me again, this time on the cheek before I feel my feet touch the floor.

For the next few minutes, we circle the room exchanging hugs and best wishes for the upcoming year. It reminds me of square dancing in the fifth grade. You dance with one person and then turn to another, constantly changing partners until …

Chase is right in front of me.

He opens his arms to me. My first thought is to punch him in the gut, but then I realize if I stay mad at him forever, I may never move on. I have to work with this guy so I need to fix it. Sure, he's a total dick for what he did, but holding a grudge forever makes it seem like I'm holding on to him. And I'm done with the past. I know I'm over Chase. I don't feel that yearning for him anymore, or even the pain of what he did.

I've really moved on.

I get it now.

Finally.

So I open my arms to him too, and we embrace. It feels a lot like a goodbye to my past. Like I'm finally letting go. I don't feel sad. What I feel is more like relief, that I'm free from his hold on me. I'm free to start fresh this year, and not be tied up with all the nonsense of Chase.

I release my hold on him and try to step back. I look up at him and smile a farewell. At least, it's what I feel like I'm doing. Chase doesn't get it though because he takes this as his chance to plant a smackdown on me with his lips mashed into mine. I put my hands on his shoulders to push him back, but then I just relax in the moment. If I wasn't sure before—even though I *was* pretty fucking sure—I know now it's totally over. Chase's lips are totally smothered all over mine right now—his mouth is closed, thank God—and I feel nothing. I let it continue to be sure, but still … nothing. Not a damn thing. Zilch. No wobbly knees, no tingling in my thighs, no heat penetrating down there. No love making my heart go pitter-patter. Nothing. Zip.

It's over.

We finally separate. I pat his chest and tell him, "Thank you, Chase. That was just what I needed." I give him one last smile and turn to walk away forever—metaphorically speaking though, because I will still see him at work on Monday. But when I turn, I see Matty, who does not look too happy to see me.

He doesn't say anything. He walks away, and as I hurry to follow him, Mel stops me.

"Did I just see you kissing Chase?" she asks, with a disgusted look on her face.

"Yeah, but it's not what you think."

"I've heard that before. What the shithole, Shel?"

"I'll explain to you later. Right now, I need to talk to Matty," I reply.

I wander around outside but there is no sign of him. I look throughout the house, but he's not there either. The car, maybe he went to the car.

I grab my coat and head outside. I walk past many houses and when I get to where we're parked, he's not there either. I must have missed him inside.

When I get back to the party, I see Mel first.

"I can't find Matty," I tell her.

"He left," she says.

"What? No he didn't. His car is still here," I explain.

"He gave your brother his keys and got a ride with John." She throws her arm around me and squeezes. "He's pretty upset. You kissed *Chase*? Of all fucking people?"

I roll my eyes. "I didn't kiss Chase. He kissed me."

"He said he heard you tell Chase you needed him," she continues.

"Oh son of a mother lover. Matty should know better. He didn't hear me say those exact words. Can you get Ty? I wanna go home." The tears are threatening to break free and I want to get out of here before I cause a scene, or a scandal. I can just see the headlines at work on Monday. No thank you.

I can't believe Matty is choosing now to act like a punk. I didn't say I needed Chase. He needs to clean out his ears. He doesn't know what the hell he's talking about. He just took off and didn't give me a chance to explain. Un-fucking-believable. I thought he had confidence in me. In us.

What bullshit?

He just ran away.

By the time I get home, I'm seething mad. I don't allow myself to be sad and weepy about Matty leaving me hanging. I'm just *pissed* he left me hanging. I could ring his stupid gorgeous neck right now.

I toss around in bed, which seems like a sea of never-ending space without him here. I look at the clock and it's only been about fifteen minutes since I've been lying here. It feels like time is standing still. The minutes on the clock can't seem to turn fast enough. It's just after one and the Lady Antebellum booty call song starts playing in my head. I fight the urge to sing it aloud, knowing I'll probably start crying if I do.

Sure, I'm alone and I'm drunk and I want to call him. But I'm not going to. Fuck him. I'm not going to go out in the middle of the night and look for him. I did once already, only to find he left my ass there. Without a single word. He just left.

But I am going to text him.

Well I guess it was only a matter of time before you left me too.

I wait. Five minutes. Ten minutes. No texts back.

So I send another:

It's just too bad you didn't stick around long enough for me to tell you what I figured out tonight.

I wait again.

Nothing.

Last text:

I guess you'll never know.

Fucker.

I love you …

I stare at the text on my screen for a long time. But instead of sending it, I back space thirteen times and erase the whole damn thing.

Chapter Nineteen

The first day back after winter break always sucks ass. Nobody ever wants to be here. Not the kids, and not even the teachers. It almost feels like the first day all over again. It takes a while to get back in the groove of things. To remember old routines, and for some students, I have to remember their names.

Even worse is the fact I still haven't spoken to Matty. I went from absolutely pissed off to painfully sad, and now I'm just completely irritated he's being such a baby. He has no idea what he saw and he's not even taking the time to figure it out.

I thought maybe he'd meet me in the parking lot as usual and we'd talk on our way to class. But nothing. Then, I thought maybe he'd stop by during lunch. But nothing. I even stayed after school for an extra thirty minutes in hopes he'd visit once all the students went home. Yet, again nothing.

On my way to my car, I hear a student whisper to another, "Did you hear Ms. Gelson and Mr. Marino are back together?" I want to stop and set them straight, but I don't. *This* is really the talk on campus?

Mel comes over to watch me drag ass all night, wondering how I'm going to fix this. Or if I even want to. She's dragging ass just as much as I am. She misses my brother, and so do I.

"Want another beer?" she asks.

"Do you have to ask?" I try sarcasm, hoping it will snap me out of my funk.

She brings me another bottle and plops herself down next to me.

"See, I told you this wouldn't work. I should have never gotten involved with him in the first place. I knew this was gonna happen. Now, not only do I not have him as a whatever he was, but I don't have him as a friend either. Matty sucks."

"Don't be such a pussy, Shel. First, things are gonna work out. He just needs a minute to understand what happened. Second, if he's gonna be a pussy too, then you don't need him. As a ... whatever it is he was ... or as a friend. Screw him."

This doesn't make me feel any better.

It's Tuesday morning. I arrive and walk to my classroom alone, again. His car was in the parking lot already, which makes me a little bitchy since he didn't wait. Thankfully, being a teacher is like being an actor.

From bell to bell, I can put on a smiley face and pretend I'm in another world. But those seven minutes in between classes really suck when I check my messages, and there's nothing. Or when I check my email, and the only message I have is from my department chair talking about Friday's meeting. I take a quick glance at my cell—one message from Mel checking to see if I've made contact yet. Nope.

Nothing.

I meet Mel in the staff lounge for lunch. I guess I shouldn't be surprised to find Matty's not here.

"I'm gonna kick his ass to Sunday when I see him," I tell her when I reach the table.

She shoves a handful of Doritos in her mouth. "No doubt. I thought for sure he'd be here."

I start to gnaw on some carrots in frustration. "Wanna come over again tonight?" I ask her.

"Girl, we need to chill. This past year of man trouble has really done me in. My party liver can't keep up. I'm like a case of wine away from AA, and you're probably even closer than I am."

For the first time since the new year, I laugh. Out loud.

"You're so right. I was brushing my teeth this morning and I was still burping beer."

"Maybe he'll call tonight," she says, with a weak smile.

But he doesn't.

I'm getting sad.

Wednesday. Rinse, wash, and repeat from the day before.

In the morning, he's not waiting for me.

At lunch, he's MIA.

After school, I wait like a dumb ass again.

In the evening, still no Matty.

I'm even sadder. I now know the definition of misery.

Thursday. The same. And now …

I'm fucking mad as hell.

When Friday morning rolls around and Matty's car is not in the parking lot when I get to work, I wonder if I should wait for him. I decide against it. Instead, I sneak into his classroom. I leave a large mocha latte and a supersized Rice Krispies Treat on his desk, along with a sticky note that reads:

If you don't come and see me TODAY, your ass is gonna be sorry when I find you myself.

He doesn't show to our staff meeting. Or at lunch.

My student aide tells me, "My friend told me Mr. Fuller has a picture of you on his desk and he's been staring at it all week. He'll come around." She squeezes my hand on the way out and it amazes me the kids are so in tune with what's going on around here. He has a picture of me. And he's been looking at it. Should be a good sign, right?

Okay buddy, it's after school. Now or never. Well, not never. If he doesn't show, it just means I have to go looking for his dumb ass. He doesn't get to say all those wonderful things to me and make me feel the way I do, and then just walk away when he thinks he sees something he really didn't. Sure, it probably wasn't the best idea to let Chase kiss me, but I wouldn't change it for anything. It just solidified my already disappearing feelings for Chase and gave me the closure I needed to move forward. Now, if Matty would just let me explain.

I'm sitting at my computer entering in grades when I hear the door screech open. A giddy smile spreads over my face, as I swivel my chair around to see him.

Son of a bizatch. It's Chase.

My smile extinguishes.

"Sorry to interrupt," he says, taking a step forward.

"Don't worry about it. I was just expecting someone," I say, waving him off. It's been over an hour since school's been out. He's not coming.

"Fuller didn't show?" he asks. How does he know? Damn it. The whole effing school probably knows he's not talking to me.

"Nope," I tell him, but I'm not interested in talking about it with him. The sooner I get rid of him, the better. "What's up, Chase?"

"I was thinking about New Year's Eve, and I realized I screwed things up for you." He pauses. "You were trying to tell me something and I didn't get it then, but I do now." He sits on one of the student desks. "You were saying goodbye, weren't you?"

I amble toward him slowly and sit on my desk facing him. I nod my head in agreement. "I wasn't absolutely sure I was ready to move on until then. But when you kissed me, I knew."

"I guess I knew, too." He scratches his head. "Summer and I are back together." Surprisingly, it doesn't bother me in the slightest to hear this. "She kept on telling me I wasn't over you. And even though I tried to reassure her, maybe I didn't believe it myself. But then we kissed, and it wasn't like it used to be. It was just … "

"Blah," I finish his thought. He smiles. "I know. It was weird. I didn't feel anything." Then I realize how bad it sounds. "No offense," I quickly say.

"Shelly, I don't want us to hate each other anymore. I think we had a great relationship all those years, but it just wasn't meant to be forever."

"I could never hate you, Chase. I'm grateful for the time we had together," I say. "I've known you my whole life. We grew up together. I think we've finally come to the point where we're really ready to move on. I'm assuming you explained this to Summer?"

He nods. "I had to email her because she wouldn't talk to me. But she understands now." He grins at me mischievously. "I think you and Mel would really like her, if you gave her a chance."

"I think you'd like Matty too, if you gave him a chance," I flash the same grin right back.

"I do like Fuller. I always have. He's cool. Maybe he just rubbed me the wrong way because I kinda knew you'd end up with him. You two are perfect for each other. I'll be totally cool with him from now on. You'll see."

"Now, if I could just get him to be in the same room with me, I could fix all this. He saw you kiss me, and he took it the wrong way. I haven't talked to him since." My eyes well up and I put my head down to try to calm my emotions.

"Don't worry about it, Shel." He stands, and gives me a hug. "Summer and I are proof things will work themselves out."

"I hope so," I sniffle into his chest.

My door flings open and I really must have the worst luck in the entire fucking world. Once again, Matty catches me in Chase's arms.

He puts his hands up like WTF. "You know, I was already in my car and I decided to come back. I guess I was right in thinking I should have just gone home," he practically spits the words out.

"Oh son of a beeyotch, Matty, you have the worst timing ever," I say, rolling my eyes for good measure.

He turns to leave but Chase shouts, "Fuller, don't leave. Stay here and talk to her. I think you'll want to hear what she has to say."

Just then, my door opens for the third time and the familiar sound of heels comes tapping in.

"Well hello, everyone," Summer says.

"Hi, Summer," I say, as I hop off my desk and start to move toward her. "Nice to see you. I'm really happy everything worked out for you two."

She smiles and I have this overwhelming urge to hug her. So I do. Thankfully, she doesn't punch me. She hugs me back and says, "I'm sure things will work out for you too."

We back away from each other, and I run my fingers through my hair. I glance at Matty and he looks so confused, it's adorable.

Summer gestures to the door. "You ready, Chase?"

"Sure am," he says. He bends down and kisses my cheek. "Good luck." Then he sticks out his hand to Matty, who still looks puzzled but shakes Chase's hand anyway.

"Bye, guys, see ya later," I say as they leave.

Matty points at the door, "What the hell was that?"

I smile at him. "What are you talking about?" I ask, facetiously.

"You just hugged Summer McGallian." He's still pointing at the door.

I shrug. "We're friends."

"Since when?" He puts his hand to my forehead. "Are you feeling okay? Is it the flu?" Thank you Jesus, he's joking. This is going to work.

"Since she discovered I'm not in love with her boyfriend." He runs his fingertips along the side of my face and brushes my hair back. "And since Chase explained to her I've moved on just like he has."

"But what about the party?" he asks, putting his hands to his sides.

"Chase and I kissed, briefly and it was just a peck. But I think it was more out of curiosity—for both of us—to see if there was something still between us. And we both figured out what we already knew. Our feelings for each other no longer exist. I didn't feel one thing when he kissed me. He may as well have been a stranger. There was nothing."

"And what about what you said? You needed him."

I roll my eyes in frustration. "You need to use Q-tips, Matty. What I said was 'I needed that.' Meaning, I needed *that* to move on, to say goodbye to him. And he understood, but you just left and didn't give me the chance to explain. You bailed on me."

Matty runs his fingers through his hair, and then puts his hands on his hips. "You scared me, Shel. When you went out with the other guys, I wasn't worried in the slightest. There was never a doubt in my mind you'd come back to me. But with Chase, it was different. When I saw you guys together, I was crushed. I assumed the worst. I guess I always felt like I couldn't compete with him and the history you have together."

I shake my head, and can't help but laugh.

"What's so funny?"

"You!" I shout. "You don't get it Mr. Fuller. There's no competition. And if there was, you'd win every time."

He tilts his head, still looking perplexed.

"For you being such a smart ass, you sure are dumb." I stretch my arms up and clasp my hands around his neck. "Matt Fuller, I love you. Now kiss me, you fool."

He cups my face in his hands and touches his lips to mine. Our lips lock together several times, before our tongues slide against each other rekindling the fire that had gone out for a week. Matty traces his tongue across my top lip and catches my bottom lip between his, sucking softly and playfully, and sending tingles all over my body. Then he lifts me in a tight squeeze, as my feet dangle in the air, and he plants quick smooches all over my face and throat. He nuzzles his face in my neck and the feel of his warm breath on my skin is so great I let out a hushed moan.

"You really love me, huh?" he asks, grinning.

"Yes, I do." I smile at him, my feet still off the ground.

"It's a good thing I wasn't drinking a Bud Light at the bar that night," he tries to say with the utmost seriousness, but it doesn't work.

"It wouldn't have mattered." I peck at his lips again. "You could've been drinking a Lucky Lager and I'd still love you."

"What about a wine cooler?" he laughs.

"Now, let's not get crazy." I giggle.

He sets me down and brushes my hair away from my face with his finger tips.

"You know what this means, don't you?" I ask.

He knows exactly what this means.

"Getting naked and having my way with you on your desk is probably out of the question, huh?"

I rest my palms on his strong chest. "Probably." We grin at each other.

"The car?"

"Why don't you just shut up and take me home, Mr. Fuller," I say to him.

"One thing," he pauses. I gaze up at him, and he gently brushes his lips against mine for a few seconds. "I love you too."

Chapter Twenty

It's date night.

Again.

But this time I really want to go. I'm not going to pout as I get dressed. I'm not second-guessing my motives. The idea of going out on a real date with my new boyfriend couldn't make me feel any happier.

It's funny, really. Since last week when Matty and I finally confessed our love for each other—well, I finally told him I loved him, he's been telling me he loves me for months—he hasn't gone home. But this morning, after breakfast, he kissed me goodbye and was out the door. What a goof. He wants to pick me up and that won't work if we both get ready at my house. So he went home.

The radio is blaring a mix of dance music, slow songs, and country throughout my house. I love setting the player to random picks and just being surprised by what comes through the speakers. After spending over an hour in the shower washing, exfoliating and moisturizing, my body feels silky smooth. It helps I shaved my legs from the tops of my thighs all the way down to my toes. I'd been doing this already, but I took special care today so I wouldn't miss a spot. If Matty decides tonight is the night, I'm going to be ready for him.

Now that I'm in love with him, I thought we would have been screwing like horny teenagers whose parents were on vacation, but my boyfriend—I like saying it—has this odd sense of honor and thinks we should continue to wait awhile longer. He wants to show me how much he respects me by taking things slowly. I've never wanted anyone to respect me less. He's really driving me crazy. I thought it was always the woman who wouldn't give it up.

In Matty's case, I think his reluctance might also have something to do with my house and my bed. While it was okay for us to do everything but make love in my bed before, I'm not so sure he wants to take our relationship to the next level in the same bed I slept in with Chase for so many years. Understandable, I know. But I refuse to do it at his place with three roommates roaming around, two of them being other teachers who work with us. His place reminds me of a frat house, except his room, which is all tidy and neat. I should have suspected considering the way he cleans my house and clears the table within minutes of us finishing a meal.

My place is out and so is his.

I think we're going to have to go old school and get a room somewhere. Can you imagine? A grown man, and a grown woman, having to book a hotel room to have sex. Will we have to get a room every time?

Matty will be at my door in thirty minutes. My hair is flowing down my back in loose curls. My makeup is applied lightly in warm tones to match my green eyes. I've never been one to get flashy with my makeup and I don't want to start now. He likes my natural look. I apply a thin layer of nude lip gloss and look at myself in the mirror. Fitted jeans, a flirty black tank dips low in the front under a charcoal gray crocheted cardigan. My heeled boots will give me a little height, maybe enough to make the top of my head clear Matty's shoulders. Maybe.

Dangly silver earrings pierce my lobes, and a strand of tiny crystals surrounds my neck.

There, I'm done. Ready for my date with my boyfriend.

A knock at my door tells me I'm right on time. I knew he'd be early.

I open my door, and Matty stands before me with a bouquet of orange Gerbera daisies, my favorite flower.

"You're so sweet," I tell him, taking the fresh flowers from his hands and accepting his kiss on my lips.

"I thought all this nice guy stuff was gonna get thrown out the window as soon as I told you I loved you."

"Nope, get used to it, baby." He kisses the top of my head. "This is me. You're stuck with it."

I roll me eyes, sarcastically. "Well, I guess I can manage."

In the kitchen, I clip the stems of the flowers and place them in a vase. When I'm finished, Matty and I are practically skipping down my walkway to his car.

"Where to?" I ask him.

"Where do you think?" he grins.

"Well if I knew, why would I ask?" I smile at him.

"To your happiest place on earth," he says. I tilt my head and beam at him. I couldn't be happier with his choice of restaurants. "I figure they have a hundred different choices of beer, two Sunday night games, plenty of non-vegetarian choices of food, and air conditioning."

"Oh, Matty, this is gonna be the best effing date I've ever had," I cry out. "I'm gonna get a Guinness."

"And I'm gonna get a Black and Tan."

"Perfect," I tell him, leaning over his center console to press my lips to his.

Just perfect.

Third time *is* a charm.

My first date was with Jacob. Then Jackson.

And now Matty.

My luck finally turned around.

Chapter Twenty One

"Rally day, baby," I tell Matty as he brushes his teeth and I brush my hair.

He spits in the sink, and turns on the water to rinse. He wipes his mouth dry with a washcloth, and whips around so he's facing me. With the sight of his bronze skin, fresh from the shower, and smelling so clean, I can't help but press my mouth to his chest. He cradles my head in his hand, grasping the hair I just rid of knots. "You're gonna make us late, baby," he murmurs in my ear. The hum of his deep voice makes me want to call in sick and cuddle with him in bed all day.

"Like you care. You hate rallies." I continue to kiss his neck and slide down to nip at his abs and his sides, running my fingertips along the waistband of his boxer briefs.

"I think you're the only one who likes rally days. You and Mel anyway." He lifts my chin from his belly and bends down to cover my mouth with his. "You're insatiable, you know that?"

"You haven't given me anything to satisfy my … needs," I whine. Both of us chuckle.

He takes my breasts in his hands and hunches over to suck on the skin plumping over the cups of my bra. "Oh really," he says. "Nothing?"

"Okay, not nothing." My fingers run through his hair and I let out a moan when I feel the suction of his lips get harder against my nipple that he managed to free.

"That's what I thought." He stands up straight, smacks me in the ass, and says, "Now hurry up. We still need to have breakfast."

"Breakfast my ass, you tease," I scoff at him. "I'll eat a Pop Tart."

I watch his tight ass walk away before I take my time getting ready, dressing myself in a hot pink V-neck sweater and a pair of jeans. I even bust out my pink Chucks for the occasion. This is one of my favorite rallies of the year. I loved it when I was in high school. I think that's when I fell in love with football, playing powder puff—girls flag football—for the Sadie Hawkins game. The boys wear cheerleading uniforms and perform a choreographed dance while the crowd goes wild.

And then there's the dance after the game.

I asked Matty to be my date for the dance tonight. He wasn't too thrilled to chaperone but if I have to be there, so does he.

"You look cute, Shel," Matty says as we walk hand-in-hand to the car. Carpooling is great. I never have to drive, which is spectacular because I've always wanted a chauffeur. Especially one who thinks I'm cute.

The rally went smoothly and my students weren't complete animals for the rest of the day. A thirty-minute rally can really make the students do things they'd never do. Like toilet papering the quad, or spray painting "Seniors Rule" all over the school, as if defacing their own school goes down as the ultimate pledge of school spirit.

But my kids are cool. None of them were fighting, they all looked sober, and very few ditched class. Can't say that to be true of my aide, Meg. Matty and Chase said their aides, Travis and Keesha, were MIA too, so I know they went to the Steel Grille. I remember those days. Not much has changed around here since I walked the halls of Carver High.

"You ready to go?" Mel asks, popping her head in my classroom.

"Yeah," I tell her, packing the last of the projects in my bag. "I'm just waiting for Matty to get here."

"He's coming down the hall right now, let's go beeyotch," she yelps, looking around like a crack addict to see if anyone heard her. I think she's safe. Very few kids are on campus this late.

"You ready for the game?" I ask her. "I think the juniors are going to kill the seniors this year. They have been practicing like crazy, even at the local parks when practice is over here."

"I know, they're gonna kill it," Mel agrees.

Matty catches up with us and rests his arm on my shoulder.

"When Mel and I were in eleventh grade, The Program was popular." He looks at me confused. "You know that movie about college football, when one of the guys on the defensive line goes wacko on steroids."

He nods, "Oh yeah, yeah, I remember."

Mel continues the story, "Well our coaches were crazy like that. Not on drugs or anything, but wild. They called us *aminals*. Why not *animals*? I have no idea. But we painted our faces for the game just like they did in the movie and the ASB class posted signs all over the place with our signature Aminal word. We were bad ass."

"Yes, we were," I tell her, putting my hand up for a high five.

Mel slaps my hand. "That is until the juniors stomped on our asses our senior year."

"Why you gotta bring up old shit, Melly Belly?"

The three of us crack up, until Mel starts snorting.

"Sounds like you had some good times at this school," Matty says.

"Yep, we sure did. I love how the traditions have been carried on. This is a special place," I tell him.

Mel nods in agreement.

"I'm sorry," I tell Matty, leaning into him as we make it to the car. "I'm sure you're sick of hearing about our walks down memory lane."

"No way," he says, putting his fingers through my hair. "I know how much this stuff means to you, more than you know."

He opens the car door for me. I look at him and pucker my lips. He bends down and touches his lips to mine.

"You guys make me sick," Mel says, making gagging noises.

"Oh shut it and get in the car, you Aminal!"

At the Yard House before the game, my mood goes from fantastic to craptastic as we walk in and see my parents waiting for a table. Surprise is not a strong enough word to express my thoughts when I see my mother standing there in a pair of jeans and Carver T-shirt.

Matty breaks the silence, going to my parents first and offering them his hand. "Mr. and Mrs. Gelson, what a surprise," he says.

"Oh, Matt, you can call me Sandy. I think we're beyond the formal exchanges by now." My mother lifts her arms to give him a hug. Is she on drugs? Did someone slip her a roofie?

Matty reciprocates her hug and offers his hand to my dad.

"Matt, good to see you again. Would you guys like to join us for dinner?" he asks.

Oh no. Oh no.

"Hello, Daddy," I interrupt, sliding my arm around his waist for a hip hug. "We're in a hurry to get back to work. We have to chaperone a game tonight so we're just going to eat at the bar."

My mother stares me down. "Hi, Mother, you look very casual today."

"Your dad and I went for a walk this afternoon and decided to stop for dinner on the way home. Since this is one of the beer establishments you rave about, I didn't think it necessary to go home and change." She blinks her eyes at me like she's looking for my approval. Since when?

"You look great, totally ready to throw back a few," I joke with her.

"Hi, guys," Mel says, sneaking in to say hello to my parents. My mother smiles at the greeting and my dad hugs Mel, ruffling her hair.

"Well then, I guess we'll see you later. I'll call you. Maybe we can get together for lunch or something," I quickly hug my parents, and try to get Matty and Mel to do the same.

"Sounds good, princess," my dad says.

"That would be lovely," my mother adds.

"Great seeing you again," Matty offers the last words before we make our way into the bar area and meet up with Chase and Summer.

"Hey," I tell them as we all squeeze in a booth.

"Did you just see your parents out there?" Chase asks.

"Don't remind me," I tell him.

"They can't be that bad," Summer says.

There's silence as the four of us look at her.

"Well, my mom is," I clarify.

Matty shakes his head. "No, she was pretty nice tonight."

Mel chomps on the chips in the center of the table. "She likes you Matt. She even told you to call her Sandy."

"And she gave you a hug," I scoff at him.

"She hugged you?" Chase asks, like he can't believe it.

Matty's eyes dart from mine to Mel's to Chase's and back to mine. "What? That's not normal."

"No…" we all say in unison.

The waitress interrupts us to take our orders of appetizers and one beer each. We can't go to a school function hammered. When we were in high school, we went to these very same functions more than just tipsy. But, we're adults now and have to be responsible.

It seems like an odd combination to have the five of us at one table, but over the last month, we have all learned to get along and for the most part, enjoy each other's company. I still sense some irritation between Mel and Summer, but overall things are good. She's not as funny as us and she takes herself way too seriously, but she's a perfect match for Chase. She seems to make him happy and her reputation for flirting with all the male staff members has diminished so maybe she's changed. They look like a couple in love and I'm happy for them.

Mel doesn't look so happy though. I know she misses my brother. All her talk about Brazilian wax jobs, and being a cheetah went out the window as soon as he became her Christmas present. I knew she wouldn't be the same once he left. I know they try to email and talk on the phone, but it's not the same as being able to hold the one you love whenever you want to. I wish my brother would just suck it up and come home. I know he wants to. But he has really established himself up there and I don't know if he wants to start over. Well, he wouldn't be starting over completely. This is his home.

I'm just not sure he will make that sacrifice for her.

My biggest fear is she's going to take off and relocate to be with Ty.

I'd kill her if she left me, even if it was for my brother.

Game time.

I have my licorice. I have my Diet Coke.

Come on ladies … kickoff time.

Okay, so they're not going to kick the ball but let's get the show on the road.

I'm not happy about being stuck on the field. I like the view from the bleachers better but the powers that be just put us where they need us. At least, the five of us are stationed on the sidelines together. And we can all keep Summer out of everyone's way.

The juniors are on the other side of the field and it's a bummer we can't switch. We all have student aides who are juniors but they were stuck doing work for ASB so they can't play. I feel bad for them but they don't seem bothered by it. They appear to be having a good time. It's funny how we managed to snag up three best friends and their two little boy sidekicks. The goofballs, Travis and Josh, joined the student government class just to be close to their women.

"Those cheerleaders are funny," Matty says in my ear.

I look over at the boys covered in makeup, pink wigs falling off their heads, cheering away.

"I could totally see you cheering in a skirt," I yell over the noise.

He laughs. "Yeah, I probably would have." He glances at them again, shaking his head. "Thanks for getting me out here, Shel. It's a lot more fun once you know about all the traditions and history here. I don't think I ever paid attention before."

"Yeah, I know. You always sign up to work track meets." I roll me eyes. Track meets—really?

"Hey, don't knock it till you try it. The Fat Man Race is worth it." We meet eyes and crack up.

"Do I even want to know?"

"You'll have to go with me sometime," he shouts.

"Done."

We watch the juniors spank the seniors, completely shutting them out for the first part of the game.

Matty puts his hand on my shoulder. "Hey, I'll be right back. I gotta take a leak and I wanna be back for the half-time show."

"Okay." He kisses the top of my head and jogs off the field.

"Damn, Matty's taking forever," I shout to Mel. "He's gonna miss the crowning."

Mel rolls her eyes at me. "Like he cares. He's probably in the parking lot drinking beer with Chase." I look around. He's gone too.

"Those bastards. Matty was just saying he didn't want to miss it."

"Was that before or after you chopped off his balls and put them in your purse?" she teases me.

She's probably right.

"Ms. Cruz, Ms. Gelson, Ms. McGallian, we need your help," a little mousy girl calls out to us.

"Okay, hon, whatcha need?" Mel asks her.

"We need one teacher to stand with each one of the guys. There's a rumor something might go down so we need to have more teachers out there. One of the guys found out his girl cheated on him with one of the other guys. It's dumb, but it would make the principal feel better."

"All right, all right," Mel says. And the three of us walk onto the field, spreading out with two other staff members till we're all paired up with one of the boys.

Dumb. These losers are going to fight about some girl on their big night. If I knew which two were the culprits I'd tell them what idiots they are.

The National Anthem blares through the speakers, and I put my hand to my chest. Looking toward the gates and the sidelines, Matty still isn't anywhere in sight. Well, I guess if I was a dude, the high school king's court halftime show wouldn't be on my top ten list of events to oversee.

Bummer though. I wanted him to see how cute it is when the Tiger runs around the field before kneeling down in front of the winner and crowning the King. It's always so exciting to see the parents react and the cheers in the crowd.

Oh, here comes the Tiger now.

"I'm Too Sexy," sings through the speakers and the Tiger shakes her booty, and swings her tail around. How cute.

Here she comes. She's doing her fake out moves.

Is it the first prince?

Nope.

She dances near the prince on the right.

Nope.

The one in the middle.

Nope.

Oh, his mom looks so disappointed.

She's going Mel's way. Her prince is going to win.

Nope.

Oh shit … the kid I'm next to is going to win.

But the Tiger is not kneeling in front of the prince. Can't she see out of that big head?

She's standing in front of me.

Mel walks over to me and points to the bleachers.

Oh. My. God.

A giant sign spreads from one end to the other and it has to be at least four feet tall.

It reads:

Ms. G, Will You Marry Mr. Fuller?

Tears fill my eyes as I look down at the Tiger kneeling before me.

"Matty?" His name barely escapes my mouth.

My dad appears behind the Tiger and starts to lift off his mask.

Oh goodness. I look at Mel to tell me this is real. Tears stream down her face, as my brother holds her in his arms. Tyler. He's here.

I look back at Matty, kneeling, smiling, tears in his eyes, and I can't believe I love him more than I did already. He sheds his giant paw gloves and my mother places something in his hands.

He holds up a square chocolate covered gourmet Rice Krispies Treat.

"Will you marry me, Shelly Gelson?"

I look closer and sticking out from the middle of the dessert is a very impressive diamond ring.

"Oh, hell yes, Matt Fuller. Hell frickin' yes!"

He takes the ring out, gives the treat to Mel, and rises to his feet.

"I love you, Shel," he says, his beautiful blue eyes sparkling through a sea of tears.

"And I love you, Matty."

He slides the ring on my finger for a perfect fit.

Just like us.

Epilogue

It's my wedding day.

Impatient me is not a fan of long engagements, and neither is Matty, so just a few months after his amazing and well-planned proposal, we're already getting hitched.

Spring break is always a good time for weddings. We will get married today, and then tomorrow, we're setting sail on a cruise for a week.

My mother tried to talk us out of it, of course. I mean, how can she possibly plan a wedding fit for a debutante in just two months. When Matty reminded her I'm a far cry from a southern belle, she backed off. My mother loves him, and he knows exactly how to handle her without her even knowing it. Matty has really taken a liking to my mother, probably because he misses his own. His mother died when he was in college, and he never knew his dad. So my family has just gobbled him up, my brother especially. I'm starting to think they're having an internet affair, constantly emailing each other or posting lame videos on each other's Facebook pages. They even connect through their video game consoles, wearing headsets, speaking into microphones, and blasting each other to pieces.

Mel comes into the dressing room. "Are you ready, Shel?"

"Definitely," I tell her, taking one last look in the full-length mirror. My hair has been curled and pulled to the side in a loose ponytail. My makeup is soft as usual. But I really love my dress. I feel like a princess. A heart-shaped strapless dress in satin is fitted past my hips before it spreads out into a full gown with layers of tulle underneath. Beads and lace cover the upper part of the dress and the lights will help them to sparkle as I walk down the aisle.

"You look stunning, Shelly," she says, a lone tear rolling down her cheek.

"Shut it," I tell her softly. "You're gonna ruin your makeup."

We both smile.

"You're first." I gesture to the door, and she walks out holding a bouquet of orange Gerbera daisies. My own bouquet is similar to hers, just a bit bigger with all white daisies. My mom almost had a stroke when I refused roses. Daisies are my thing.

I watch Mel walk out the door, and I'm so grateful I have her as my best friend, my sister.

Matty and I are having only two people in our wedding—my maid of honor and his best man. Mel and Tyler, the two most important people in our lives.

But ... our guest list is a bit larger, like the size of a school. We decided to do something that's never been done before.

When I walk down the aisle to meet Matty, I will be walking down the aisle of our school auditorium. It's time to make some new memories at my school, and the venue couldn't be more beautiful.

We invited the entire staff, and most of our students, including some special ones we had in the past. Neither one of us has a large family so the bulk of our guests are from work.

Maybe this is one reason workplace relationships *shouldn't* be frowned upon, because if they weren't, we'd all be invited to a lot more parties.

"It's time, princess," my daddy says. He holds out his hand to me. "I'm very happy for you, Shelly. You have found yourself a good man. I wish you many years of happiness." He kisses my cheek, and wraps my hand around the crook of his arm.

"Thanks, Daddy," I murmur. I release a deep breath and tell him, "Let's do this."

The doors fly open and I can hear the bridal procession begin.

Here I come, Matt Fuller.

I lock eyes with his the whole way, and we smile. I notice the creases in the corners of his eyes are magnified with happiness and his baby blues sparkle in the spotlight.

When I reach him, he takes my hands in his and the joy I feel is overwhelming.

We say our vows, exchange rings, and when my husband kisses me for the first time, I shiver with excitement as tears stream down my face.

"I'm so glad you fell in love with me, Shelly."

"And I'm glad you were so confident that I would."

He kisses me again before we turn around to see our family, friends, and students.

The minister says, "I now introduce to you for the very first time: Mr. and Mrs. Matthew Fuller."

As we make our way out of the auditorium, I think back to the evening on the football field and can't believe Matty did all that for me. He actually pulled it off and I had absolutely no idea. After the surprise engagement, we all went back to my parent's house, where I learned Matty had visited my parents to ask for my hand in marriage. From that moment, my parents accepted him into our family with full hearts and open arms.

Talk about new traditions. Maybe Matty started one. Maybe next year, someone will follow his lead and propose marriage on the fifty yard line with a Rice Krispies snack and a giant sign. Our aides rolled up the banner for us and it's like a foot in diameter squished in the corner of our closet. But I had to keep it.

We bought a three-bedroom house together close to work. We got lucky on a thirty-day escrow and have been living there for two weeks, taking care to christen every room with our lovemaking.

We never made it to the dance the night of the engagement, but we did make it to a fancy hotel with a Jacuzzi tub, a giant bed, and plenty of wall space.

It's crazy I'm even thinking about this now. How many other "just married" brides walk back down the aisle smiling at their guests thinking about the first time she made love to her brand spanking new husband? Not many, I'd guess. Leave it to me.

But I can't help it.

When we entered our hotel room on our engagement night, we both knew what was going to happen. There wasn't a doubt in our minds. Matty plopped our bags down on the leather bench seat at the foot of the king-sized bed. He looked at me with his hands on his hips and grinned.

I smiled back, wondering how long it would take for us to get naked.

He stepped toward me, pushing his chest to mine, till I backed up against a wall.

"How's this?" he had asked.

"It'll work," I answered, remembering The Notebook.

He covered my mouth with his, and kissed me deeply, our tongues tangled together, my palms were pressed flat against the wall holding me steady, and Matty's fingers weaved in my hair. Without touching him, the pressure of his kiss had my senses on high alert. He sucked hard on my bottom lip before dragging his mouth down my neck, and yanking open my hot pink cardigan. Buttons popped off along the way, and he cupped my right breast in one hand as he lifted my shirt with his other.

With a moistened kiss planted to my belly, I could almost hear a sizzle as his tongue flitted across my skin. He unfastened the buttons on my jeans with one hand, and with each press of his lips on my navel, and my hips, my pants slid down my waist and then my thighs.

When Matty pulled down my black panties, he traced the path with his warm tongue and I almost came right then, but he stopped me.

"Oh, no you don't," he said. "We haven't even gotten to the good part."

"Shit, Matty, I don't know if I can handle anymore," I told him, through heavy breaths.

With a quick kiss pressed to my sex, he stood to lift me and pin me against the wall. I could feel his erection rubbing against me and I wanted nothing more than his jeans to disappear. It was as if Matty could hear me because he put me down and without ever removing his lips from mine, kicked off his shoes, yanked off his pants and boxer briefs, and dropped them to the floor.

My hand shot to his shaft, my fingers strummed along his smooth skin and I had the impulse to bend down and take him into my mouth in one big gulp. I felt him slide across my tongue as my mouth opened, and my lips closed around him, just one slow glide down his length, and one pulsing glide up. He gasped when the wet suction of my lips lingered on his head, and I squeezed my fingernails into his ass.

Then, I let him go, and our lips found each other once more.

He lifted me again and I tried to raise my legs to wrap around his core, but I couldn't. My jeans and shoes were still on and we laughed. He found the hem of one of my pant legs and yanked it over my shoe. I shook my foot loose from one side of my panties, and his hands dropped from my ass to my thighs. The next time when he propelled me against the wall, my legs were free to encircle him.

Within seconds, I felt Matty plunge inside me. He didn't tease me with just a little at a time, he went hard and deep and my eyes almost popped out of my head as I took him in all at once.

I gasped *ohmygod*, groaned and moaned, all at the same time.

Matty buried his head in my neck, breathing heavily, and said, "Sorry, I didn't mean to do it like that."

"It's okay. It's great actually, but..." I managed to say, digging my pink high-top Chucks into his backside. "This can't be comfortable for you."

With Matty still pulsing inside me, we continued the conversation. "This is a lot more difficult than it looks. What's her name wasn't wearing skinny jeans and a pair of Converse in the movie," he said through a chuckle.

"Take me to the bed, Matty," I told him.

"Not so fast, Shel." He didn't say anything else, he just went to work popping off my shoes, my socks, and peeling off the rest of my jeans and panties. He pulled his shirt over his head while I got rid of my tee and bra.

Finally, we were both naked.

"Let's try this again," he had said. And with those few words, I felt my temperature rise and my muscles tighten with desire all over again.

He pushed me back against the wall, slid his hand down my side until he lifted my thigh toward his hip. I hooked my arms around his neck and he lifted me just like before. Only this time, nothing stood in our way.

With my ass cupped in his strong grip, Matty rocked into me, shattering me like nothing I ever expected. My gaze never left his as he slid in and out of me with slow, deep strokes that I felt from the tips of my toes to the little hairs on the back of my head.

Just when I thought it couldn't get any better, Matty backed away from the wall, carrying me with him and lowered me to the bed.

He stood there, gorgeous and chiseled like a freaking sex god and all I could think was this man is mine and I can't wait for him to be inside me again.

In a flash of movement I wasn't expecting, I was on my elbows and knees. Matty's erection teased at my flesh from behind. I reached down and guided him inside, and he thrust his hips as I backed into him slow and steady. I explored the action, allowing my fingers to feel him sliding in and out. When I grasped his balls in my hand, I backed into him harder, this time circling my hips in tune with each of his strokes.

I gasped *ohmygod*, groaned and moaned, all at the same time. Again.

Matty withdrew from me, and grasped my ass tightly, holding on like he was willing himself to hang on just a bit longer.

I dropped to my stomach and rolled over so I could see him again.

He kissed my nose and told me he loved me.

I sat up and pushed him down so he was flat on his back and I could straddle him. It was my turn. I stroked him a few times before I lowered myself onto his length. I pressed my breasts to his chest and he traced his hands up and down my back, the pads of his fingertips sending tingles like pin pricks across my body.

The rotation of my hips allowed me to grind my most sensitive part against him while he plunged deeper and deeper into the heart of my sex. Matty's hands squeezed my hips, and I noticed his teeth biting down on the corner of his bottom lip. The intense look on his face did me in. I could only last for a minute or so more before I collapsed on his chest, feeling the pulse between my legs tighten in spasms as we both released.

Matty cupped my face in his hands and pulled me to him for our first after sex kiss. It was peck after peck to my lips, my neck, my throat, my chest, before I rolled over next to him.

We both sighed, and I thought, I could definitely get used to this. This man is all mine. Forever.

Of course, I was the first to say something. "Holy son of a sex fest," I had cried out, still panting like I just finished the LA marathon. He chuckled, and I continued. "I so didn't expect our first time to last so long."

He chuckled again, and ran his fingers through his dampened hair. "I kinda shot one off this morning in the shower." He paused, and touched a gentle kiss to my nose. "To get ready for tonight."

"Well, thank you," I said, cracking up too. We spooned for the rest of the evening, and woke up early in the morning for another round of lovemaking to make up for all the time I'd wasted before telling the man, who I'd soon marry, I loved him.

And now, leaving this auditorium hand-in-hand with my best friend, and now husband, I just can't help but smile with such giddy satisfaction.

It finally happened.

I finally found a man who loves me enough to nail me against the wall.

The end.

Dear Readers,

Thank you so much for giving Against the Wall a shot. I really loved delving into the lives of these young and fun teachers, and I hope you did too.

Please take time to rate and/or review Against the Wall on Amazon, Barnes & Noble, Goodreads, Smashwords, and your other retails store sites. Your words mean so much to me, and to the success of this book.

In the spirit of addictive social media, spread the word. Tweet about Against the Wall. You can also follow me on Twitter (@juliepbooks) or add me as a friend on Facebook (facebook.com/juliepbooks).

Keep turning the pages for a preview of Mel and Tyler's story. Their story, Between The Sheets, is available now. Also, look for the third book in the series in the Spring of 2013.

Yours truly,
Julie Prestsater

Between The Sheets

Against The Wall #2

"Can I have this dance, pretty lady?" Tyler holds out his hand, one side of his mouth rising in a sexy grin.

I glance up at him, trying to resist his adorable appeal. "Lady huh? Do I look fifty to you?"

"Come on now, Mel. Don't be such a smart ass. Isn't it customary for the best man to dance with the maid of honor?" He rests his hands on his hips and smiles.

"Well, if I must." I stand, with a sigh, and he engulfs my teeny hand in his strong grip. I've never felt more safe and loved before in my entire life than when I'm with Tyler. This is what this man does to me. With the slightest touch, my insides swirl around like the spin cycle of a washing machine. But the unease isn't all about the sparks flying between us. I'm just plain sad. I only have one week with him and then he's going back home. How can I get that out of my mind long enough to enjoy the time we do have together? It doesn't seem possible.

When we reach the hard wood dance floor, he takes my right hand in his, and wraps his other arm around me, resting his palm slightly above my bottom. I can feel his embrace get tighter as he leans down to nuzzle my neck. Inhaling his familiar scent, I get lightheaded and brace myself against his chest so I don't slither down his body into a boneless pile of skin.

I don't think I can ever love anyone more than I love Tyler. I've loved him almost my entire life. I've waited just as long for him to hold me like this and my heart aches knowing it will soon be over, again.

How many times can I really put myself through this? When he left after winter break, I'll admit it—I cried. Shelly doesn't know that and neither does Tyler. They both think I'm this strong Latina woman with tough skin like the beef jerky I eat from the little liquor store near work.

I did get over my divorce rather quickly. That was easy though. The mother trucker was cheating on me with some nasty ass blond bimbo from work. As if I was going to waste my time fretting over a man who never had enough time for me, yet he had plenty to be screwing some colleague on his cherry wood desk at his office. No thank you. Seeing your husband and his mistress all wrapped up with your very own eyes does a lot for the recovery of a broken heart.

But damn me for not being able to resist my best friend's brother. I'd kept him at arm's length in high school—mostly—and in college, but recently, at the first opportunity, we're doing the wild thing in Shelly's spare bedroom. I wonder if she's noticed she needs a new mattress in there. Those springs are way too squeaky.

The song plays on. Adele wailing about someone who did her wrong. This is so not wedding music. If I wasn't so happy for my best friend and her Marky Mark Calvin Klein underwear model look alike of a husband, I'd want to slit my wrists.

Tyler loosens his grip. "What are you thinking about, Melly Belly?" Gosh I used to hate it when people called me that. But with Tyler, it's like a sweet love song whispering in my ears.

"I'm thinking about how depressing this song is," I tell him, looking up into his almond-shaped green eyes.

He chuckles. "Yeah, pretty grim for a wedding, huh?"

"More appropriate for a funeral."

"Wedding. Funeral. Aren't they synonymous? I'm sure Matt feels like his life is ending right now."

When I smack him in the chest, he throws his head back with a big belly laugh causing all the guests who were enjoying the sad song to look our way. He snuggles me close again, still giggling in my ear. I can actually feel the goofball shaking with laughter and it makes my heart melt even more.

"You guys look like you're having way too much fun over here. You been hittin' the bar without me, Mel?" Shelly asks.

"Oh no, your brother here is just full of jokes." I punch him in the arm. Then I tell her what he said. Matt laughs along with him until Shel swings her trademark backhand into his chest. That's my girl.

"Let's go get a drink," Shel says, linking her arm in mine. "These two knuckleheads can dance with each other."

I can't help but crack up when Shel orders a beer at the bar. Here she is, in this gorgeous gown, beautiful hair, and stunning makeup, looking like the belle of the ball, elegant from head to toe. And she has a bottle of Newcastle in her hand. Not even a glass. The bartender offered and she sneered at him like he was crazy, as if he offended her.

She takes a swig and lets out a big "Ahh" sound.

"Nice, Shel. Very lady like," I tease her.

"Oh excuse me," she snickers. "Let me put my pinky up. Is that better?"

We both laugh.

"Here's to a life full of love, happiness, and wild sex against the wall?" I toast to her.

She clinks her bottle of beer against my rather large glass of Stella Rosa sweet red wine.

"How about just wild sex anywhere? Against the wall sounds hot and sexy and all, but it's not that practical. Downright uncomfortable if you ask me. We've tried."

My bestie is way too frickin' funny. Just when I thought my night was headed south, she comes up with this goofy shit and I can't help but laugh and smile.

"Thanks Shel."

"For what?"

"Just because."

I don't have the heart to ruin her day with my misery. I doubt she'd want to hear about how crappy I feel about her brother leaving me yet again. The first time, I thought I could handle it. Then when he came back for Valentine's Day, when Matt proposed to Shelly in front of the entire school, I knew things were going to be difficult. We spent the weekend together before he went back home to San Francisco, and we've been

Skyping, talking on the phone, and texting ever since. But that can only do so much. My heart aches for him the moment he's gone and my body yearns for his touch.

I should really just shut up and enjoy the week we have together before we go back to work.

"Hey," Shel says, startling me.

"What?"

"Do me a favor, would ya?"

"Anything for the most beautiful bride I've ever seen."

She turns to me, narrowing her eyes. This is serious.

"Promise me to forget that Tyler is leaving on Sunday. Pretend like he's not going anywhere. And just let yourself be happy." She squeezes my shoulder and pulls me toward the dance floor.

"Am I that obvious?" I question.

"I know you better than yourself. So promise."

"I promise. I swear to have a week full of happiness, love, and wild sex against the wall with your brother." I grin at her, and she raises a brow at me.

She shakes her head, saying, "TMI, Melly Belly, TMI."

We make our way back to the dance floor, drinks in hand, already bobbing to the beat.

"Now this is a song I can get down to," Ty says as we reach the guys.

"Get down on it," I tell him, listening to Kool and the Gang blaring from the speakers. "Really?"

"They just don't make songs like this anymore," Matt adds, with a chuckle.

Shelly finishes a gulp of her beer and then says, "Yeah, now the songs just say 'fuck me' and 'blow me' rather than trying to use metaphors. You really think this old song is about dancing?"

"True dat, sista," I agree with her in our ridiculous slang speak. You just never know when it's going to creep up on you, when Shel and I start talking like we're chillin' with Snoop Dog.

"Why don't you both just zip it and dance?" Ty jokes. He shimmies closer to me, and takes the glass from my hand. After setting it down on a nearby table, he struts his way back over to me, where he grabs both of my hands in his and starts swaying them back and forth. He turns me around, his hands squeezing my hips. I back myself up into his lap, and we spend the rest of the night grinding and freaking like a bunch of high schoolers at prom. Good thing there aren't any chaperones around to break us apart.

The reception is coming to a close and Matt and Shel are getting ready to make their departure. I still can't believe they've stayed as long as they have. I would've been gone a long time ago and been doing some serious damage back in the hotel room. But, I'm glad she did stay. Dancing and singing with her all night has brought back so many memories. It felt just like old times.

I can still picture our sophomore homecoming dance like it was yesterday. My date was a total dickhead and he left me hanging. Ryan only asked me to make his ex-girlfriend jealous. I wish I would've known that before I said yes. When we got to the dance, the ex got all possessive and wanted nothing to do with her own date. She just had to pick the dance as the place to stake her claim and ask Ryan to get back together. Ty and his date were fairing just as well as I was. His date was only interested in dancing with her girlfriends the entire night and she totally ignored him. I wanted to slap her and tell her she didn't know what she was thinking not taking advantage of her time with such an awesome and gorgeous guy. I would have totally given my entire collection of New Kids on the Block buttons and posters to go anywhere on a date with Tyler at that time. Not that I would have ever admitted it.

Tyler saw me holding up the wall while watching Shel and her high school sweetheart, Chase, dance pressed against each other like their life depended on it. Those two were so cute at the time. They looked into each other's eyes, smiling, leaning in for a peck every so often, while they danced to song after song. They wouldn't have cared if I joined them, but watching them was so much more fun. Or heart breaking, maybe, because I wished more than anything to have a relationship like theirs. Maybe it was a good thing that I didn't. Shelly sure as hell didn't marry Chase today, thank you very much.

Just when I thought I might burst with jealousy, Ty came over and threw his arm around me. Even then, he was so much taller than I was, so I looked up into his bright happy eyes and he lifted the side of his mouth in a soft smile. He knew I was feeling down. He never asked me, but he knew. He pulled me into a side hug, squeezing my shoulder and resting his head on mine.

"My date ditched me, Melly Belly," he had said, pouting his lips jokingly. "Will you save my reputation of being a stud and dance with me?"

We walked out on that dance floor, and he pretended he wouldn't rather be with anyone else other than me. He never mentioned anything about how my asshole date left me in the lurch. He made it seem like he was the one who needed saving, when in reality, he could've had any other girl there.

Instead, he was mine.

For the night.

Just like now.

But this time, I get a week before he turns back into a pumpkin.

About the Author

This is Julie's first adult romance novel. She has also written five young adult books. Against The Wall is actually a spinoff from her teen series. The Double Threat novels focus on the high school years of Megan Miller, who is Shelly Gelson's student aide. If you haven't already, check them out. The entire Double Threat series—*So I'm a Double Threat, Double Threat My Bleep, Double Time, and Double Threats Forever*—is available now. Julie is also the author of *You Act So White*, a multicultural teen novel about staying true to one's self in the face of peer pressure and racial tension. Julie recently released another adult romance, *More Than A Friend Request*—a short, sweet, and sexy read.

Acknowledgments

I'd like to send a major shout out to my mama, Dolores Aguilera. I don't know what I'd do without her endless support and multiple reads. I love you. To my bestie since the fourth grade, Lyndsi "Sausages" Hanley, thanks so much for all the feedback and taking time out of your busy schedule to edit ATW. Having you around since the fourth grade has finally paid off. HAHA. JK! I love you. And to, Christina Houser, thank you so very much for your enthusiasm for my writing. Your exceptional feedback and editing skills have been invaluable. Thank you for allowing me to drop off pages and pages of severely jacked up writing and turning it into something readable.

Finally, I'd like to thank my family for their undying support. While you may joke about me having a laptop permanently attached to my body, your words of encouragement are always heard and appreciated. Love you, guys.

Made in the USA
Charleston, SC
15 August 2015